The Haynes
Small Engine Repair Manual

by Curt Choate
and John H Haynes
Member of the Guild of Motoring Writers

The Haynes Workshop Manual
for small engine repair

(8B4 – 10340)
(1666)

ABCDE
F

2

Haynes Publishing Group
Sparkford Nr Yeovil
Somerset BA22 7JJ England

Haynes North America, Inc
861 Lawrence Drive
Newbury Park
California 91320 USA

Acknowledgements

We are grateful for the help and cooperation of Briggs & Stratton Corporation for supplying the four-stroke engine operating cycle illustrations. We also want to thank Tecumseh Products Company for assistance with technical information and certain illustrations.

© **Haynes North America, Inc. 1990**

With permission from J. H. Haynes & Co. Ltd.

A book in the **Haynes Automotive Repair Manual Series**

Printed in the USA

ISBN 1 85010 666 5

Library of Congress Catalog Card Number 90-81408

While every attempt is made to ensure that the information in this manual is correct, no liability can be accepted by the authors or publishers for loss, damage or injury caused by any errors in, or omissions from, the information given.

Contents

Contents

Introduction

There are literally millions of small engines in the garages, sheds and basements of homes all across America today. Some estimates are as high as five or six engines per household. They're mounted on lawn mowers, garden tillers, generators, air compressors, pumps, mini-bikes, go-carts and various other types of equipment and recreational vehicles . . . and many of them are badly neglected – in need of some type of maintenance or repair (often both). Since they're required to operate in hostile conditions (dust, heat, overloading and in many cases without proper lubrication), it's a tribute to the designers, as well as those who have a part in the manufacturing processes, that they perform as well and last as long as they do! However, you don't have to be guilty of neglecting the small engines in your possession, now that Haynes Publications, the world's largest publisher of automotive repair manuals, has made available this repair manual covering the most popular and widely used small engines from the leading manufacturers. Its proven approach, featuring easy-to-follow, step-by-step troubleshooting, maintenance and repair procedures, profusely illustrated with photographs taken in our own shop, has been refined over the years in our do-it-yourself automotive and motorcycle repair manuals.

The purpose of this manual is to help you maintain and repair small gas engines. It can do so in several ways. It can help you decide what work must be done, even if you choose to have it done by a repair shop, it provides information and procedures for tune-ups and routine maintenance and it offers diagnostic and repair procedures to follow when trouble occurs.

It's hoped you'll use the manual to tackle the work yourself. For many jobs, doing it yourself may be quicker than arranging an appointment to get the machinery into a shop and making the trips to drop it off and pick it up. More importantly, a lot of money can be saved by avoiding the expenses the shop must pass on to you to cover labor and overhead costs. An added benefit is the sense of satisfaction and accomplishment you feel after doing the job yourself. We also hope that as you gain experience and confidence working on small engines, you'll decide to move on to simple motorcycle, car or truck maintenance and repair jobs. When you do, Haynes can supply you with virtually all the service information you'll need.

Haynes small engine repair manual

How to use this repair manual

The manual is divided into several chapters. Each chapter is sub-divided into well-defined sections, many of which consist of consecutively numbered Paragraphs (usually referred to as "Steps", since they're normally part of a maintenance or repair procedure). If the material is basically informative in nature, rather than a step-by-step procedure, the Paragraphs aren't numbered.

The first five chapters contain material that applies to all engines, regardless of manufacturer. The remaining chapters cover specific material related to the individual brand engines only. Since most people are initially exposed to practical mechanics working on small engines, comprehensive chapters covering tool selection and usage, safety and general shop practices have also been included. *Be sure to read through them before beginning any work.* All specifications are included in an Appendix at the end of the manual.

The term "see illustration" (in parentheses), is used in the text to indicate that a photo or drawing has been included to make the information easier to understand (the old cliche "a picture is worth a thousand words" is especially true when it comes to how-to procedures). Also, every attempt is made to position illustrations directly opposite the corresponding text to minimize confusion. The two types of illustrations used (photographs and line drawings) are referenced by a number preceding the caption. Illustration numbers denote chapter and numerical sequence within the chapter (i.e. 3.4 means Chapter 3, illustration number four in order).

The terms "Note", "Caution" and "Warning" are used throughout the text with a specific purpose in mind – to attract the reader's attention. A "Note" simply provides information required to properly complete a procedure or information which will make the procedure easier to understand. A "Caution" outlines a special procedure or special steps which must be taken when completing the procedure where the Caution is found. Failure to pay attention to a Caution can result in damage to the component being repaired or the tools being used. A "Warning" is included where personal injury can result if the instructions aren't followed exactly as described.

Note: *Even though extreme care has been taken during the preparation of this manual, neither the publisher nor the author can accept responsibility for any errors in, or omissions from, the information given.*

Engine types and manufacturers included

The information in this repair manual is restricted to single-cylinder, air-cooled engines rated up to five horsepower, normally used to power lawn mowers, garden tillers, generators, air compressors, pumps and other types of commonly available equipment. The following manufacturers/engine types are included – for a complete list of engines, by model designation, refer to the chapter with the specific repair information for the particular manufacturer:

Briggs & Stratton single-cylinder four-strokes (side valve only)

Tecumseh single-cylinder four-strokes (side valve only)

Tecumseh single-cylinder two-strokes

Sears Craftsman single-cylinder four-strokes (side valve only)

Sears Craftsman single-cylinder two-strokes

Honda single-cylinder four-strokes (side valve)

Honda single-cylinder four-strokes (OHV)

How to identify an engine

To determine what repair information and specifications to use, and to purchase replacement parts, you'll have to be able to accurately identify the engine you're working on. Every engine, regardless of manufacturer, comes from the factory with a model number stamped or cast into it or a tag attached to it somewhere **(see illustration)**. The most common location is on the shroud used to direct the cooling air around the cylinder (look for the recoil starter – it's normally attached to the shroud as well). On some engines, the model number may be stamped or cast into or attached to the main engine casting and may not be visible, especially if the engine is dirty. To identify an engine from a known manufacturer covered in this manual, refer to the chapter with the specific repair information for the particular manufacturer.

If you can't find a model number or tag, you can determine if the engine is a two or four stroke (which will help a dealer decide what engine model you're dealing with) using one or more of the following quick checks:

● Look for a cap used to check the oil level and add oil to the engine – if the engine has a threaded or friction fit cap or plug that's obviously intended for adding oil to the crankcase **(see illustration)**, it's a four-stroke (the

The engine model/serial number is usually located on the cooling shroud (as shown here), but it may be located on the main engine casting

Four-stroke engines will have an oil level check/fill plug like this one somewhere on the lower part of the engine

Two-stroke engines require oil to be mixed with the gas for lubrication

The muffler on a four-stroke engine will look something like this

cap may be marked "Engine oil" or "Oil fill" and may have an oil level dipstick attached to it as well).

● Look for instructions to mix oil with the gas – if the engine requires oil in the gasoline **(see illustration)**, it's a two-stroke.

● Look for a muffler near the cylinder head – if the muffler (usually a canister-shaped device with several holes or slots in the end) is threaded into or bolted to the engine near one end **(see illustration)**, it's a four-stroke. Two-stroke engines have exhaust ports on the cylinder itself, near the center.

● Use the recoil starter to feel for compression strokes – detach the wire from the spark plug and ground it on the engine, then slowly operate the recoil starter. If you can feel resistance from cylinder compression every revolution of the crankshaft, the engine is a two-stroke. If compression resistance is felt every other revolution, the engine is a four-stroke.

Buying parts

The best place (and sometimes the only place) to buy parts for any small engine is the dealer that sells and repairs the engine brand or the equipment the engine is mounted on. Some auto parts stores also stock small engine parts, but they normally carry only tune-up and maintenance items. Look in the yellow pages of your telephone directory under "Small engines" and "Lawn and garden equipment" for a list of dealers in your area.

Always purchase and install name-brand parts. Most manufacturers market new, complete replacement engines and also what is termed a "short block". A short block is a brand new engine sub-assembly that includes the main crankcase casting, piston, rings and connecting rod, valves and related components, cylinder and camshaft. If you purchase one, you'll have to bolt on the external parts, such as the cylinder head, magneto, carburetor, fuel tank and recoil starter/cooling shroud. A short block typically costs about half as much as a complete new engine and approximately twice as much as a new crankshaft. If you have an engine that's worn out, severely damaged or that requires more work than you're willing to invest, a short block – or an entire new engine – may be the best alternative to an overhaul or major repairs.

Be sure to have the engine model and serial number available when buying parts and, if possible, take the old parts with you to the dealer. Then you can compare the new with the old to make sure you're getting the right ones. Keep in mind that parts may have to be ordered, so as soon as you realize you're going to need something, see if it's in stock and allow extra time for completing the repair if parts must be ordered.

You may occasionally be able to purchase used parts in usable condition and save some money in the process. A reputable dealer normally won't sell substandard parts, so don't hesitate to inquire about used components.

1 Setting up shop

Finding a place to work

Before considering what tools to collect, or how to use them, a safe, clean, well-lit place to work should be located. If anything more than routine maintenance is going to be done, some sort of special work area is essential. It doesn't have to be particularly large, but it should be clean, organized and equipped especially for doing mechanic work. It's understood, and appreciated, that many home mechanics don't have a good workshop or garage available and end up servicing or repairing an engine out of doors; however, an overhaul or major repairs should be completed in a sheltered area with a roof (the main reason is to prevent parts from collecting dirt, which is abrasive and will cause wear if it finds its way into an engine).

The workshop building

The size, shape and location of a shop building is usually dictated by circumstances rather than personal choice. Ideally, every do-it-yourselfer would have a spacious, clean, well-lit building specially designed and equipped for working on everything from small engines on lawn and garden equipment to cars and other vehicles. In reality, however, most of us must be content with a corner of the garage or basement or a small shed in the backyard.

As mentioned above, anything beyond minor maintenance and adjustments in nice weather should be done indoors. The best readily-available building would be a typical one or two car garage, preferably one that's detached from the house. A garage provides ample work and storage space and room for a large workbench. With that in mind, it must be pointed out that even the most extensive job possible on the typical small engine could – if necessary – be done in a small shed or corner of a garage. The bottom line is you'll have to make do with whatever facilities you have and adapt your workshop and methods of work to it.

Whatever the limitations of your own proposed or existing workshop area are, spend some time considering its potential and drawbacks – even a well-established workshop will benefit from occasional reorganization. Most do-it-yourselfers find that lack of space causes problems; this can be overcome to a great extent by carefully planning the locations of benches and storage facilities. The rest of this Section will cover some of the options available when setting up or reorganizing a workshop. Perhaps the best approach when designing a shop is to look at how others do it. Try approaching a local repair shop owner and asking to see his shop; note how work areas, storage and lighting are arranged, then try to scale it down to fit your own shop space, finances and needs.

General building requirements

A solid concrete floor is probably the best surface for any shop area used for mechanic work. The floor should be as even as possible and must also be dry. Although not absolutely necessary, it can be improved by applying a coat of paint or sealer formulated for concrete surfaces. This will make oil spills and dirt easier to remove and help cut down on dust – always a problem with concrete. A wood floor is less desirable and may sag or be damaged by the weight of equipment and machinery. It can be reinforced by laying sheets of thick plywood or chipboard over the existing surface. A dirt floor should be avoided at all costs, since it'll produce abrasive dust, which will be impossible to keep away from internal engine components. Dirt floors are also as bad as gravel or grass when it comes to swallowing up tiny dropped parts such as ball bearings and small springs.

Walls and ceilings should be as light as possible. It's a good idea to clean them and apply a couple of coats of white paint. The paint will minimize dust and reflect light inside the workshop. On the subject of light, the more natural light there is the better. Artificial light will also be needed, but you'll need a surprising amount of it to equal ordinary daylight.

A normal doorway is just wide enough to allow all but the biggest pieces of machinery and equipment through, but not wide enough to allow it through easily. If possible, a full-size garage door (overhead or hinged at each side) should allow access into the shop. Steps (even one of them) can be difficult to negotiate – make a ramp out of wood to allow easier entry if the step can't be removed.

Make sure the building is adequately ventilated, particularly during the winter. This is essential to prevent condensation problems and is also a vital safety consideration where solvents, gasoline and other volatile liquids are being stored and used. You should be able to open one or more windows for ventilation. In addition, opening vents in the walls are desirable.

Storage and shelving

All the parts from a small engine can occupy more space than you realize when its been completely disassembled – some sort of organized storage is needed to avoid losing them. In addition, storage space for hardware, lubricants, solvent, rags, tools and equipment will also be required.

If space and finances allow, install metal shelf units along the walls. Arrange the shelves so they're widely spaced near the bottom to take large or

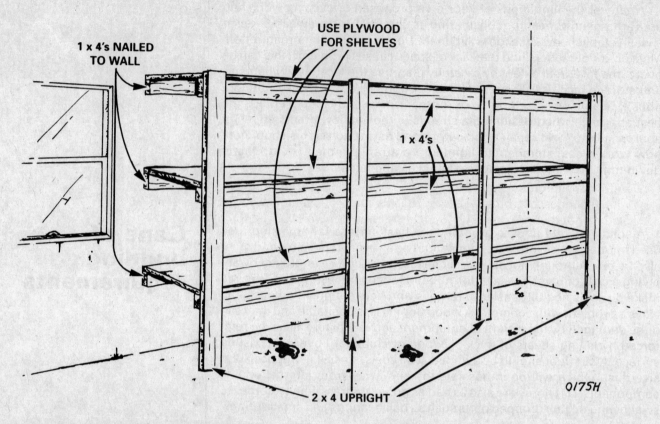

1 x 4's NAILED
TO WALL

USE PLYWOOD
FOR SHELVES

1 x 4's

2 x 4 UPRIGHT

0175H

1.1 Since they're relatively inexpensive and can be designed to fit available space, homemade wooden shelves may be the best choice for shop storage – however, keep in mind the obvious fire hazard they will become

heavy items. Metal shelf units are expensive, but they make the best use of available space. An added advantage is the shelf positions are not fixed and can be changed if necessary.

A cheaper (but more labor intensive) solution is to build shelves out of wood **(see illustration 1.1)**. Remember that wooden shelves must be much heftier than metal shelves to carry the same weight and the shelf positions are difficult to change. Also, wood absorbs oil and other liquids and is obviously a much greater fire hazard.

Small parts can be stored in plastic drawers or bins mounted on metal racks attached to the wall. They're available from most lumber and home centers as well as hardware stores. The bins are available in various sizes and normally have slots for labels.

Other containers can be used in the shop to keep storage costs down, but try to avoid round tubs, which waste a lot of space. Glass jars are often recommended as cheap storage containers, but they can easily get broken. Cardboard boxes are adequate for temporary use, but eventually the bottoms tend to drop out of them, especially if they get damp. Most plastic containers are useful, however, and large ice cream pails are invaluable for keeping small parts together during a rebuild or major repairs (collect the type that has a cover that snaps into place). Old metal cake pans, bread pans and muffin tins also make good storage containers for small parts.

Electricity and lights

Of all the useful shop facilities, electricity is by far the most essential. It's relatively easy to arrange if the workshop is near to or part of a house and it can be difficult and expensive if it isn't. It must be stressed that safety is the number one consideration when dealing with electricity; unless you have a very good working knowledge of electrical installations, any work required to provide power and lights in the shop should be done by an electrician.

You'll have to consider the total electrical requirements of the shop, making allowances for possible later additions of lights and equipment. Don't substitute extension cords for legal and safe permanent wiring. If the wiring isn't adequate or is substandard, have it upgraded.

Careful consideration should be given to lights for the workshop (two 150-watt incandescent bulbs or two 48-inch long, 40-watt fluorescent tubes suspended approximately 48-inches above the workbench would be a minimum). As a general rule, fluorescent lights are probably the best choice for even, shadow-free lighting. The position of the lights is important; for example, don't position a fixture directly above the area where the engine (or equipment it's mounted on) will be located during work – this will cause shadows even with fluorescent lights. Attach the light or lights slightly to the rear of or to each side of the workbench or work area to provide even lighting. A portable "trouble-light" is very helpful for use when overhead lights are inadequate. Note that if solvents, gasoline or other flammable liquids are present, which is usually the case in a mechanic's shop, special fittings should be used to minimize the risk of fire. Also, don't use fluorescent lights above machine tools (like a drill press). The flicker produced by alternating current is especially pronounced with this type of light and can make a rotating chuck appear stationary at certain speeds – a very dangerous situation.

Tools and equipment needed

Fire extinguisher

Since the use, maintenance and repair of any gasoline engine requires fuel to be handled and stored, buy a good-quality fire extinguisher before doing any maintenance or repair procedures (**see illustration 1.2**). Make sure it's rated for flammable liquid fires, familiarize yourself with its use and be sure to have it checked/recharged at regular intervals. Refer to Chapter 2 for safety-related information – warnings about the hazards of gasoline and other flammable liquids are included there.

1.2   Have a fire extinguisher designed for use on flammable liquid fires handy and know how to use it!

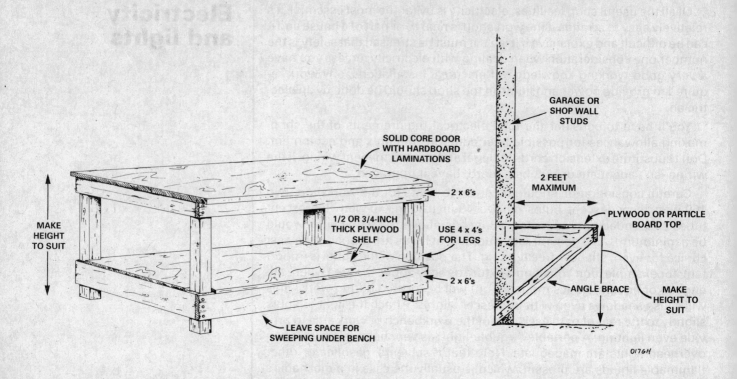

1.3 A sturdy, inexpensive workbench can be constructed from 2 x 6's

Workbench

A workbench is essential – it provides a place to lay out parts and tools during repair procedures, which means they'll stay clean longer, and it's a lot more comfortable than working on a floor or the driveway. This very important piece of shop equipment should be as large and sturdy as space and finances will allow. Although many types of benches are commercially available, they're usually quite expensive and don't nec- essarily fit into the available space as well as custom-built ones will. An excellent free-standing bench frame can be fabricated from slotted angle-iron or Douglas fir lumber (use 2 x 6's rather than 2 x 4's) **(see illustration 1.3)**. The pieces of the frame can be cut to any required size and bolted together. A 30 or 36 by 80-inch wood, solid-core door with hardboard surfaces, available at any lumber or home center, makes a nice bench top and can be turned over to expose the fresh side if it gets damaged or worn out.

If you're setting up shop in a garage, a sturdy bench can be assembled very quickly by attaching the bench top frame pieces to the wall with angled braces, effectively using the wall studs as part of the framework. Regardless of the type of frame you decide to use for the workbench, be sure to position the bench top at a comfortable working height and make sure everything is level. Shelves installed below the bench will make it more rigid and provide useful storage space.

One of the most useful pieces of equipment – and one that's usually associated with the workbench – is a vise. Size isn't necessarily the most important factor to consider when shopping for one; the quality of materials used and workmanship is. Good vises are very expensive, but as with any-

1.4   A bench vise is one of the most useful pieces of equipment you can have in the shop

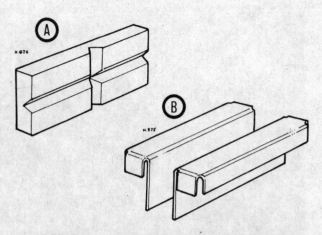

1.5   Some jobs will require engine parts to be held in the vise – to avoid damage to the parts from the hardened vise jaws, use commercially available fiberglass or plastic "soft jaws" (A) or fabricate inserts from 1/8-inch thick aluminum to fit over the jaws (B)

thing else, you get what you pay for. Buy the best quality vise you can afford and make sure the jaws will open at least four inches. Purchase a set of soft jaws to fit the vise as well (they're used to grip engine parts that could be damaged by the hardened vise jaws) (see illustrations 1.4 and 1.5).

Many small engine manufacturers also distribute a special fixture to hold engines during disassembly and reassembly. Equipment of this type is undoubtedly very useful, but outside the scope of most home workshops. In practice, most do-it-yourselfers will have to make do with a selection of wood blocks that can be used to prop the engine up on a bench. They can be arranged as required so the engine is supported in almost any position. An engine stand can also be fabricated from short lengths of 2 x 4 lumber and lag bolts, screws or nails (see illustration 1.6). When using wood blocks or a homemade engine stand, it's a good idea to have a helper available to assist in steadying the engine while fasteners are loosened or tightened. In some situations, the engine can be clamped in a vise, but be very careful not to damage the crankcase or cylinder castings.

Engine stands

1.6   A handy engine stand can be made from short lengths of 2 x 4 lumber and lag bolts or nails

Haynes small engine repair manual

1.7   A Black & Decker Workmate comes in very handy for holding an engine while working on it – the quick-release clamping feature makes it easy to change the engine's position quickly

Adjustable workbenches, like the Black & Decker Workmate, can also be very useful for holding an engine while it's being worked on **(see illustration 1.7)**. You probably won't want to buy one just for working on a lawn mower engine, but if you already have one, it can easily be adapted for use as a holding fixture.

Air compressor

Although it isn't absolutely necessary, an air compressor can make many tasks in the shop much easier and enable you to do a better job. (How else can you easily remove debris from the engine's cooling fins, dry off parts after cleaning them with solvent or blow out all the tiny passages in a carburetor?) If you can afford one, you'll wonder how you ever got along without it. In addition to supplying compressed air for cleaning parts, a compressor – if it's large enough – can also be used to power air tools, which are now widely available and quite inexpensive and can take

1.8   Although it's not absolutely necessary, an air compressor can make many jobs easier and produce better results, especially when air-powered tools are available to use with it

much of the drudgery out of mechanical repair jobs **(see illustration 1.8)**. For example, an impact wrench (and special impact sockets) can be invaluable when it comes time to remove the large nut that holds a lawn mower blade or the magneto flywheel to the end of the crankshaft. On the down side, the cost involved, the need for maintenance on the equipment and additional electrical requirements must be considered before equipping your shop with compressed air.

A selection of good mechanic's tools is a basic requirement for anyone who plans to maintain and repair small gasoline engines. For someone who has few tools, if any, the initial investment might seem high, but when compared to the spiraling costs of routine maintenance and repairs, it's a wise one; besides, most of the tools can also be used for other types of work. Keep in mind that this chapter simply lists the tools needed for doing the work – Chapter 2 explains in greater detail what to look for when shopping for tools and how to use them correctly.

To help the reader decide which tools are needed to perform the tasks detailed in this manual, two tool lists have been compiled: Routine maintenance and minor *repair* and *Repair and overhaul*. A separate section related to special factory tools is also included, but only the most serious do-it-yourselfers will be interested in reading about, purchasing and using them. Illustrations of most of the tools on each list are also included.

Hand tools

Haynes small engine repair manual

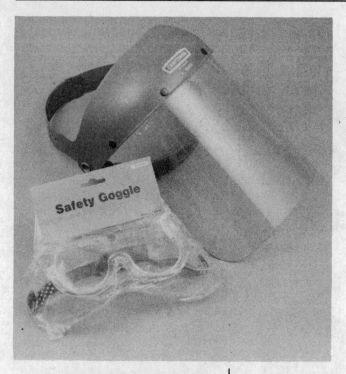

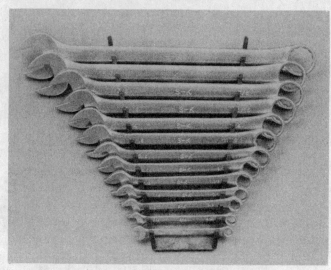

1.10   Combination wrenches – buy a set with sizes from 1/4 to 7/8-inch or 6 to 19 mm

1.9   One of the most important items you'll need in the shop is a face shield/safety goggles – fortunately, it'll also be one of the least expensive

The newcomer to mechanic work should start off with the *Routine maintenance and minor repair* tool kit, which is adequate for simple jobs. Then, as confidence and experience increase, you can tackle more difficult tasks, buying additional tools as they're needed. Eventually the basic kit will be built into the *Repair and overhaul* tool set. Over a period of time, the experienced do-it-yourselfer will assemble a set of tools complete enough for most repair and overhaul procedures and may begin adding special factory tools when it's felt the expense is justified by the frequency of use or the savings realized by not taking the equipment in to a shop for repair.

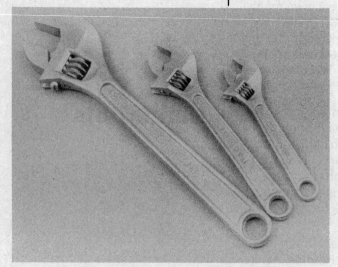

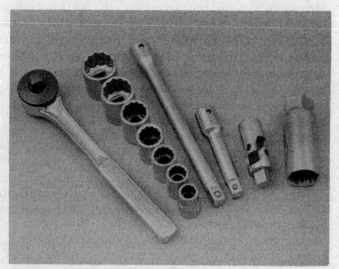

1.11   Adjustable wrenches are very handy – just be sure to use them correctly or you can damage fasteners by rounding off the hex head

1.12   A 3/8-inch drive socket set with interchangeable accessories will probably be used more often than any other tool(s) (left-to-right; ratchet, sockets, extensions, U-joint, spark plug socket) – don't buy a cheap socket set!

1.13   A spark plug adjusting tool will have several wire gauges for measuring the electrode gap and a device used for bending the side electrode to change the gap – make sure the one you buy has the correct size wire to check the spark plug gap on your engine

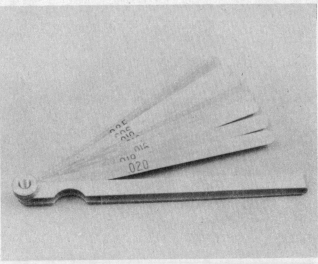

1.14   Feeler gauge sets have several blades of different thicknesses – if you need it to adjust ignition points, make sure the blades are as narrow as possible and check them to verify the required thickness is included

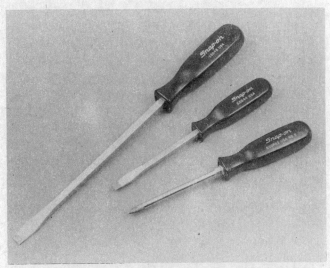

1.15   The routine maintenance tool kit should have 5/16 x 6-inch and 3/8 x 10-inch standard screwdrivers, as well as a no. 2 x 6-inch Phillips

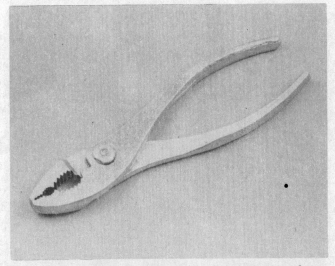

1.16   Common slip-joint pliers will be adequate for almost any job you end up doing

Routine maintenance and minor repair tools

The tools on this list should be considered the minimum required for doing routine maintenance, servicing and minor repair work (**see illustrations 1.9 through 1.22**). Incidentally, if you have a choice, it's a good idea to buy combination wrenches (box-end and open-end combined in one wrench); while more expensive than open-end ones, they offer the advantages of both types. Also included is a complete set of sockets which, though expensive, are invaluable because of their versatility (many types of interchangeable accessories are available). We recommend 3/8-inch drive over 1/2-inch drive for general small engine maintenance and repair, although a 1/4-inch drive set would also be useful (especially for igni-

1.17 A shallow pan (for draining oil/cleaning parts with solvent), a wire brush and a medium size funnel should be part of the routine maintenance tool kit

1.18 To remove the starter clutch used on some Briggs & Stratton engines, a special tool (which is turned with a wrench) will be needed

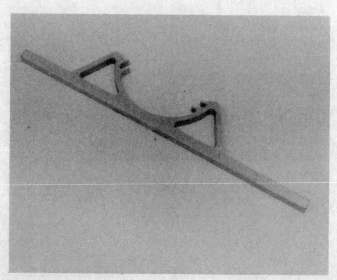

1.19 Briggs & Stratton also sells a special flywheel holder for use when loosening the nut or starter clutch

1.20 The flywheel on a Briggs & Stratton engine can be removed with a puller (shown here) . . .

tion and carburetor work). Buy 6-point sockets, if possible, and be careful not to purchase sockets with extra thick walls – they can be difficult to use when access to fasteners is restricted.

Safety goggles/face shield
Combination wrench set (1/4 to 7/8-inch or 6 to 19 mm)
Adjustable wrench – 10-inch
Socket set (6-point)
Reversible ratchet

Extension – 6-inch

Universal joint

Spark plug socket (with rubber insert)

Spark plug gap adjusting tool

Feeler gauge set

Standard screwdriver (5/16-inch x 6-inch)

Standard screwdriver (3/8-inch x 10-inch)

Phillips screwdriver (no. 2 x 6-inch)

Combination (slip-joint) pliers – 6-inch

Oil can

Fine emery cloth

Wire brush

Funnel (medium size)

Drain pan

Starter clutch wrench*

Flywheel holder*

Flywheel puller or knock-off tool*

1.21 . . . or, although it's not recommended by the factory, a knock-off tool, which fits on the end of the crankshaft (Tecumseh/Craftsman flywheels can also be removed with one of these tools)

*Although these tools are normally available exclusively through distributors/dealers (so technically they're "special factory tools"), they are included in this list because certain tune-up and minor repair procedures can't be done without them (specifically ignition point and flywheel key replacement on most Briggs & Stratton, Tecumseh and Craftsman engines). The factory tools may also be available at hardware and lawn and garden stores and occasionally you'll come across imported copies of the factory tools – examine them carefully before buying them.

1.22 Many Tecumseh/Craftsman and Honda engines require a puller like the one shown here for flywheel removal

These tools are essential if you intend to perform major repairs or overhauls and are intended to supplement those in the *Routine maintenance and minor repair* tool kit **(see illustrations 1.23 through 1.49).**

The tools in this list include many which aren't used regularly, are expensive to buy, or which need to be used in accordance with their manufacturer's instructions. Unless these tools will be used frequently, it's not very economical to purchase many of them. A consideration would be to split the cost and use between yourself and a friend or neighbor.

Repair and overhaul tools

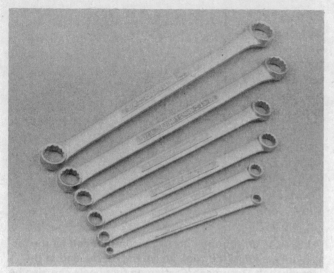

1.23 A set of box-end wrenches will complement the combination wrenches in the routine maintenance tool kit

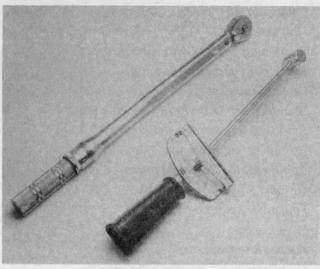

1.24 A torque wrench will be needed for tightening head bolts and flywheel nuts (two types are available: click type – left; beam type – right)

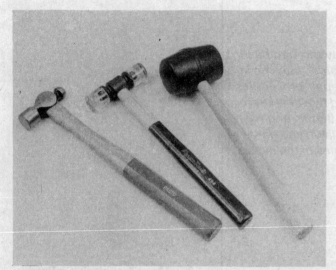

1.25 A ball-pein hammer, soft-face hammer and rubber mallet (left-to-right) will be needed for various tasks (any steel hammer can be used in place of the ball-pein hammer)

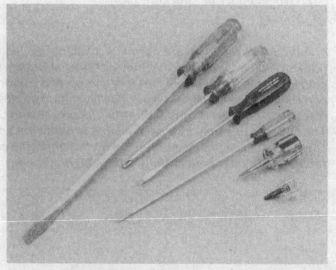

1.26 Screwdrivers come in many different sizes and lengths

Box-end wrenches
Torque wrench (same size drive as sockets)
Ball pein hammer – 12 oz (any steel hammer will do)
Soft-face hammer (plastic/rubber)
Standard screwdriver (1/4-inch x 6-inch)
Standard screwdriver (stubby – 5/16-inch)
Phillips screwdriver (no. 3 x 8-inch)
Phillips screwdriver (stubby – no. 2)
Hand impact screwdriver and bits

1.27   A hand impact screwdriver (used with a hammer) and bits can be very helpful for removing stubborn, stuck screws (or screws with deformed heads)

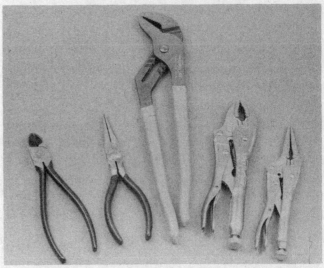

1.28   As you can afford them, arc-joint, needle-nose, Vise-grip and wire cutting pliers should be added to your tool collection

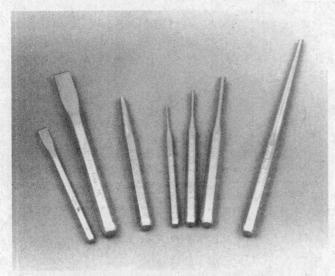

1.29   Cold chisels, center punches, pin punches and line-up punches (left-to-right) will be needed sooner or later for many jobs

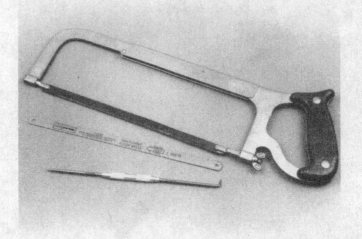

1.30   A scribe is used for making lines on metal parts and a hacksaw and blades will be needed for dealing with fasteners that won't unscrew

Pliers – Vise-grip
Pliers – needle-nose
Wire cutters
Cold chisels – 1/4 and 1/2-inch
Center punch
Pin punches (1/16, 1/8, 3/16-inch)
Line up tools (tapered punches)
Scribe
Hacksaw and assortment of blades

Haynes small engine repair manual

1.31   A gasket scraper is used for removing old gaskets from engine parts after disassembly – 3M "scrubbies" can be used to rough up the gasket surfaces prior to reassembly

1.32   Files must be used with handles and should be stored so they don't contact each other

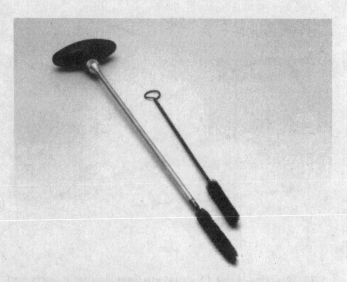

1.33   A selection of nylon/metal brushes is needed for cleaning passages in engine and carburetor parts

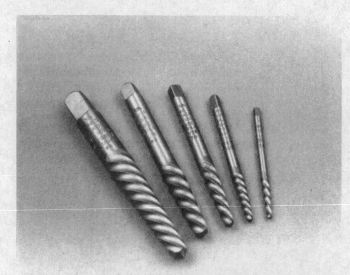

1.34   Special tools called E-Z outs are used to remove broken-off screws and bolts from engine parts

Gasket scraper
Steel rule/straightedge – 12-inch
A selection of files
A selection of brushes for cleaning small passages
E-Z out (screw extractor) set

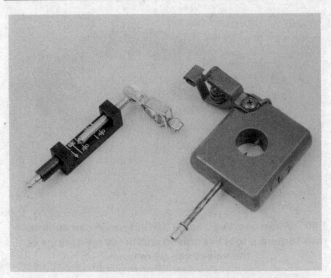

1.35 A spark tester (for checking the ignition system) can be purchased at an auto parts store (left) or fabricated from a block of wood, a large alligator clip, some nails, screws and wire and the cap end of an old spark plug (right)

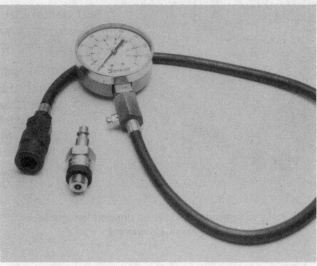

1.36 Although not required by most small engine manufacturers, a compression gauge can be used to check the condition of the piston rings and valves (two types are commonly available: The screw-in type – shown here – and the type that's held in place by hand pressure)

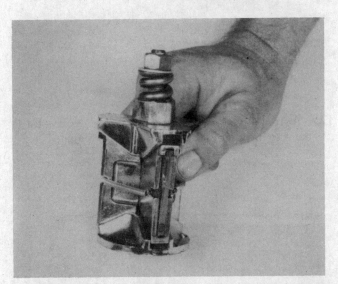

1.37 A ridge reamer is needed to remove the carbon/wear ridge at the top of the cylinder so the piston will slip out

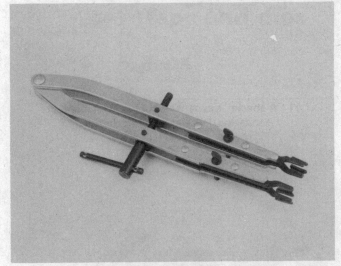

1.38 A valve spring compressor like this is required for side valve Briggs & Stratton engines

Spark tester
Compression gauge
Ridge reamer
Valve spring compressor

1.39   A valve lapping tool will be needed for any four-stroke engine overhaul

1.40   Some overhead valve (OHV) four-stroke engines may require a tool like this to compress the springs so the valves can be removed

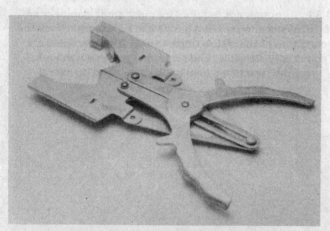

1.41   A special inexpensive tool is available for removing/installing piston rings

1.42   Piston ring compressors come in many sizes – be sure to buy one that will work on your engine

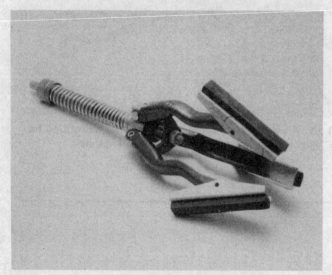

1.43   A cylinder surfacing hone can be used to clean up the bore so new rings will seat, but it won't resize the cylinder

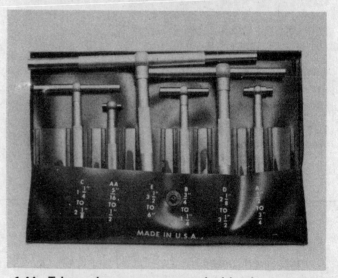

1.44   Telescoping gauges are used with micrometers or calipers to determine the inside diameter of holes (like the cylinder bore) to see how much wear has occurred

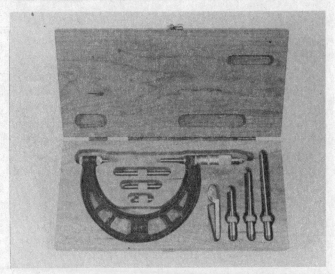

1.45 Micrometers are needed for precision measurements to check for wear – they're available in two styles: The mandrel type, shown here, which has one frame and interchangeable mandrels which allow for measurements from 0 to 4-inches, and . . .

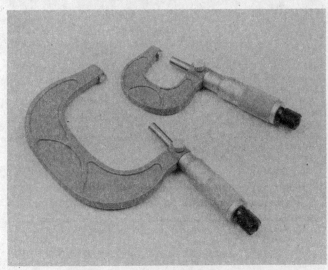

1.46 . . . individual fixed-mandrel micrometers that are capable of making measurements in one inch increments (0 to 1, 1 to 2, 2 to 3, etc.)

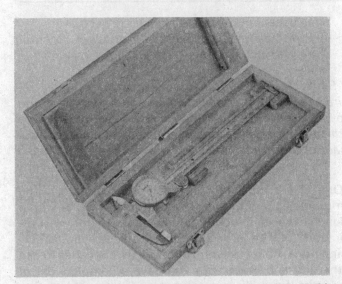

1.47 Vernier or dial calipers (shown here) can be used in place of micrometers for most checks and can also be used for depth measurements

1.48 A dial indicator can be used for end play checks on crankshafts and camshafts

Valve lapping tool
Piston ring removal and installation tool
Piston ring compressor
Cylinder hone
Telescoping gauges
Micrometer(s) and/or dial/Vernier calipers
Dial indicator

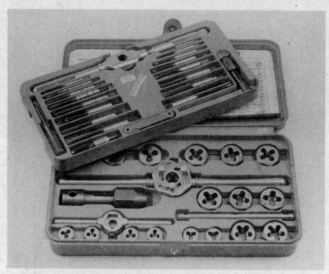

1.49   A tap-and-die set is very handy for cleaning and restoring threads

1.50   Some Tecumseh/Craftsman two-stroke engines require a no. 6 Torx socket for removal of the connecting rod bolts during an engine overhaul

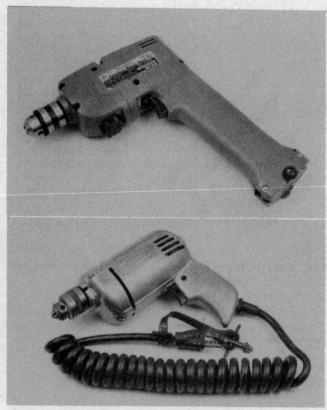

1.51   An electric drill (both 115-volt AC and cordless types are shown here), . . .

Tap and die set
Torx socket(s)**

** Some Tecumseh/Craftsman two-stroke engines require a Torx socket (size E6) to remove the connecting rod cap bolts **(see illustration 1.50)**. If you're overhauling one of these engines, purchase a socket before beginning the disassembly procedure.

One of the most indispensable tools around is the common electric drill **(see illustration 1.51)**. One with a 3/8-inch capacity chuck should be sufficient for most repair work – it'll be large enough to power a cylinder surfacing hone. Collect several different wire brushes to use in the drill and make sure you have a complete set of sharp bits (for drilling metal, not wood) **(see illustration 1.52)**. Cordless drills, which are extremely versatile because they don't have to be plugged in, are now widely available and relatively inexpensive. You may want to consider one, since it'll obviously be handy for non-mechanical jobs around the house and shop.

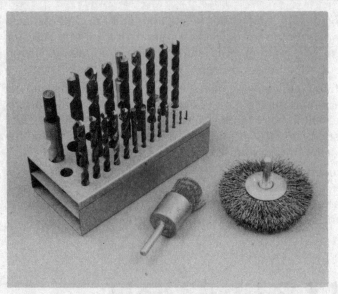

1.52 . . . a set of good-quality drill bits and wire brushes of various sizes will find many uses in the shop

1.53 Another almost indispensable piece of equipment in a mechanic's shop is a bench grinder (with a wire wheel mounted on one arbor) – make sure it's securely bolted down and never use it with the tool rests or eye shields removed!

Another very useful piece of equipment is a bench-mounted grinder (see illustration 1.53). If a wire wheel is mounted on one end and a grinding wheel on the other, it's very handy for cleaning up fasteners, sharpening tools and removing rust from parts. Make sure the grinder is fastened securely to the bench or stand, always wear eye protection when using it and never grind aluminum parts on the grinding wheel.

Buying tools

For the do-it-yourselfer just starting to get involved in small engine maintenance and repair, there are a number of options available when purchasing tools. If maintenance and minor repair is the extent of the work to be done, the purchase of individual tools is satisfactory. If, on the other hand, extensive work is planned, it would be a good idea to purchase a modest tool set. A set can usually be bought at a substantial savings over the individual tool prices (and they often come with a tool box). As additional tools are needed, add-on sets, individual tools and a larger box can be purchased to expand the tool selection. Building a tool set gradually allows the cost to be spread over a longer period of time and gives the mechanic the freedom to choose only tools that will actually be used.

Tool stores and small engine distributors or dealers will often be the only source of some of the overhaul and special factory tools needed, but regardless of where tools are bought, try to avoid cheap ones (especially when buying screwdrivers, wrenches and sockets) because they won't last very long. The expense involved in replacing cheap tools will eventually be greater than the initial cost of quality tools. Read Chapter 2 for an in-depth, detailed look at choosing and using tools.

Haynes small engine repair manual

Storage and care of tools

Good tools are expensive, so it makes sense to treat them with respect. Keep them clean and in usable condition and store them properly. Always wipe off dirt, grease and metal chips before putting them away. Never leave tools lying around in the work area.

Some tools, such as screwdrivers, pliers, wrenches and sockets, can be hung on a panel mounted on the garage or workshop wall, while others should be kept in a tool box or tray. Measuring instruments, gauges, cutting tools, etc. must be carefully stored where they can't be damaged by weather or impact from other tools.

When tools are used with care and stored properly, they'll last a very long time. However, even with the best of care, tools will wear out if used frequently. When a tool is damaged or worn out, replace it; subsequent jobs will be safer and more enjoyable if you do.

Special factory tools

Each small engine manufacturer provides certain special tools to distributors and dealers for use when overhauling or doing major repairs on their engines. The distributors and dealers often stock some of the tools for sale to do-it-yourselfers and independent repair shops. A good example would be tools like the starter clutch wrench, flywheel holder and flywheel puller(s) supplied by Briggs & Stratton, which are needed for relatively simple procedures such as ignition point and flywheel key replacement (they're required to get the flywheel off for access to the ignition parts). If the special tools aren't used, the repair either can't be done properly or the engine could be damaged by using substitute tools. Fortunately, the tools mentioned are not very expensive or hard to find.

Other special tools, like bushing drivers, bushing reamers, valve seat and guide service tools, cylinder sizing hones, main bearing repair sets, etc. are prohibitively expensive and not usually stocked for sale by dealers. If repairs requiring such tools are encountered, take the engine or components to a dealer with the necessary tools and pay to have the work done, then reassemble the engine yourself.

Haynes small engine repair manual

 **General shop practices**

Safety first!

Like it or not, a workshop can be a dangerous place. Electricity, especially if it's misused or taken for granted, is potentially harmful in an environment that's often damp. Hand and power tools, if misused, present opportunities for accidents and stored gasoline, solvents, lubricants and chemicals are a very real fire risk.

There's no way to make a shop totally safe (as long as people and potentially hazardous equipment/materials are involved) – the topic of safety really must focus on minimizing the risk of accidents by following safe shop practices (primary safety) and using the correct clothing and equipment to minimize injury in the event of an accident (secondary safety). The subject of safety is large and could easily fill a chapter on its own. To keep the subject within reasonable bounds – and because few people will bother to read an entire chapter on safety – its been confined here, initially, to a set of rules (Additional notes appear in the text and captions, where necessary, throughout the manual.)

The rest of this section covers some of the more important and relevant safety topics, but isn't intended to be definitive. Read through it, even if you've done mechanic work for years without scraping a knuckle. It should be emphasized that the most important piece of safety equipment of all is the human brain – try to get into the habit of thinking about what you're doing, and what could go wrong. A little common sense and foresight can prevent the majority of workshop accidents.

Safety rules

Professional mechanics are trained in safe working procedures. Regardless of how eager you are to start working on an engine or piece of equipment, take the time to read through the following list. As mentioned above, lack of attention, no matter how brief, can result in an accident. So can failure to follow certain simple safety precautions. The possibility of an accident will always exist, and the following points aren't intended to be a comprehensive list of all dangers; they are intended, however, to make you aware of the risks involved in mechanic work and encourage a safety-conscious approach to everything you do.

Haynes small engine repair manual

2.1   Before doing any checks or maintenance on a small engine that require you to turn the blade attached to the crankshaft, detach the wire from the spark plug and position it out of the way!

2.2   Store and transport gas in an approved metal or plastic container only – never use a glass bottle!

DON'T start the engine before checking to see if the drive is in Neutral (where applicable).

DON'T turn the blade attached to the engine unless the spark plug wire has been detached from the plug **(see illustration 2.1)** and positioned out of the way!

DON'T use gasoline for cleaning parts – ever!

DON'T store gasoline in glass containers – use an approved metal or high-impact plastic gasoline container only **(see illustration 2.2)**!

DON'T store, pour or spill gasoline near an open flame or devices such as a stove, furnace, or water heater which utilizes a pilot light or devices that can create a spark.

DON'T smoke when filling the fuel tank!

DON'T fill the fuel tank while the engine is running. Allow the engine to cool for at least two minutes before refueling.

DON'T refuel equipment indoors where there's poor ventilation. Outdoor refueling is preferred.

DON'T operate the engine if a gasoline odor is present.

DON'T operate the engine if gasoline has been spilled. Move the machine away from the spill and don't start the engine until the gas has evaporated.

DON'T crank an engine with the spark plug removed **(see illustration 2.3)**. If the engine is flooded, open the throttle all the way and operate the starter until the engine starts.

DON'T attempt to drain the engine oil until you're sure its cooled so it won't burn you.

DON'T touch any part of the engine or muffler **(see illustration 2.4)** until its cooled down enough to avoid burns.

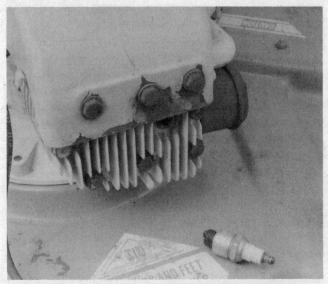

2.3   Don't try to clear a flooded engine by removing the spark plug and cranking the engine – the gasoline vapors coming out of the plug hole could be ignited

2.4   The cooling fins and muffler can get extremely hot!

2.5   Wrenches that don't fit snugly on the fastener can result in skinned knuckles, cuts and bruises

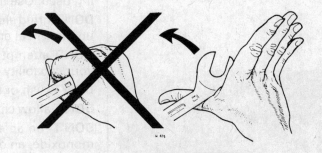

2.6   Always pull on a wrench when loosening a fastener – if you can't pull on it, push with your hand open as shown here

DON'T siphon toxic liquids, such as gasoline, by mouth or allow them to remain on your skin.

DON'T allow spilled oil or grease to remain on the floor – wipe it up before someone slips on it.

DON'T use loose fitting wrenches (**see illustration 2.5**) or other tools that may slip and cause injury.

DON'T push on wrenches when loosening or tightening nuts or bolts. Always try to pull the wrench towards you (**see illustration 2.6**). If the situation calls for pushing the wrench away, push with an open hand to avoid scraped knuckles if the wrench slips.

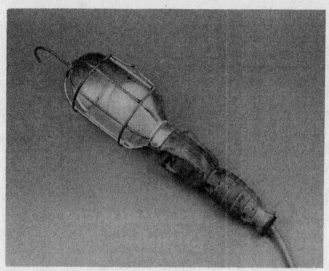

2.7 Never use an unshielded light bulb in the shop – special "trouble-lights" designed to prevent broken bulbs and the accompanying safety hazards are commonly available

2.8 Do not run the engine with the air cleaner removed

2.9 Always wear eye protection when using power tools!

DON'T use unshielded light bulbs in the shop, especially if gasoline is being used. Use an approved "trouble-light" only **(see illustration 2.7).**

DON'T grind aluminum parts on a grinding wheel – the aluminum can load up the wheel and cause it to come apart!

DON'T attempt to lift a heavy piece of equipment which may be beyond your capability – get someone to help you.

DON'T rush or take unsafe shortcuts to finish a job.

DON'T allow children on or around equipment when you're working on it.

DON'T run an engine in an enclosed area. The exhaust contains carbon monoxide, an odorless, colorless, deady poisonous gas.

DON'T operate an engine with a build-up of grass, leaves, dirt or other combustible material in the muffler area.

DON'T use equipment on any forested, brush-covered, or grass-covered unimproved land unless the engine has a spark arrester installed on the muffler.

DON'T run an engine with the air cleaner or cover (directly over the carburetor air intake) removed **(see illustration 2.8).**

DON'T store lubricants and chemicals near a heater or other sources of heat or sparks.

DO wear eye protection when using power tools such as a drill, bench grinder, etc. **(see illustration 2.9).**

DO keep loose clothing and long hair well out of the way of moving parts.

DO wear steel-toe safety shoes when working on equipment on a bench. If heavy parts are dropped or fall, they won't crush your toes.

DO get someone to check on you periodically when working alone.

DO carry out work in a logical sequence and make sure everything is correctly assembled and tightened.

DO keep lubricants, chemicals and other fluids tightly capped and out of the reach of children and pets.

Gasoline

Remember – gasoline is extremely flammable! Never smoke or have any kind of open flames or unshielded light bulbs around when working on an engine in the shop. The risk doesn't end there however – a spark caused by an electrical short-circuit, by two metal surfaces striking each other, or even static electricity built up in your body under certain conditions, can ignite gasoline vapors, which in a confined space are highly explosive. As mentioned above, DO NOT, under any circumstances, USE GASOLINE FOR CLEANING PARTS; use an approved safety solvent only! Also, DO NOT STORE GASOLINE IN A GLASS CONTAINER – use an approved metal or plastic container only

Fire

Always have a fire extinguisher suitable for use on fuel and electrical fires handy in the garage or workshop. Never try to extinguish a gasoline or electrical fire with water! Have the fire department phone number posted near the telephone!

Fumes

Certain fumes are highly toxic and can quickly cause unconsciousness and even death if inhaled to any extent. Gasoline vapor falls into this category, as well as vapors from some cleaning solvents. Draining and pouring of such volatile fluids should be done in a well-ventilated area, preferably outdoors.

When using cleaning fluids and solvents, read the instructions on the container carefully. Never use materials from unmarked containers.

Don't run the engine in an enclosed space such as a garage; exhaust fumes contain carbon monoxide, which is extremely poisonous. If you need to run the engine, always move it outside.

Household current

When using an electric power tool, trouble-light, etc., which operates on household current, always make sure the cord is correctly connected to the plug and properly grounded **(see illustration 2.10)**. Don't use such items in damp conditions and, again, don't create a spark or apply excessive heat in the vicinity of fuel or fuel vapor. Never string extension cords together to supply electricity to an out of the way place.

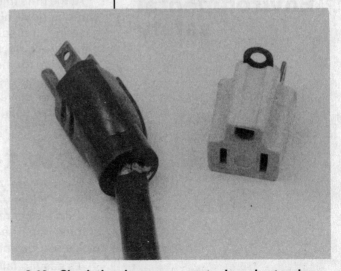

2.10 Check the plugs on power tools and extension cords to make sure they're securely attached, with no burned or frayed wires, and use an adapter to ground the plug at the outlet if necessary

Haynes small engine repair manual

Spark plug voltage

A severe electric shock can result from touching certain parts of the ignition system (such as the spark plug wire) when the engine is running or being cranked, particularly if components are damp or the insulation is defective. If an electronic ignition system is involved, the secondary system voltage is much higher and could prove fatal.

Keep it clean

Get in the habit of taking a regular look around the shop, checking for potential dangers. The work area should always be kept clean and neat – all debris should be swept up and disposed of as soon as possible. Don't leave tools lying around on the floor.

Be very careful with oily rags. If they're left in a pile, it's not uncommon for spontaneous combustion to occur, so dispose of them properly in a covered metal container.

Check all equipment and tools for security and safety hazards (like frayed cords). Make necessary repairs as soon as a problem is noticed – don't wait for a shelf unit to collapse before fixing it.

Accidents and emergencies

These range from minor cuts and skinned knuckles to serious injuries requiring immediate medical attention. The former are inevitable, while the latter are, hopefully, avoidable or at least uncommon. Think about what you would do in the event of an accident. Get some first aid training and have an adequate first aid kit somewhere within easy reach.

Think about what you would do if you were badly hurt and incapacitated. Is there someone nearby who could be summoned quickly? If possible, never work alone just in case something goes wrong.

If you had to cope with someone else's accident, would you know what to do? Dealing with accidents is a large and complex subject, and it's easy to make matters worse if you have no idea how to respond. Rather than attempt to deal with this subject in a superficial manner, buy a good First Aid book and read it carefully.

Environmental safety

At the time this manual was being written, several state and Federal regulations governing the storage and disposal of oil and other lubricants, gasoline and solvents – petroleum-based substances in general – were pending (contact the appropriate government agency or your local auto parts store for the latest information). Be absolutely certain that all materials are properly stored, handled and disposed of. Never pour used or leftover oil or solvents down the drain or dump them on the ground. Also, don't allow volatile liquids to evaporate – keep them in sealed containers.

How to buy and use tools

Chances are you already own some of the tools in the lists included in Chapter 1. Many of them are the same ones needed for home maintenance and simple car repairs. This chapter will cover the types of tools to buy, assuming you'll need more, and how to use them properly so the repairs you tackle will be enjoyable and successful.

It's easy to fall into the trap of thinking you should only purchase individual, high-quality tools, gradually expanding your tool set as needs change and finances allow. This is good advice on the subject, and is normally suggested in how-to books and magazine articles, but it's difficult to follow through on. For starters, a glance through any mechanic's tool collection will reveal a very mixed assortment of tools. You'll usually find top-quality, lifetime guaranteed items alongside cheap tools purchased on the spur of the moment from many sources.

There seems to be a law governing the contents of tool boxes that dictates any expensive, well-made and indispensable tool will get lost or "disappear" very quickly, but during your short ownership of it, it'll never break, slip or damage fasteners. Conversely, a cheap, ill-fitting and poorly made tool will be with you for life, even when you thought you had thrown it away. It'll never quite fit properly and will probably drive you crazy.

Although this is a broad generalization, it does happen in the real world. There are some very methodical and organized people out there who unfailingly clean and check each tool after use, before hanging it back up on the pegboard hook or placing it in its special drawer in the tool box. While there are few who practice this disciplined treatment of tools, there's no denying it's the correct approach and should be encouraged.

There are also those to whom the idea of using the correct tool is completely foreign and who will cheerfully tackle the most complex overhaul procedures with only a set of cheap open-end wrenches of the wrong type, a single screwdriver with a worn tip, a large hammer and an adjustable wrench. This approach is undeniably wrong and should be avoided – but while it often results in damaged fasteners and components, people often get away with it.

It's a good idea to strive for a compromise between these two extremes and, like most mechanics, cultivate a vision of the ideal workshop that's tempered by economic realities. This will inevitably lead to a mixed assortment of tools and seems to end up as the controlling factor in most workshops.

In this chapter we'll also try to give you some kind of idea when top-quality tools are essential and where cheaper ones will be adequate. As a general rule, if tools will be used often, purchase good-quality ones – if they'll be used infrequently, lower quality ones will usually suffice.

If you're unsure about how much use a tool will get, the following approach may help. For example, if you need a set of combination wrenches but aren't sure which sizes you'll end up using most, buy a cheap or medium-priced set (make sure the jaws fit the fastener sizes marked on them). After some use over a period of time, carefully examine each tool in the set to assess its condition. If all the tools fit well and are undamaged, don't bother buying a better set. If one or two are worn, replace them with high-quality items – this way you'll end up with top-quality tools where they're needed most and the cheaper ones are sufficient for occasional use. On rare occasions you may conclude the whole set is poor quality. If so, buy a better set, if necessary, and remember never to buy that brand again.

The best place to buy hand tools is an auto parts store, tool store or the tool department at your nearest Sears store. You may not find cheap tools, but you should have a large selection to choose from and expert advice will be available. Take the tool lists in Chapter 1 with you when shopping for tools and explain what you want to the salesperson. Sources to steer clear of, at least until you have experience judging quality, are mail order suppliers (other than Sears or those selling name-brands) and flea markets. Some of them offer good value for the money, but most carry cheap, imported tools of dubious quality. Tools, like any other consumer product, are often counterfeited in the Far East. The resulting tools can be acceptable or, on the other hand, they might be unusable. Unfortunately, it can be hard to judge by looking at them.

Finally, consider buying secondhand tools from garage sales or used tool outlets. You may have limited choice in sizes, but you can usually determine from the condition of the tools if they're worth buying. You can end up with a number of unwanted or duplicate tools, but it's a cheap way of putting a basic tool kit together, and you can always sell off any surplus tools later.

Buying wrenches and sockets

Wrenches of varying quality are available and cost is usually a good indication of quality – the more they cost, the better they are. In the case of wrenches, it's important to buy high-quality tools. Your wrenches will be some of the most often used tools in the shop, so buy the best you can afford.

Buy a set with the sizes outlined in Chapter 1. The size stamped on the wrench (see illustration 2.11) indicates the distance across the nut or bolt head (or the distance between the wrench jaws), in inches, not the diameter of the threads on the fastener. For example, a 1/4-inch bolt will almost always have a 7/16-inch hex- head – the size of the wrench required to loosen or tighten it. In the case of metric tools, the number is in millimeters. At the risk of confusing the issue, it should be mentioned the relationship between thread diameter and hex size doesn't always hold true; in some applications, an unusually small hex may be used, either for reasons of limited space around the fastener or to discourage over-tightening. Conversely, in some areas, fasteners with a disproportionately large hex-head may be encountered.

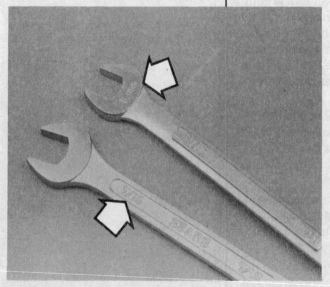

2.11   Wrench sizes are clearly stamped on the ends or handle

Wrenches tend to look similar, so it can be difficult to judge how well they're made just by looking at them. As with most other purchases, there are bargains to be had, just as there are overpriced tools with well-known brand names. On the other hand, you may buy what looks like a good set of wrenches only to find they fit badly or are made from poor-quality steel.

With a little experience, it's possible to judge the quality of a tool by looking at it. Often, you may have come across the brand name before and have a good idea of the quality. Close examination of the tool can often reveal some hints as to its quality. Prestige tools are usually polished and chrome-plated over their entire surface, with the working faces ground to size. The polished finish is largely cosmetic, but it does make them easy to keep clean. Ground jaws normally indicate the tool will fit well on fasteners.

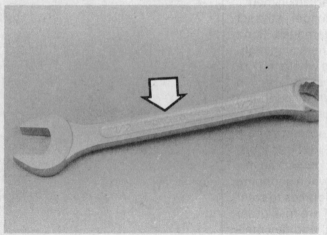

2.12   Look for the words "chrome vanadium" or "forged" when trying to determine wrench quality

A side-by-side comparison of a high-quality wrench with a cheap equivalent is an eye opener. The better tool will be made from a good-quality material, often a forged/chrome-vanadium steel alloy (see illustration 2.12).

This, together with careful design, allows the tool to be kept as small and compact as possible. If, by comparison, the cheap tool is thicker and heavier, especially around the jaws, it's usually because the extra material is needed to compensate for its lower quality. If the tool fits properly, this is not necessarily bad – it is, after all, cheaper – but in situations where it's necessary to work in a confined area, the cheaper tool may be too bulky to fit.

The open-end wrench is the most common type, due mainly to its general versatility. It normally consists of two open jaws connected by a flat handle section. The jaws usually vary by one size, with an occasional overlap of sizes between consecutive wrenches in a set. This allows one wrench to be used to hold a bolt head while a similar-size nut is removed. A typical fractional size wrench set might have the following jaw sizes: 1/4 x 5/16, 3/8 x 7/16, 1/2 x 9/16, 9/16 x 5/8 and so on.

Typically, the jaw end is set at an angle to the handle, a feature which makes them very useful in confined spaces; by turning the nut or bolt as far as the obstruction allows, then turning the wrench over so the jaw faces in the other direction, it's possible to move the fastener a fraction of a turn at a time **(see illustration 2.13)**. The handle length is generally determined by the size of the jaw and is calculated to allow a nut or bolt to be tightened sufficiently by hand with minimal risk of breakage or thread damage (though this doesn't apply to soft materials like brass or aluminum).

Common open-end wrenches are usually sold in sets and it's rarely worth buying them individually unless it's to replace a lost or broken tool from a set. Single tools invariably cost more, so check the sizes you're most likely to need regularly and buy the best set of wrenches you can afford in that range of sizes. If money is limited, remember that you'll use open-end wrenches more than any other type – it's a good idea to buy a good set and cut corners elsewhere.

A box-end wrench consists of a ring-shaped end with a 6-point (hex) or 12-point (double hex) opening **(see illustration 2.14)**. This allows the tool to fit on the fastener hex at 15 (12-point) or 30-degree (6-point) intervals. Normally, each tool has two ends of different sizes, allowing an overlapping range of sizes in a set, as described for open-end wrenches.

Although available as flat tools, the handle is usually offset at each end to allow it to clear obstructions near the fastener, which is normally an advantage. In addition to normal length wrenches, it's also possible to buy long handle types to allow more leverage (very useful when trying to loosen rusted or seized nuts). It is, however, easy to shear off fasteners if not careful, and sometimes the extra length impairs access.

As with open-end wrenches, box-ends are available in varying quality, again often indicated by finish and the amount of metal around the ends. While the same criteria should be applied when selecting a set of box-end wrenches, if your budget is limited, go for better quality open-end wrenches and a slightly cheaper set of box-ends.

Open-end wrenches

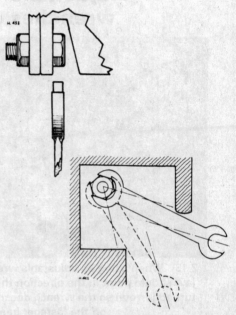

2.13   Open-end wrenches are the most versatile for general use

Box-end wrenches

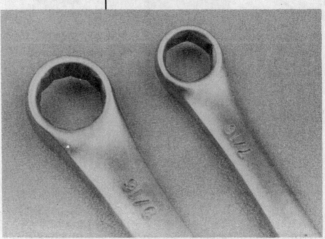

2.14   Box-end wrenches are available in both 6 and 12-point openings – if you have a choice, buy 6-point wrenches

Combination wrenches

These wrenches combine a box-end and open-end of the same size in one tool and offer many of the advantages of both. Like the others, they're widely available in sets and as such are probably a better choice than box-ends only. They're generally compact, short-handled tools and are well suited for small engine repairs, where access is often restricted.

Adjustable wrenches

These tools come in a wide variety of shapes and sizes with various types of adjustment mechanisms. The principle is the same in each case – a single tool that can handle fasteners of various sizes. Adjustable wrenches are not as good as single-size tools and it's easy to damage fasteners with them. However, they can be an invaluable addition to any tool kit – if they're used with discretion. **Note:** *If you attach the wrench to the fastener with the movable jaw pointing in the direction of wrench rotation* (**see illustration 2.15**), *an adjustable wrench will be less likely to slip and damage the fastener head.*

The most common adjustable wrench is the open-end type with a set of parallel jaws that can be set to fit the head of a fastener. Most are controlled by a threaded spindle, though there are various cam and spring-loaded versions available. Don't buy large tools of this type; you'll rarely be able to find enough clearance to use them. The sizes specified in Chapter 1 are best suited to small engine repair work.

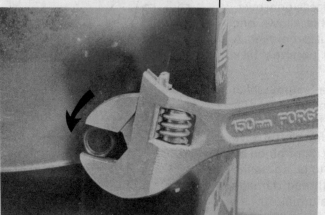

2.15   When using an adjustable wrench, the movable jaw should point in the direction the wrench is being turned (arrow) so the wrench doesn't distort and slip off the fastener head

Socket sets

A refined version of the box-end wrench, interchangable sockets consist of a forged steel alloy cylinder with a hex or double hex formed inside one end. The other end is formed into the square drive recess that engages over the corresponding square end of various socket drive tools.

Sockets are available in 1/4, 3/8, 1/2 and 3/4-inch drive sizes. Of these, a 3/8-inch drive set is most useful for small engine repairs, although 1/4-inch drive sockets and accessories may occasionally be needed.

The most economical way to buy sockets is in a set. As always, quality will govern the cost of the tools. Once again, the "buy the best" approach is usually advised when selecting sockets. While this is a good idea, since the end result is a set of quality tools that should last a lifetime, the cost is so high it's difficult to justify the expense for home use. Go shopping for a socket set and you'll be confronted with a vast selection, so stick with the recommendations in Chapter 1.

As far as accessories go, you'll need a ratchet, at least one extension (buy a three or six inch size), a spark plug socket and maybe a T-handle or breaker bar. Other desirable, though less essential items, are a speeder handle, a U-joint, extensions of various other lengths and adaptors from one drive size to another (**see illustration 2.16**).

2.16   Many accessories are available in each drive size for use with sockets (left to right: Breaker bar, sliding T-handle, speed handle and 3/8 to 1/4-inch drive adapter)

2.17   Deep sockets are handy for loosening/tightening recessed bolts and nuts threaded onto long bolts or studs

2.18   Standard and Phillips screwdriver bits, Allen-head and Torx drivers are available for use with ratchets and other socket drive tools

Some of the sets you find may combine drive sizes; they're well worth having if you find the right set at a good price, but avoid being dazzled by the number of pieces.

Above all, be sure to completely ignore any label that reads "86-piece Socket Set"; this refers to the number of pieces, not to the number of sockets (and in some cases even the metal box and plastic insert are counted in the total!).

Apart from well-known and respected brand names, you'll have to take a chance on the quality of the set you buy. If you know someone who has a set that has held up well, try to find the same brand, if possible. Take a few nuts and bolts with you and check the fit in some of the sockets. Check the operation of the ratchet. Good ones operate smoothly and crisply in small steps; cheap ones are coarse and stiff – a good basis for guessing the quality of the rest of the pieces.

One of the best things about a socket set is the built-in provision for expansion. Once you have a basic set, you can purchase extra sockets when needed and replace worn or damaged tools. There are special deep sockets for reaching recessed fasteners or to allow the socket to fit over a projecting bolt or stud **(see illustration 2.17)**. You can also buy screwdriver, Allen and Torx bits to fit various drive tools (they can be very handy in some applications) **(see illustration 2.18)**. Most socket sets include a special deep socket for spark plugs. They have rubber inserts to protect the spark plug porcelain insulator and hold the plug in the socket to avoid burned fingers.

Torque wrenches

Torque wrenches compliment the socket set, since they require the use of a socket so a fastener can be tightened accurately to a specified torque figure. To attempt an engine overhaul without a torque wrench is to invite oil leaks, distortion of the cylinder head, damaged or stripped threads or worse.

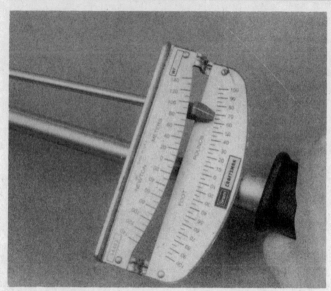

2.19 A simple, inexpensive, deflecting beam torque wrench will be adequate for small engine repairs – the torque figure is read off the scale near the handle

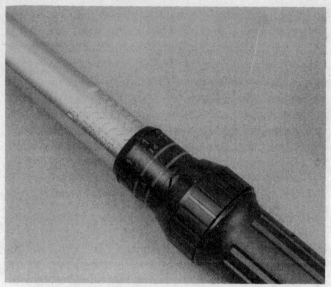

2.20 "Click" type torque wrenches can be set to "give" at a pre-set torque, which makes them very accurate and easy to use

The cheapest type of torque wrench consists of a long handle designed to bend as pressure increases. A long pointer is fixed to the drive end and reads off a scale near the handle as the fastener is tightened (see illustration 2.19). This type of torque wrench is simple and usually accurate enough for most jobs. Another version is the pre-set or "click" type. The torque figure required is dialed in on a scale before use (see illustration 2.20). The tool gives a positive indication, usually a loud click and/or a sudden movement of the handle, when the desired torque is reached. Needless to say, the pre-set type is far more expensive than the beam type – you alone can decide which type you need. For occasional use, go for the cheaper beam type.

Torque wrenches are available in a variety of drive sizes and torque ranges for particular applications. For small engine use, the range required is lower than for cars or trucks; 0 to 75 ft-lbs should be adequate. However, if you anticipate doing car repairs in the future, you may want to take that into consideration when buying a torque wrench – try to settle on one that'll be usable for both.

Impact drivers

The impact driver belongs with the screwdrivers, but it's mentioned here since it can also be used with sockets (impact drivers normally are 3/8-inch square drive). An impact driver works by converting a hammer blow on the end of its handle into a sharp twisting movement. While this is a great way to jar a seized fastener loose, the loads imposed on the socket are excessive. Use sockets only with discretion and expect to have to replace damaged ones occasionally.

Using wrenches and sockets

In the last section we looked at some of the various types of wrenches available, with a few suggestions about building up a tool collection without bankrupting yourself. Here we're more concerned with using the tools in actual work. Although you may feel it's self-explanatory, it's worth some thought. After all, when did you last see instructions for use supplied with a set of wrenches?

Before you start tearing an engine apart, figure out the best tool for the job; in this instance the best wrench for a hex-head fastener. Sit down with a few nuts and bolts and look at how various tools fit the bolt heads.

A good rule of thumb is to choose a tool that contacts the largest area of the hex-head. This distributes the load as evenly as possible and lessens the risk of damage. The shape most closely resembling the bolt head or nut is another hex, so a 6-point socket or box-end wrench is usually the best choice **(see illustration 2.21)**. Many sockets and box-end wrenches have double hex (12-point) openings. If you slip a 12-point box-end wrench over a nut, look at how and where the two are in contact. The corners of the nut engage in every other point of the wrench. When the wrench is turned, pressure is applied evenly on each of the six corners **(see illustration 2.22)**. This is fine unless the fastener head was previously rounded off or is made of extremely poor quality (soft) material. If so, the corners will be damaged and the wrench will slip. If you encounter a damaged bolt head or nut, always use a 6-point wrench or socket if possible. If you don't have one in the right size, choose a 12-point wrench or socket that fits securely and proceed carefully.

If you slip an open-end wrench over a hex-head fastener, you'll see the tool is in contact on two faces only **(see illustration 2.23)**. This is acceptable provided the tool and fastener are both in good condition. The need for a snug fit between the wrench and nut or bolt explains the recommendation to buy good-quality open-end wrenches. If the wrench jaws, the bolt head or both are damaged, the wrench will probably slip, rounding off and distorting the head. In some applications, an open-end wrench is the only possible choice due to limited access, but always check the fit of the wrench on the fastener before attempting to loosen it; if it's hard to get at with a wrench, think how hard it will be to remove after the head is damaged.

The last choice is an adjustable wrench or self-locking plier/wrench (Vise-Grips). Use these tools only when all else has failed. In some cases, a self-locking wrench may be able to grip a damaged head that no wrench could deal with, but be careful not to make matters worse by damaging it further.

Bearing in mind the remarks about the correct choice of tool in the first place, there are several things worth noting about the actual use of the tool. First, make sure the wrench head is clean and undamaged. If the fastener is rusted or coated with paint, the wrench won't fit correctly. Clean off the head and, if it's rusted, apply some penetrating oil. Leave it to soak in for a while before attempting removal.

It may seem obvious, but take a close look at the fastener to be removed before using a wrench. On many mass-produced machines, one end of a fastener may be fixed or captive, which speeds up initial assembly and usually makes removal easier. If a nut is installed on a stud or a bolt threads into a captive nut or tapped hole, you may have only one fastener to deal with. If, on the other hand, you have a separate nut and bolt, you'll have to hold the bolt head while the nut is removed. In some areas this can be difficult, particularly where engine mount bolts are involved. In this type of situation you

Which wrench?

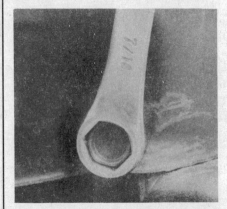

2.21   A 6-point box-end wrench or socket contacts the nut or bolt head entirely, which spreads out the force and tends to prevent rounded-off corners

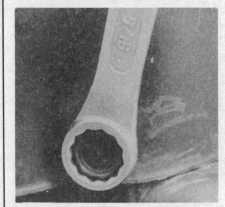

2.22   A 12-point box-end wrench or socket only contacts the nut or bolt head near the corners and concentrates the force at specific points, which leads to rounded-off fasteners and a frustrated mechanic

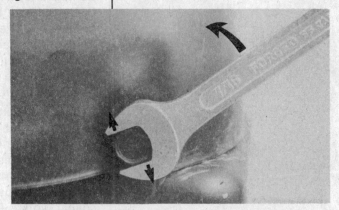

2.23   Open-end wrench jaws tend to spread apart when loosening tight fasteners and can quickly damage a nut or bolt

may need an assistant to hold the bolt head with a wrench, while you remove the nut from the other side. If this isn't possible, you'll have to try to position a box-end wrench so it wedges against some other component to prevent it from turning.

Be on the lookout for left-hand threads. They aren't common, but are sometimes used on the ends of rotating shafts to make sure the nut doesn't come loose during engine operation. If you can see the shaft end, the thread type can be checked visually. If you're unsure, place your thumbnail in the threads and see which way you have to turn your hand so your nail "unscrews" from the shaft. If you have to turn your hand counterclockwise, it's a conventional right-hand thread.

Beware of the upside-down fastener syndrome. If you're loosening an oil drain plug on the under side of a mower deck, for example, it's easy to get confused about which way to turn it. What seems like counterclockwise to you can easily be clockwise (from the plug's point of view). Even after years of experience, this can still catch you once in a while.

In most cases, a fastener can be removed simply by placing the wrench on the nut or bolt head and turning it. Occasionally, though, the condition or location of the fastener may make things more difficult. Make sure the wrench is square on the head. You may need to reposition the tool or try another type to obtain a snug fit. Make sure the engine you're working on is secure and can't move when you turn the wrench. If necessary, get someone to help steady it for you. Position yourself so you can get maximum leverage on the wrench.

If possible, locate the wrench so you can pull the end towards you. If you have to push on the tool, remember that it may slip, or the fastener may move suddenly. For this reason, don't curl your fingers around the handle or you may crush or bruise them when the fastener moves; keep your hand flat, pushing on the wrench with the heel of your thumb. If the tool digs into your hand, place a rag between it and your hand or wear a heavy glove.

If the fastener doesn't move with normal hand pressure, stop and try to figure out why before the fastener or wrench is damaged or you hurt yourself. Stuck fasteners may require penetrating oil, heat or an impact driver or air tool.

Using sockets to remove hex-head fasteners is less likely to result in damage than if a wrench is used. Make sure the socket fits snugly over the fastener head, then attach an extension, if needed, and the ratchet or breaker bar. Theoretically, a ratchet shouldn't be used for loosening a fastener or for final tightening because the ratchet mechanism may be overloaded and could slip. In some instances, the location of the fastener may mean you have no choice but to use a ratchet, in which case you'll have to be extra careful.

Never use extensions where they aren't needed. Whether or not an extension is used, always support the drive end of the breaker bar with one hand while turning it with the other. Once the fastener is loose, the ratchet can be used to speed up removal.

Pliers

Generally speaking, three types of pliers are needed when doing mechanic work: Slip-joint, arc-joint or "Channel-lock" and Vise-Grips. Although somewhat limited in use, needle-nose pliers and side (wire) cutters should be included if your budget will allow it.

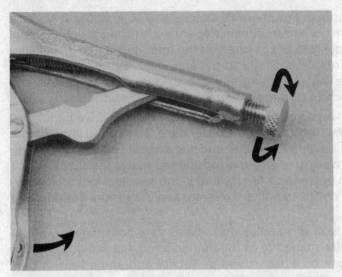

2.24 Vise-Grips are adjusted with the knurled bolt, then the handles are closed to lock the jaws on the part

2.25 As a last resort, you can use locking pliers to loosen a rusted or rounded-off nut or bolt

Slip-joint pliers have two open positions; a figure eight-shaped, elongated slot in one handle slips back-and-forth on a pivot pin on the other handle to change them. Good quality pliers have jaws made of tempered steel and there's usually a wire-cutter at the base of the jaws. The primary uses of slip-joint pliers are for holding objects, bending and cutting throttle wires and crimping and bending metal parts, not loosening nuts and bolts.

Arc-joint or "Channel-lock" pliers have parallel jaws that can be opened to various widths by engaging different tongues and grooves, or channels, near the pivot pin. Since the tool expands to fit many size objects, it has countless uses for small engine and equipment maintenance. Channel-lock pliers come in various sizes. The medium size is adequate for general work; small and large sizes are nice to have as your budget permits. You'll use all three sizes frequently.

Vise-Grips (a brand name) come in various sizes; the medium size with curved jaws is best for all-around work. However, buy a large and small one if possible, since they're often used in pairs. Although this tool falls somewhere between an adjustable wrench, a pair of pliers and a portable vise, it can be invaluable for loosening and tightening fasteners – it's the only pliers that should be used for this purpose.

The jaw opening is set by turning a knurled knob at the end of one handle. The jaws are placed over the head of the fastener and the handles are squeezed together, locking the tool onto the fastener (**see illustration 2.24**). The design of the tool allows extreme pressure to be applied at the jaws and a variety of jaw designs enable the tool to grip firmly even on damaged heads (**see illustration 2.25**). Vise-Grips are great for removing fasteners rounded off by badly-fitting wrenches.

As the name suggests, needle-nose pliers have long, thin jaws designed for reaching into holes and other restricted areas. Most needle-nose, or long-nose, pliers also have wire cutters at the base of the jaws.

Look for these qualitiies when buying pliers: Smooth operating handles and jaws, jaws that match up and grip evenly when the handles are closed, a nice finish and the word "forged" somewhere on the tool.

Haynes small engine repair manual

Screwdrivers

Screwdrivers come in innumerable shapes and sizes to fit the various screw head designs in common use. Regardless of the tool quality, the screwdrivers in most tool boxes rarely fit the intended screw heads very well. This is attributable not only to general wear, but also to misuse. Screwdrivers make very tempting and convenient pry bars, chisels and punches, uses which in turn make them very bad screwdrivers.

A screwdriver consists of a steel blade or shank with a drive tip formed at one end. The most common tips are standard (also called straight slot and flat-blade) and Phillips. The other end has a handle attached to it. Traditionally, handles were made from wood and secured to the shank, which had raised tangs to prevent it from turning in the handle. Most screwdrivers now come with plastic handles, which are generally more durable than wood.

The design and size of handles and blades vary considerably. Some handles are specially shaped to fit the human hand and provide a better grip. The shank may be either round or square and some have a hex-shaped bolster under the handle to accept a wrench to provide more leverage when trying to turn a stubborn screw. The shank diameter, tip size and overall length vary too. As a general rule, it's a good idea to use the longest screwdriver possible, which allows the greatest possible leverage.

If access is restricted, a number of special screwdrivers are designed to fit into confined spaces. The "stubby" screwdriver has a specially shortened handle and blade. There are also offset screwdrivers and special screwdriver bits that attach to a ratchet or extension.

Standard screwdrivers

These are used to remove and install conventional slotted screws and are available in a wide range of sizes denoting the width of the tip and the length of the shank (for example: A 3/8 x 10-inch screwdriver is 3/8-inch wide at the tip and the shank is 10-inches long). You should have a variety of screwdrivers so screws of various sizes can be dealt with without damaging them. The blade end must be the same width and thickness as the screw slot to work properly, without slipping. When selecting standard screwdrivers, choose good quality tools, preferably with chrome moly, forged steel shanks. The tip of the shank should be ground to a parallel, flat profile (hollow ground) and not to a taper or wedge shape, which will tend to twist out of the slot when pressure is applied **(see illustration 2.26)**.

All screwdrivers wear in use, but standard types can be reground to shape a number of times. When reshaping a tip, start by grinding the very end flat at right angles to the shank. Make sure the tip fits snugly in the slot of a screw of the appropriate size and keep the sides of the tip parallel. Remove only a small amount of metal at a time to avoid overheating the tip and destroying the temper of the steel.

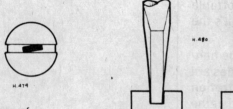

Misuse of a screwdriver – the blade shown is both too narrow and too thin and will probably slip or break off

The left-hand example shows a snug-fitting tip. The right-hand drawing shows a damaged tip which will twist out of the slot when pressure is applied

2.26 Standard screwdrivers – wrong size (left), correct fit in screw slot (center) and worn tip (right)

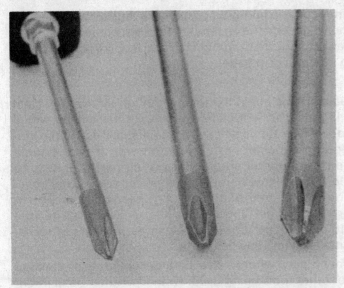

2.27 The tip size on a Phillips screwdriver is indicated by a number from 1 to 4, with 1 being the smallest (left – no. 1; center – no. 2; right – no. 3)

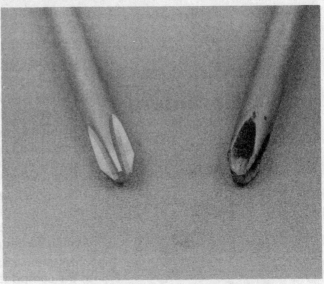

2.28 New (left) and worn (right) Phillips screwdriver tips

Phillips screwdrivers

Some engines have Phillips screws that are installed during initial assembly with air tools and are next to impossible to remove later without ruining the heads, particularly if the wrong size screwdriver is used. Be sure to use only Phillips type screwdrivers on them; other cross-head patterns are available, but they won't work on Phillips screws.

The only way to ensure the tools you buy will fit properly, is to take a couple of screws with you to make sure the fit between the screwdriver and fastener is snug. If the fit is good, you should be able to angle the blade down almost vertically without the screw slipping off the tip. Use only screwdrivers that fit exactly – anything else is guaranteed to chew out the screw head instantly.

The idea behind all cross-head screw designs is to make the screw and screwdriver blade self-aligning. Provided you aim the blade at the center of the screw head, it'll engage correctly, unlike conventional slotted screws, which need careful alignment. This makes the screws suitable for machine installation on an assembly line (which explains why they're usually so tight and difficult to remove). The drawback with these screws is the driving tangs on the screwdriver tip are very small and must fit very precisely in the screw head. If this isn't the case, the huge loads imposed on the small flats of the screw recess simply tear the metal away, at which point the screw ceases to be removable by normal methods. The problem is made worse by the normally soft material chosen for screws.

To deal with these screws on a regular basis, you'll need high-quality screwdrivers with various size tips so you'll be sure to have the right one when you need it. Phillips screwdrivers are sized by the tip number and length of the shank (for example: A number 2 x 6-inch Phillips screwdriver has a number 2 tip – to fit screws of only that size recess – and the shank is 6-inches long). Tip sizes 1, 2 and 3 should be adequate for small engine repair work (see illustration 2.27). If the tips get worn or damaged, buy new screwdrivers so the tools don't destroy the screws they're used on (see illustration 2.28).

Haynes small engine repair manual

Here's a tip that may come in handy when using Phillips screwdrivers – if the screw is extremely tight and the tip tends to back out of the recess rather than turn the screw, apply a small amount of valve lapping compound to the screwdriver tip so it will grip better.

Hammers

You'll need at least one ball-pein hammer, although almost any steel hammer will work in most cases. A ball-pein hammer has a head with a conventional cylindrical face at one end and a rounded ball end at the other and is a general-purpose tool found in almost any type of shop. It has a shorter neck than a claw hammer and the face is tempered for striking punches and chisels. A fairly large hammer is preferred over a small one. Although it's possible to find small ones, you won't need them very often and it's much easier to control the blows from a heavier head. As a general rule, a single 12 or 16-ounce hammer will work for most jobs, though occasionally larger or smaller ones may be useful.

A soft-face hammer is used where a steel hammer could cause damage to the component or other tools being used. A steel hammer head might crack an aluminum part, but a rubber or plastic hammer can be used with more confidence. Soft-face hammers are available with interchangeable heads (usually one made of rubber and another made of relatively hard plastic). When the heads are worn out, new ones can be installed. If finances are really limited, you can get by without a soft-face hammer by placing a small hardwood block between the component and a steel hammer head to prevent damage.

Hammers should be used with common sense; the head should strike the desired object squarely and with the right amount of force. For many jobs, little effort is needed – simply allow the weight of the head to do the work, using the length of the swing to control the amount of force applied. With practice, a hammer can be used with surprising finesse, but it'll take a while to achieve. Initial mistakes include striking the object at an angle, in which case the hammer head may glance off to one side, or hitting the edge of the object. Either one can result in damage to the part or to your thumb, if it gets in the way, so be careful. Hold the hammer handle near the end, not near the head, and grip it firmly but not too tightly.

Check the condition of your hammers on a regular basis. The danger of a loose head coming off is self-evident, but check the head for chips and cracks too. If damage is noted, buy a new hammer – the head may chip in use and the resulting fragments can be extremely dangerous. It goes without saying that eye protection is essential whenever a hammer is used.

Punches and chisels

These tools are used along with a hammer for various purposes in the shop. Drift punches are often simply a length of round steel bar used to drive a component out of a bore in the engine or equipment it's mounted on. A typical use would be for removing or installing a bearing or bushing. A drift of the same diameter as the bearing outer race is placed against the bearing and tapped with a hammer to drive it in or out of the bore. Most manufacturers offer special drifts for the various bearings in a particular engine. While they're useful to a busy dealer service department, they are prohibitively expensive for the do-it-yourselfer who may only need to use them once. In such cases, it's better to improvise. For bearing removal and installation it's usually possible to use a socket of the appropriate diameter to tap the bearing in or out; an unorthodox use for a socket, but it works.

Smaller diameter drift punches can be purchased or fabricated from steel bar stock. In some cases, you'll need to drive out items like corroded engine mounting bolts. Here, it's essential to avoid damaging the threaded end of the bolt, so the drift must be a softer material than the bolt. Brass or copper is the usual choice for such jobs; the drift may be damaged in use, but the thread will be protected.

Punches are available in various shapes and sizes and a set of assorted types will be very useful. One of the most basic is the center punch, a small cylindrical punch with the end ground to a point. It'll be needed whenever a hole is drilled. The center of the hole is located first and the punch is used to make a small indentation at the intended point. The indentation acts as a guide for the drill bit so the hole ends up in the right place. Without a punch mark the drill bit will wander and you'll find it impossible to drill with any real accuracy. You can also buy automatic center punches. They're spring loaded and are pressed against the surface to be marked, without the need to use a hammer.

Pin punches are intended for removing items like roll pins (semi-hard, hollow pins that fit tightly in their holes). Pin punches have other uses, however. You may occasionally have to remove rivets or bolts by cutting off the heads and driving out the shanks with a pin punch. They're also very handy for aligning holes in components while bolts or screws are inserted.

Of the various sizes and types of metal-cutting chisels available, a simple cold chisel is essential in any mechanic's workshop. One about 6-inches long with a 1/2-inch wide blade should be adequate. The cutting edge is ground to about 80-degrees **(see illustration 2.29),** while the rest of the tip is ground to a shallower angle away from the edge. The primary use of the cold chisel is rough metal cutting – this can be anything from sheet metal work (uncommon on small engines) to cutting off the heads of seized or rusted bolts or splitting nuts. A cold chisel can also be useful for turning out screws or bolts with messed up heads.

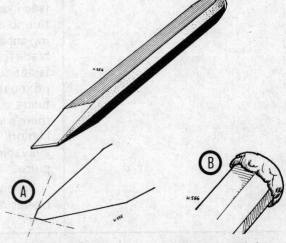

2.29   A typical general purpose cold chisel – note the angle of the cutting edge (A), which should be checked and resharpened on a regular basis; the mushroomed head (B) is dangerous and should be filed to restore it to its original shape

All of the tools described in this section should be good quality items. They're not particularly expensive, so it's not really worth trying to save money on them. More significantly, there's a risk that with cheap tools, fragments may break off in use – a potentially dangerous situation.

Even with good quality tools, the heads and working ends will inevitably get worn or damaged, so it's a good idea to maintain all such tools on a regular basis. Using a file or bench grinder, remove all burrs and mushroomed edges from around the head. This is an important task because the build-up of material around the head can fly off when it's struck with a hammer and is potentially dangerous. Make sure the tool retains its original profile at the working end, again, filing or grinding off all burrs. In the case of cold chisels, the cutting edge will usually have to be reground quite often because the material in the tool isn't usually much harder than materials typically being cut. Make sure the edge is reasonably sharp, but don't make the tip angle greater than it was originally; it'll just wear down faster if you do.

The techniques for using these tools vary according to the job to be done and are best learned by experience. The one common denominator is the fact they're all normally struck with a hammer. It follows that eye protection should be worn. Always make sure the working end of the tool is in contact with the part being punched or cut. If it isn't, the tool will bounce off the surface and damage may result.

Hacksaws

A hacksaw consists of a handle and frame supporting a flexible steel blade under tension. Blades are available in various lengths and most hacksaws can be adjusted to accommodate the different sizes. The most common blade length is 10-inches.

Most hacksaw frames are adequate and since they're simple tools, there's not much difference between brands. Try to pick one that's rigid when assembled and allows the blade to be changed or repositioned easily.

The type of blade to use, indicated by the number of teeth per inch (TPI) **(see illustration 2.30)** is determined by the material being cut. The rule of thumb is to make sure at least three teeth are in contact with the metal being cut at any one time **(see illustration 2.31)**. In practice, this means a fine blade for cutting thin sheet materials, while a coarser blade can be used for faster cutting through thicker items such as bolts or bar stock. It's worth noting that when cutting thin materials it's helpful to angle the saw so the blade cuts at a shallow angle. This way more teeth are in contact and there's less chance of the blade binding and breaking or teeth being broken off. This approach can also be used when a fine enough blade isn't available; the shallower the angle, the more teeth are contacting the workpiece.

When buying blades, choose a well-known brand. Cheap, unbranded blades may be perfectly acceptable, but you can't tell by looking at them.

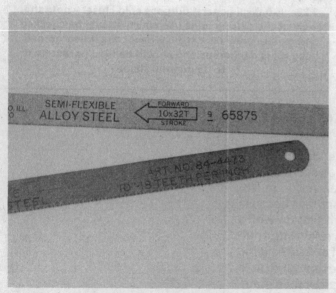

2.30   Hacksaw blades are marked with the number of teeth per inch (TPI) – use a relatively coarse blade for aluminum and a fine blade for steel

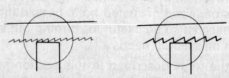

When cutting thin materials, check that at least three teeth are in contact with the workpiece at any time. Too coarse a blade will result in a poor cut and may break the blade. If you do not have the correct blade, cut at a shallow angle to the material

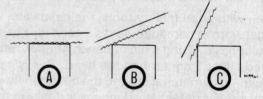

The correct cutting angle is important. If it is too shallow (A) the blade will wander. The angle shown at (B) is correct when starting the cut, and may be reduced slightly once under way. In (C) the angle is too steep and the blade will be inclined to jump out of the cut

2.31   Correct procedure for use of a hacksaw

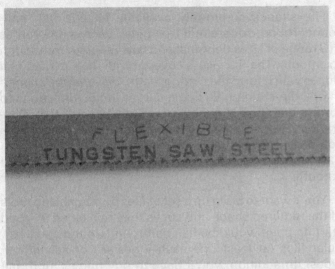

2.32 Good quality hacksaw blades will be marked like this

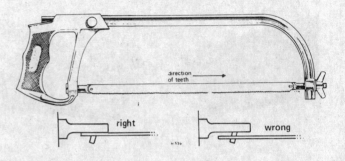

2.33 Correct installation of a hacksaw blade – the teeth must point away from the handle and butt against the locating lugs

Poor quality blades will be insufficiently hardened on the teeth edge and will dull quickly. Most reputable brands will be marked "Flexible High Speed Steel" or something similar, giving some indication of the material they're made of (see illustration 2.32). It is possible to buy "unbreakable" blades (only the teeth are hardened, leaving the rest of the blade less brittle).

In some situations, a full-size hacksaw is too big to allow access to a frozen nut or bolt. Sometimes this can be overcome by turning the blade 90-degrees – most saws allow this to be done. Occasionally you may have to position the saw around an obstacle and then install the blade on the other side of it. Where space is really restricted, you may have to use a handle that clamps onto a saw blade at one end. This allows access when a hacksaw frame would not work at all and has another advantage in that you can make use of broken off hacksaw blades instead of throwing them away. Note that because only one end of the blade is supported, and it's not held under tension, it's difficult to control and less efficient when cutting.

Before using a hacksaw, make sure the blade is suitable for the material being cut and installed correctly in the frame (see illustration 2.33). Whatever it is you're cutting must be securely supported so it can't move around. The saw cuts on the forward stroke, so the teeth must point away from the handle. This might seem obvious, but it's easy to install the blade backwards by mistake and ruin the teeth on the first few strokes. Make sure the blade is tensioned adequately or it'll distort and chatter in the cut and may break. Wear safety glasses and be careful not to cut yourself on the saw blade or the sharp edge of the cut.

Files

Files come in a wide variety of sizes and types for specific jobs, but all of them are used for the same basic function of removing small amounts of metal in a controlled fashion. Files are used by mechanics mainly for deburring, marking parts, removing rust, filing the heads off rivets, restoring threads and fabricating small parts.

2.34   Files will be either single-cut (left) or double-cut (right) – generally speaking, use a single cut file to produce a very smooth surface; use a double-cut file to remove large amounts of material quickly

File shapes commonly available include flat, half-round, round, square and triangular. Each shape comes in a range of sizes (lengths) and cuts ranging from rough to smooth. The file face is covered with rows of diagonal ridges which form the cutting teeth. They may be aligned in one direction only (single cut) or in two directions to form a diamond-shaped pattern (double-cut) **(see illustration 2.34)**. The spacing of the teeth determines the file coarseness, again, ranging from rough to smooth in five basic grades: Rough, coarse, bastard, second-cut and smooth.

You'll want to build up a set of files by purchasing tools of the required shape and cut as they're needed. A good starting point would be flat, half-round, round and triangular files (at least one each – bastard or second-cut types). In addition, you'll have to buy one or more file handles (files are usually sold without handles, which are purchased separately and pushed over the tapered tang of the file when in use) **(see illustraation 2.35)**. You may need to buy more than one size handle to fit the various files in your tool box, but don't attempt to get by without them. A file tang is fairly sharp and you almost certainly will end up stabbing yourself in the palm of the hand if you use a file without a handle and it catches in the workpiece during use. Adjustable handles are also available for use with files of various sizes, eliminating the need for several handles **(see illustration 2.36)**.

Exceptions to the need for a handle are fine swiss pattern files, which have a rounded handle instead of a tang. These small files are usually sold in sets with a number of different shapes. Originally intended for very fine work, they can be very useful for use in inaccessible areas. Swiss files are normally the best choice if piston ring ends require filing to obtain the correct end gap.

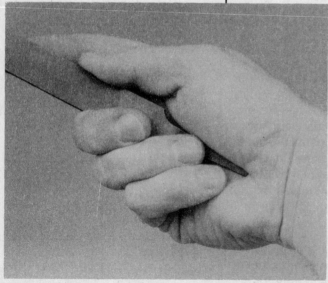

2.35   Never use a file without a handle – the tang is sharp and could puncture your hand

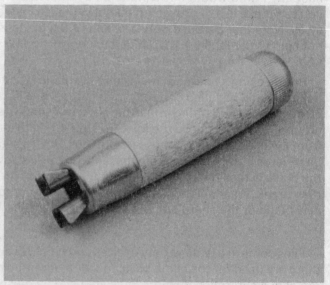

2.36   Adjustable handles that will work with many different size files are also available

The correct procedure for using files is fairly easy to master. As with a hacksaw, the work should be clamped securely in a vise, if needed, to prevent it from moving around while being worked on. Hold the file by the handle, using your free hand at the file end to guide it and keep it flat in relation to the surface being filed. Use smooth cutting strokes and be careful not to rock the file as it passes over the surface. Also, don't slide it diagonally across the surface or the teeth will make grooves in the workpiece. Don't drag a file back across the workpiece at the end of the stroke – lift it slightly and pull it back to prevent damage to the teeth.

Files don't require maintenance in the usual sense, but they should be kept clean and free of metal filings. Steel is a reasonably easy material to work with, but softer metals like aluminium tend to clog the file teeth very quickly, which will result in scratches in the workpiece. This can be avoided by rubbing the file face with chalk before using it. General cleaning is done with a file card or a fine wire brush. If they're kept clean, files will last a long time – when they do eventually dull, they must be replaced; there is no satisfactory way of sharpening a worn file.

Drills are often needed to remove rusted or broken off fasteners, enlarge holes and fabricate small parts.

Drilling operations are done with twist drills, either in a hand drill or a drill press. Twist drills (or drill bits, as they're often called) consist of a round shank with spiral flutes formed into the upper two-thirds to clear the waste produced while drilling, keep the drill centered in the hole and finish the sides of the hole.

The lower portion of the shank is left plain and used to hold the drill in the chuck. In this section, we'll cover only parallel shank drill bits **(see illustration 2.37)**. There is another type of bit with the plain end formed into a special taper designed to fit directly into a corresponding socket in a heavy-duty drill press. These drills are known as Morse Taper drills and are used primarily in machine shops.

At the cutting end of the drill, two edges are ground to form a conical point. They're generally angled at about 60-degrees from the drill axis, but they can be reground to other angles for specific applications. For general use, the standard angle is correct – this is how drill bits are sold.

When buying bits, purchase a good-quality set (sizes 1/16 to 3/8-inch). Make sure they're marked "High Speed Steel" or "HSS", which indicates they're hard enough to withstand continual use in metal; many cheaper, unmarked bits are suitable only for use in wood or other soft materials. Buying a set ensures the right size bit will be available when it's needed.

Twist drills and drilling equipment

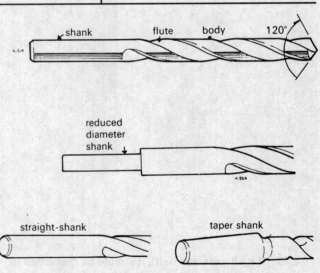

2.37   A typical drill bit (top), a reduced shank bit (center) and a tapered shank bit (bottom right)

Twist drill sizes

Twist drills are available in a vast array of sizes, most of which you'll never need. There are three basic drill sizing systems: Fractional, number and letter **(see illustration 2.38)** (we won't get involved with the fourth system, which is metric sizes).

Fractional sizes start at 1/64-inch and increase in increments of 1/64-inch. Number drills range in descending order from 80 (0.0135-inch), the smallest, to 1 (0.2280-inch), the largest. Letter sizes start with A (0.234-inch), the smallest, and go through Z (0.413-inch), the largest.

This bewildering range of sizes means it's possible to drill an accurate hole of almost any size within reason. In practice, you'll be limited by the size of chuck on your drill (normally 3/8 or 1/2-inch). In addition, very few stores stock all sizes, so you'll have to shop around for the nearest available size to the one you need.

2.38   Drill bits in the range most commonly used are available in fractional sizes (left) and number sizes (right) so almost any size hole can be drilled

Sharpening twist drills

Like any tool with a cutting edge, twist drills will eventually get dull **(see illustration 2.39)**. How often they'll need sharpening depends to some extent on whether they're used correctly. A dull twist drill will be obvious in use. A good indication of the condition of the cutting edges is to watch the waste emerging from the hole being drilled. If the tip is in good condition, two even spirals of waste metal will be produced; if this fails to happen or the tip gets hot, it's safe to assume that sharpening is required.

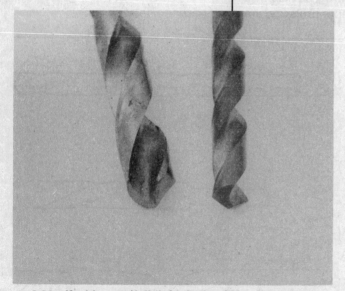

2.39   If a bit gets dull (left), it should be discarded or resharpened so it looks like the one on the right

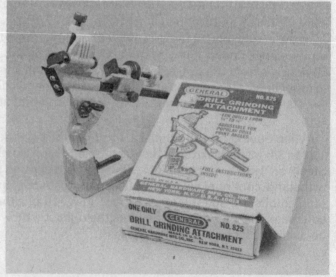

2.40   Inexpensive drill bit sharpening jigs for use with a bench grinder are widely available – even if you use it infrequently to resharpen drill bits, it'll pay for itself quickly

With smaller size drill bits – under about 1/8-inch – it's easier and more economical to throw the worn bit away and buy another one. With larger (more expensive) sizes, sharpening is a better bet. When sharpening twist drills, the included angle of the cutting edge must be maintained at the original 120-degrees and the small chisel edge at the tip must be retained. With some practice, sharpening can be done freehand on a bench grinder, but it should be noted that it's very easy to make mistakes. For most home mechanics, a sharpening jig that mounts next to the grinding wheel should be used so the drill is held at the correct angle **(see illustration 2.40)**.

Drilling equipment

Tools to hold and turn drill bits range from simple, inexpensive hand-operated or electric drills to sophisticated and expensive drill presses. Ideally, all drilling should be done on a drill press with the workpiece clamped solidly in a vise. These machines are expensive and take up a lot of bench or floor space, so they're out of the question for many do-it-yourselfers. An additional problem is the fact that many of the drilling jobs you end up doing will be on the engine itself or the equipment it's mounted on, in which case the tool has to be taken to the work.

The best tool for the home shop is an electric drill with a 3/8-inch chuck. As mentioned in Chapter 1, both cordless and AC drills (that run off household current) are available. If you're purchasing one for the first time, look for a well-known, reputable brand name and variable speed as minimum requirements. A 1/4-inch chuck, single-speed drill will work, but it's worth paying a little more for the larger, variable speed type.

All drills require a key to lock the bit in the chuck. When removing or installing a bit, make sure the cord is unplugged to avoid accidents. Initially, tighten the chuck by hand, checking to see if the bit is centered correctly. This is especially important when using small drill bits that can get caught between the jaws. Once the chuck is hand tight, use the key to tighten it securely – remember to remove the key afterwards!

Drilling and finishing holes

Preparation for drilling

If possible, make sure the part you intend to drill in is securely clamped in a vise. If it's impossible to get the work to a vise, make sure it's stable and secure. Drill bits often catch during drilling – this can be dangerous, particularly if the work suddenly starts spinning on the end of the drill. Obviously, there's not much chance of a complete engine or piece of equipment doing this, but you should make sure it's supported securely.

Start by locating the center of the hole you're drilling. Use a center punch to make an indentation for the drill bit so it won't wander. If you're drilling out a broken-off bolt, be sure to position the punch in the exact center of the bolt **(see illustration 2.61)**.

If you're drilling a large hole (above 1/4-inch), you may want to make a pilot hole first. As the name suggests, it will guide the larger drill bit and minimize bit wandering. Before actually drilling a hole, make sure the area immediately behind the bit is clear of anything you don't want drilled.

Drilling

When drilling steel, especially with smaller bits, no lubrication is needed. If a large bit is involved, oil can be used to ensure a clean cut and prevent overheating of the drill tip. When drilling aluminum, which tends to cling to the cutting edges and clog the drill bit flutes, use kerosene as a lubricant.

Wear safety goggles or a face shield and assume a comfortable, stable stance so you can control the pressure on the drill easily. Position the drill tip in the punch mark and make sure, if you're drilling by hand, the bit is perpendicular to the surface of the workpiece. Start drilling without applying much pressure until you're sure the hole is positioned correctly. If the hole starts off center, it can be very difficult to correct. You can try angling the bit slightly so the hole center moves in the opposite direction, but this must be done before the flutes of the bit have entered the hole. It's at the starting point that a variable-speed drill is invaluable; the low speed allows fine adjustments to be made before it's too late. Continue drilling until the desired hole depth is reached or until the drill tip emerges from the other side of the workpiece.

Cutting speed and pressure are important – as a general rule, the larger the diameter of the drill bit, the slower the drilling speed should be. With a single-speed drill, there's little that can be done to control it, but two-speed or variable speed drills can be controlled. If the drilling speed is too high, the cutting edges of the bit will tend to overheat and dull. Pressure should be varied during drilling. Start with light pressure until the drill tip has located properly in the work. Gradually increase pressure so the bit cuts evenly. If the tip is sharp and the pressure correct, two distinct spirals of metal will emerge from the bit flutes. If the pressure is too light, the bit won't cut properly, while excessive pressure will overheat the tip.

Decrease pressure as the bit breaks through the workpiece. If this isn't done, the bit may jam in the hole; if you're using a hand-held drill, it could be jerked out of your hands, especially when using larger size bits.

Once a pilot hole has been made, install the larger bit in the chuck and enlarge the hole. The second bit will follow the pilot hole – there's no need to attempt to guide it (if you do, the bit may break off). It is important, however, to hold the drill at the correct angle.

After the hole has been drilled to the correct size, remove the burrs left around the edges of the hole. This can be done with a small round file, or by chamfering the opening with a larger bit or a countersink **(see illustration 2.41)**. Use a drill bit that's several sizes larger than the hole and simply twist it around each opening by hand until any rough edges are removed.

2.41   Use a large drill bit or a countersink mounted in a tap wrench to remove burrs from a hole after drilling or enlarging it

Enlarging and reshaping holes

The biggest practical size for bits used in a hand drill is about 1/2-inch. This is partly determined by the capacity of the chuck (although it's possible to buy larger drills with stepped shanks). The real limit is the difficulty of controlling large bits by hand; drills over 1/2-inch tend to be too much to handle in anything other than a drill press. If you have to make a larger hole, or if a shape other than round is involved, different techniques are required.

If a hole simply must be enlarged slightly, a round file is probably the best tool to use. If the hole must be very large, a hole saw will be needed, but they can only be used in sheet metal and other thin materials.

Large or irregular-shaped holes can also be made in relatively thin materials by drilling a series of small holes very close together. In this case the desired hole size and shape must be marked with a scribe. The next step depends on the size bit to be used; the idea is to drill a series of almost touching holes just inside the outline of the large hole. Center punch each hole location, then drill them out. A cold chisel is used to knock out the waste material at the center of the hole, which can then be filed to size. This is a time consuming process, but it's the only practical approach for the home shop. Success is dependent on accuracy when marking the hole shape and using the center punch.

Taps and dies

Taps

Taps, which are available in inch and metric sizes, are used to cut internal threads and clean or restore damaged threads. A tap consists of a fluted shank with a drive square at one end. It's threaded along part of its length – the cutting edges are formed where the flutes intersect the threads **(see illustration 2.42)**. Taps are made from hardened steel so they'll cut threads in materials softer than what they're made of.

Taps come in three different types: Taper, plug and bottoming. The only real difference is the length of the chamfer on the cutting end of the tap. Taper taps are chamfered for the first 6 or 8 threads, which makes them easy to start but prevents them from cutting threads close to the bottom of a hole. Plug taps are chamfered up about 3 to 5 threads, which makes them a good all around tap because they're relatively easy to start and will cut nearly to the bottom of a hole. Bottoming taps, as the name implies, have a very short chamfer (1-1/2 to 3 threads) and will cut as close to the bottom of a blind hole as practical. However, to do this, the threads should be started with a plug or taper tap.

Although cheap tap and die sets are available, the quality is usually very low and they can actually do more harm than good when used on threaded holes in aluminum engines. The alternative is to buy high-quality taps if and when you need them, even though they aren't cheap, especially if you need to buy two or more thread pitches in a given size. Despite this, it's the best option – you'll probably only need taps on rare occasions, so a full set isn't absolutely necessary.

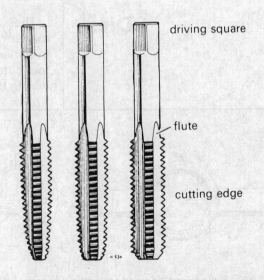

2.42   Taper, plug and bottoming taps (left-to-right)

driving square

flute

cutting edge

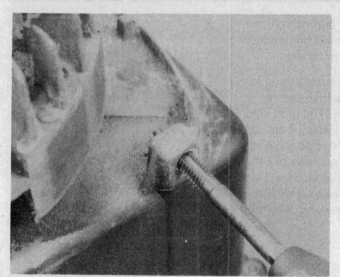

2.43   You'll run into many situations where a tap is needed to clean up or restore threads when working on small engines

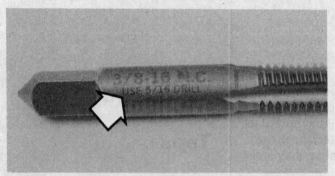

2.44   If you need to drill and tap a hole, the drill bit size to use for a given bolt (tap) size is marked on the tap

Taps are normally used by hand (they can be used in machine tools, but not when doing engine repairs). The square drive end of the tap is held in a tap wrench (an adjustable T-handle). For smaller sizes, a T-handled chuck can be used **(see illustration 2.43)**. The tapping process starts by drilling a hole of the correct diameter. For each tap size, there's a corresponding twist drill that will produce a hole of the correct size. This is important; too large a hole will leave the finished thread with the tops missing, producing a weak and unreliable grip. Conversely, too small a hole will place excessive loads on the hard and brittle shank of the tap, which can break it off in the hole. Removing a broken off tap from a hole is no fun!

The correct tap drill size is normally marked on the tap itself or the container it comes in **(see illustration 2.44)**.

Dies

Dies are used to cut, clean or restore external threads. Most dies are made from a hex-shaped or cylindrical piece of hardened steel with a threaded hole in the center. The threaded hole is overlapped by three or four cutouts, which equate to the flutes on taps and allow waste to escape during the threading process. Dies are held in a T-handle holder (called a die stock) **(see illustration 2.45)**. Some dies are split at one point, allowing them to be adjusted slightly (opened and closed) for fine control of thread clearances.

Dies aren't needed as often as taps, for the simple reason it's normally easier to install a new bolt than to salvage one. However, it's often helpful to be able to extend the threads of a bolt or clean up damaged threads with a die. Hex-shaped dies are particularly useful for mechanic work, since they can be turned

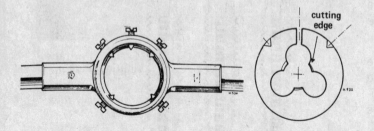

cutting edge

2.45   A die (right) is used for cutting external threads (this one is a split-type/adjustable die) and is held in a tool called a die stock (leftt)

with a wrench **(see illustration 2.46)** and are usually less expensive than adjustable ones.

The procedure for cutting threads with a die is similar to the one for taps. When using an adjustable die, the initial cut is made with the die open as far as possible. The adjustment screw is then used to reduce the diameter of successive cuts until the desired finished size is reached. As with taps, cutting oil should be used and the die must be backed off every few turns to clear waste from the cut-outs.

2.46   Hex-shaped dies are especially handy for mechanic work because they can be turned with a wrench

Pullers

During every engine overhaul, and many simple repairs, you'll often need some type of puller. The most common pullers are required for removal of the magneto flywheel from the end of the crankshaft. Other less common tasks that'll require some sort of puller include the removal of bushings and bearings. Common to all of these jobs is the need to exert pressure on the part being removed while avoiding damage to the surrounding area or components. The best way to do this is with a puller specially designed for the job.

As mentioned in Chapter 1, it's a good idea to have procedures that require a puller (other than flywheel removal) done by a dealer or repair shop, then you won't have to invest in a tool that won't be used very often.

Special pullers

A good example of a special puller is the one needed for removal of the magneto flywheel. On most engines, the flywheel fits over the tapered end of the crankshaft, where it's secured by a large nut and located by a Woodruff key. Even after the nut has been removed, you have to exert lots of pressure to draw the flywheel off the shaft. This is because the nut draws the tapered faces on the shaft and the inside of the flywheel hub together very tightly during assembly.

The method normally used to remove the flywheel requires a specially designed puller that fits over the crankshaft end and has bolts that thread into holes in the flywheel hub. After the bolts are threaded into place (they often will have to cut their own threads in the holes, but they're designed to do so), the lower nuts are tightened down against the flywheel and the upper nuts are tightened in 1/4-turn increments until the flywheel pops loose **(see illustration 2.47)**.

Flywheel "knock-off" tools are also available for Briggs & Stratton and Tecumseh engines. **Note:** *Briggs and Stratton does not endorse or recommend the use of flywheel knock-off tools on their engines, while Tecumseh does. A knock-off tool should not be used on any engine that has a ball bearing on the flywheel side of the crankshaft.* The tool is slipped over or threaded onto the end of the crankshaft until it contacts the flywheel, then it's backed off one or two turns. Moderate pressure is

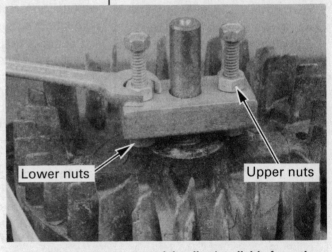

Lower nuts   Upper nuts

2.47   In most cases, a special puller (available from the engine manufacturer) will be needed for removing the flywheel – in this example (Briggs & Stratton engine shown), the puller body is slipped over the end of the crankshaft, the bolts are threaded into the flywheel holes (they may have to cut their own threads if the flywheel has never been removed before), the lower nuts are tightened against the flywheel and the upper nuts are tightened in 1/4-turn increments until the flywheel pops off the shaft taper

applied to the flywheel with a large screwdriver and the end of the knock-off tool is struck with a hammer – the blow from the hammer will usually pop the flywheel loose.

Using a puller means the pressure on the flywheel is applied where it does the most good – at the center of the hub, rather than at the edge, where it would be more likely to distort the flywheel than release the hub from the shaft taper. Read Chapter 1 to find out about specific pullers for the engines covered in this manual.

General-purpose pullers

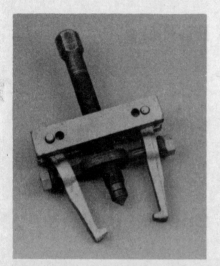

2.48   A two or three-jaw puller will come in handy for many tasks in the shop and can also be used for working on other types of equipment

You're likely to need some sort of general-purpose puller at some point in most overhauls, often where parts are seized or corroded, or where bushings or bearings must be removed. Universal two and three-jaw pullers are widely available in numerous designs and sizes.

These tools generally have jaws attached to a large center boss, which has a threaded hole to accept the puller bolt. The ends of the jaws have hooks which locate on and grip the part to be pulled off **(see illustration 2.48)**. Normally, the jaws can be reversed to allow the tool to be used on internal bushings and bearings as well. The jaws are hooked over the part being removed and the puller bolt is positioned against the end of the shaft. As the bolt is tightened, the component is drawn off the shaft.

It's possible to adapt pullers by making special jaws for specific jobs, but it'll take extra time and may not be successful. If you decide to try this approach, remember that the force should be concentrated as close to the center of the component as possible to avoid damaging it.

When using a puller, it should be assembled and a careful check should be made to ensure it doesn't snag on anything and the loads on the part to be removed are distributed evenly. If you're dealing with a part held on a shaft by a nut, loosen the nut, but don't remove it entirely. It will help prevent distortion of the shaft end under pressure from the puller bolt and will also stop the part from flying off the shaft when it comes loose.

Pullers of this type should be tightened gradually until moderate pressure is applied to the part being removed. **Caution:** *The puller bolt should never be tightened excessively or damage will occur!* Once it's under pressure, try to jar the component loose by striking the puller bolt head with a hammer. If this doesn't work, tighten the bolt a little more and repeat the procedure. The component should come off the shaft with a distinctive "pop". The puller can then be detached, the nut removed from the shaft (if applicable) and the part pulled off.

If the above approach doesn't work, it's time to stop and reconsider what you're doing. Proceed with caution – at some point a decision must be made whether it's wise to continue applying pressure in this manner. If the component is unusually tight, something will probably break before it comes off. If you find yourself in this situation, try applying penetrating oil around the joint and leaving it overnight, with the puller in place and tightened securely. In some cases, the taper will separate and the problem will resolve itself by the next morning.

If you have the necessary equipment, are skilled in its use and take the necessary safety precautions, you can try heating the component with a propane or gas welding torch. This can be a good way to release a stubborn part, but isn't recommended unless you have experience doing it. **Caution:** *This approach should be used with extreme caution on a flywheel – the heat can easily demagnetize it or cause damage to the coil windings.*

The heat should be applied to the hub area of the component to be removed, keeping the flame moving to avoid uneven heating and the risk of distortion. Keep pressure applied with the puller and make sure you're able to deal with the resulting hot component and the puller jaws if it does come free (wear gloves to protect your hands). Be very careful to keep the flame away from aluminum parts.

If all rational methods fail, don't be afraid to give up an attempt to remove something; it's cheaper than repairing a badly damaged engine. Either buy or borrow the correct tool or take the engine to a dealer and ask him to remove the part for you.

Drawbolts

A simple drawbolt extractor is easy to make and invaluable in many situations. There are no standard, commercially available tools of this type; you simply make a tool to suit a particular application. You can use a drawbolt to pull out stubborn piston pins and to remove bearings and bushings.

To make a drawbolt extractor, you'll need an assortment of threaded rods in various sizes (available at hardware stores), along with nuts to fit them. In addition, you'll need assorted washers, spacers and pieces of pipe. Don't forget to improvise where you can. A socket set can provide several sizes of spacers for short parts like bushings. For things like piston pins you'll usually need a longer piece of pipe.

Some typical drawbolt uses are shown in **illustration 2.49** – they also reveal the order of assembly of the various pieces. The same arrangement, minus the spacer, can usually be used to install a new bushing or piston pin. Using the tool is quite simple – the main thing to watch out for is to make sure you get the bushing or pin square in the bore when it's installed. Lubricate the part being pressed into place, if appropriate.

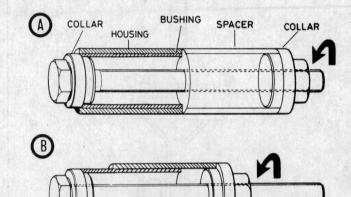

2.49 Typical drawbolt uses – in A, the nut is tightened to pull the collar and bushing into the large spacer; in B, the spacer is left out and the drawbolt is repositioned to install the new bushing

Pullers for use in blind holes

You may encounter bushings or bearings installed in blind holes in almost any engine; there are special pullers designed to deal with them as well. In the case of engine bearings, it's sometimes possible to remove them without a puller if you heat the engine or component evenly (in an oven) and tap it face down on a clean wooden surface to dislodge the bearing. If you use this method, be careful not to burn yourself when handling the heated components – wear heavy gloves! If a puller is needed, a slide-hammer with interchangeable tips is your best bet. They range from universal two or three jaw puller arrangements to special bearing pullers. Bearing pullers are hardened steel tubes with a flange around the bottom edge. The tube is split at several places, which allows a wedge to expand the tool once it's in place. The tool fits inside the bearing inner race and is tightened so the flange or lip is locked under the edge of the race.

A slide-hammer consists of a steel shaft with a stop at the upper end. The shaft carries a sliding weight, which is moved along the shaft until it strikes the stop. This allows the tool holding the bearing to drive it out of

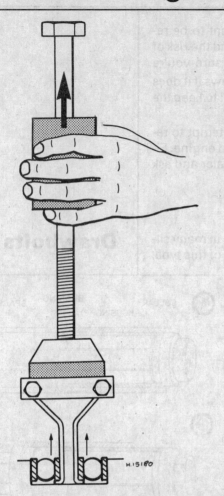

2.50   A slide hammer with special attachments can be used for removing bearings and bushings from blind holes

the bore (**see illustration 2.50**). A bearing puller set is an expensive and infrequently-used piece of equipment – to avoid the expense of buying one, as mentioned in Chapter 1, take the engine to a dealer and have the bearings/bushings replaced.

Precision measurements

During any overhaul or major repair job, you'll need certain precision measuring devices to determine the amount of wear that has occurred and whether or not a component can be reused in the rebuilt engine. In addition, some of the more basic tools, like feeler gauges, are needed for routine service and tune-up work. In this section we'll look at the most commonly-needed tools, starting with those that are considered essential, and working up to more specialized and expensive items. Some of them, such as vernier calipers and micrometers, are specialized pieces of equipment, but – unless you have someone else do the measuring for you – no substitutes are available.

Feeler gauges

These are essential for work on almost any engine. If it's a four-stroke, or has ignition points, you'll need feeler gauges to check/set the valve or ignition point clearances.

Feeler gauges normally come in sets. In smaller sets, different feeler gauges must be combined to make up thicknesses not included separately. Larger sets have a wider range of sizes to avoid this problem. Feeler gauges are available in both inch and metric sizes; they're usually marked

2.51   Feeler gauges are usually marked with inch and
metric equivalents

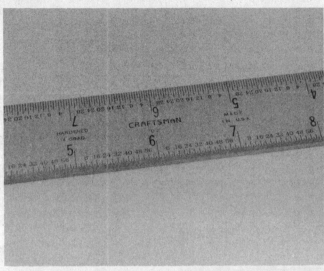

2.52   A steel rule will come in handy in any shop – if it's
a good-quality tool, it can be used for checking engine
components (like the cylinder head) for distortion

both ways **(see illustration 2.51)**. Blade-type feeler gauges are thin steel strips and are the best choice for most purposes. There are also wire-type feeler gauges, which may be preferable in some circumstances.

You'll need feeler gauges whenever you have to make an accurate measurement of a small gap (typical applications are checking valve clearances on four-stroke engines and endplay in crankshafts or camshafts). You can also use feeler gauges when checking for distortion of gasket surfaces. The cover or casting is placed, gasket surface down, on a flat plate and any gap (which indicates distortion) can be measured directly with feeler gauges.

To measure a gap with feeler gauges, slide progressively thicker blades into the gap until you find the size that fits with a slight drag as it's moved back-and-forth.

Rulers

A basic steel rule is another essential workshop item. It can be used for measurements and layout work and as a straightedge for checking warpage of gasket surfaces **(see illustration 2.52)**. Buy the best quality tool you can afford and keep it out of your toolbox or it'll soon get bent or damaged.

Dial indicators

The dial gauge, or dial indicator as it's more commonly known, consists of a short stem attached to a clock-type dial capable of indicating small amounts of movement very accurately (generally in 1/1000-inch increments). These test instruments are generally useful for checking runout in shafts and other rotating components. The gauge is attached to a holder or bracket and the stem positioned so it rests on the shaft being checked. The rotating face of the dial is set to zero in relation to the pointer, the shaft is turned and the movement of the needle noted.

Haynes small engine repair manual

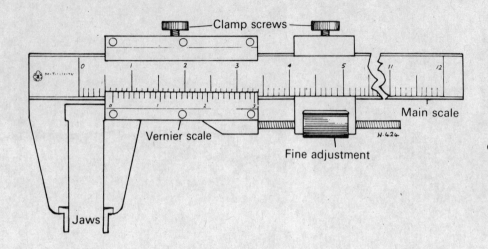

2.53   Vernier calipers can be used for both internal and external measurements

Vernier calipers

Although not strictly essential for routine work, a vernier caliper is a good investment for any workshop (if you're willing to learn how to read it accurately). The tool allows for fairly precise internal and external measurements, up to a maximum of about 6-inches or so. The object to be measured is positioned inside the external jaws – or outside the internal jaws – and the size is read off the main scale (see illustration 2.53). The vernier scale allows it to be narrowed down even more, to about 1/1000-inch. A vernier caliper allows reasonably precise measurements of a wide variety of objects, so it's a versatile piece of equipment. Even though it lacks the absolute accuracy of a micrometer, it's much cheaper to buy and can be used in more ways.

Micrometers

A micrometer is the most accurate measuring tool likely to be needed in a home shop and you could successfully argue that the cost of the tool, weighed against occasional use, makes it an unaffordable luxury. This is particularly true since individual micrometers are limited to measurements in 1-inch increments and you would need a set of two or three micrometers to be completely prepared for any measuring job.

The basic outside micrometer consists of a U-shaped metal frame covering a 1-inch size range. At one end is a precision ground stop, called the anvil, while at the other end is an adjustable stop called the spindle (see illustration 2.54). The spindle is moved in-or-out of the frame on a very precise, fine thread by a calibrated thimble, usually incorporating a ratchet to prevent damage to the threads. In use, the spindle is turned very carefully until the object to be measured is gripped very lightly between the anvil and spindle. A calibrated line on the fixed sleeve below the spindle indicates the rough size (base figure), while a more accurate measurement (down to 1/1000-inch) is calculated by adding an additional number indicated on the thimble scale to the base figure.

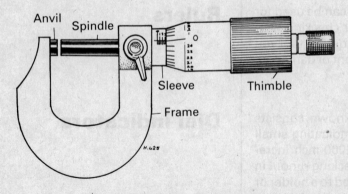

2.54   Micrometers, though expensive, are very accurate and almost indispensable when checking engine parts for wear

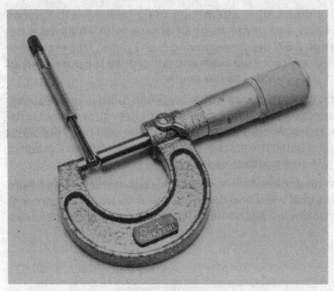

2.55 When used in conjunction with a small hole gauge . . .

2.56 . . . or a telescoping gauge, a micrometer can also make internal measurements – valve guide and cylinder bore checks are two typical examples

Micrometers are available in a wide range of sizes, starting with 0-1 inch (for small engine repair, anything over 2-3 inch is useless). There are also versions called inside micrometers, designed for making internal measurements such as cylinder bore sizes. Small hole gauges and telescoping gauges can be used along with outside micrometers to avoid the need for them (see illustrations 2.55 and 2.56).

All micrometers are precision instruments and easily damaged if misused or stored with other tools. They also require regular checks and calibration to maintain their accuracy. Given the fragile nature and high cost of these tools, as a general rule you should make do without them until you know for sure there's a definite need for them.

Basic maintenance and repair techniques

Although it was mentioned in the Environmental safety section, it's worth repeating here – sometimes waste oil, drained from the engine during normal maintenance or repairs, presents a disposal problem. To avoid pouring oil on the ground or into the sewage system, pour it into large containers, seal them with caps and take them to an authorized disposal site or service station. Plastic jugs are ideal for this purpose. **Note:** *Do not contaminate the oil with any other fluids – service stations will not accept it if you do!*

Keep a supply of old newspapers and clean rags available. Old towels are excellent for mopping up spills. Many mechanics use paper towels for most work because they're readily available and disposable. To help keep the area under the engine or equipment clean, a large cardboard box can be cut open and flattened to protect the garage or shop floor.

General repair hints

Always clean an engine before attempting to fix or service it. You can remove most of the dirt and grime from an engine with an aerosol degreaser **(see illustration 2.57)** before removing many parts. This makes the repair job much easier and more pleasant and will reduce the possibility of getting abrasive dirt particles inside the engine.

Lay parts out in the order of disassembly and keep them in order during the cleaning and inspection procedures. This will help ensure correct reassembly. Another good practice is to draw a sketch of an assembly before or while you take it apart. Then if the parts get mixed up, you'll have a guide to follow when putting them together again.

When working on an engine, look for conditions that may cause future trouble. Check for unusual wear and damage. You may be able to prevent future problems by making an adjustment or repairing a part before it fails.

2.57 Degreasers, which are normally sprayed on and rinsed off with water or solvent, are widely available at auto parts stores and will make any maintenance or repair job easier and less frustrating

Fasteners

Fasteners, basically, are nuts, bolts and screws used to hold two or more parts together. There are a few things to keep in mind when working with fasteners. Many of them require a locking device of some type (either a lock washer, locknut, locking tab or thread cement). All fasteners should be clean and straight with undamaged threads and sharp corners on the hex-head where the wrench fits. Develop the habit of replacing damaged nuts and bolts with new ones.

Rusted nuts or bolts should be treated with penetrating oil to make removal easier and help prevent breaking off the fastener. After applying the penetrating oil, let it soak in for a few minutes before trying to loosen the nut or bolt. Badly rusted fasteners may have to be chiseled off or removed with a hacksaw or special nut breaker, available at tool stores **(see illustration 2.58)**. If you mess up the recess in a Phillips screw head, make a slot in it with a hacksaw blade so a standard screwdriver can be used to remove it **(see illustration 2.59)**. The same holds true for slotted screws – if you deform the slot, use a hacksaw to

2.58 To remove a frozen or rounded-off nut, use a hacksaw to saw off one side, then open the nut with a chisel or turn it with a Vise-Grips

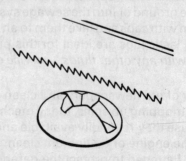

2.59 A hacksaw can be used to make a slot in a damaged Phillips screw head so it can be removed with a standard screwdriver

enlarge or deepen it and try again. It was mentioned in the tool section, but it's worth repeating here – when using a Phillips screwdriver, if the screw is extremely tight and the tip tends to back out of the recess rather than turn the screw, apply a small amount of valve lapping compound to the screwdriver tip so it'll grip better.

Flat washers and lock washers, when removed from an assembly, should always be replaced in their original locations. Discard damaged washers and replace them with new ones. Always use a flat washer between a lock washer and any soft metal surface (such as aluminum), thin sheet metal or plastic. Special locknuts can only be used once or twice before they lose their locking ability and must be replaced.

If a bolt or stud breaks off in an assembly, it can be drilled out and removed with a special tool called an E-Z out. Broken fastener removal and thread repairs are covered later in this chapter. If you don't have the tools or don't want to do it yourself, most small engine dealers and repair shops – as well as automotive machine shops – can perform these tasks.

Tightening sequences and procedures

When threaded fasteners are tightened, they're often tightened to a specific torque value (torque is basically a twisting force). Over-tightening the fastener can weaken it and cause it to break, while under-tightening can cause it to eventually come loose from engine vibration. Important fasteners, depending on the material they're made of, the diameter of the thread and, in the case of bolts, the material they're threaded into, have specific torque values, which are noted in the Specifications Section in the Appendix of this manual or in the text. Be sure to follow the torque recommendations closely. For fasteners not requiring a specific torque, use common sense when tightening them.

Fasteners laid out in a pattern (such as cylinder head bolts) must be loosened and tightened in a sequence to avoid warping the component. Initially, the bolts should go in finger-tight only. Next, they should be tightened 1/2-turn each, in a criss-cross or diagonal pattern. After each one has been tightened 1/2-turn, return to the first one and tighten each of them 1/4-turn at a time until each fastener has been tightened to the proper torque. To loosen the fasteners the procedure can be reversed.

Disassembly sequence

Engine disassembly should be done slowly and deliberately to make sure the parts go back together properly during reassembly. Always keep track of the sequence parts are removed in. Note special characteristics or marks on parts that can be installed more than one way. It's a good idea to lay the disassembled parts out on a clean surface in the order they were removed. As mentioned before, it may also be helpful to make sketches or take instant photos of components before removal.

When removing fasteners from a component, keep track of their locations. Sometimes threading a bolt back in a part, or putting the washers and nut back on a stud, can prevent mixups later. If nuts and bolts can't be returned to their original locations, they should be kept in a compartmented box or a series of small boxes. A cupcake or muffin tin is ideal for this purpose, since each cavity can hold the bolts and nuts from a particular area or sub-assembly. A pan of this type is especially helpful when working on components with very small parts (such as the carburetor and valve train). The cavities can be marked with a felt-tip pen or tape to identify the contents.

Gasket sealing surfaces

Gaskets are used to seal the mating surfaces between components and keep lubricants, fuel, vacuum or pressure contained in an assembly.

Gaskets are often coated with a liquid or paste-type gasket sealant before assembly. Age, heat and pressure can sometimes cause the two parts to stick together so tightly they're very difficult to separate. In most cases, the part can be loosened by striking it with a soft-face hammer near the joint. A regular hammer can be used if a block of wood is placed between the hammer and part. **Caution:** *Do not hammer on cast parts or parts that could be easily damaged.* With any particularly stubborn part, always recheck to make sure all fasteners have been removed.

Avoid using a screwdriver or bar to pry components apart, as they can easily mar the gasket sealing surfaces of the parts (which must remain smooth). If prying is absolutely necessary, use a piece of wood, but keep in mind that extra clean-up will be necessary if the wood splinters.

After the parts are separated, the old gasket must be carefully scraped off and the engine surfaces cleaned. Stubborn gasket material can be soaked with gasket removal solvent (available in aerosol cans) to soften it so it can be easily removed. Gasket scrapers are widely available – just be careful not to gouge the sealing surfaces if you use one. Some gaskets can be removed with a wire brush, but regardless of the method used, the mating surfaces must be left clean and smooth. If the gasket surface is scratched or gouged, then a gasket sealant thick enough to fill scratches should be used during reassembly of the components. For most applications, non-drying (or semi-drying) gasket sealant is best.

How to remove broken bolts and repair stripped threads

Removing broken-off bolts

If a bolt breaks off in the hole, a drill, drill bit and E-Z out will be required to remove it. First, select the E-Z out needed for the job (based on the bolt size), then select the drill bit required to make the hole for the E-Z out. Follow the procedure shown in the accompanying photos **(see illustrations 2.60 through 2.64).**

2.60   Before attempting to remove a broken-off bolt, apply penetrating oil and let it soak in for awhile

2.61   Use a center punch to make an indentation as close to the center of the bolt as you can

2.62   Carefully drill a hole in the bolt (hold the drill so the bit is parallel to the bolt – the bit should be about two-thirds the diameter of the bolt and the hole should be as deep as possible without going through the bolt

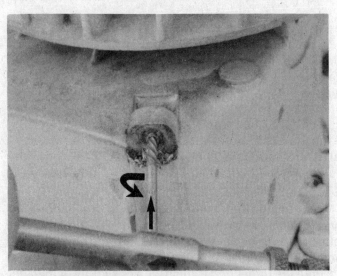

2.63   Tap the E-Z out into the hole and turn it with a die stock or adjustable wrench – keep pressure on the extractor so it doesn't turn in the hole instead of moving the bolt

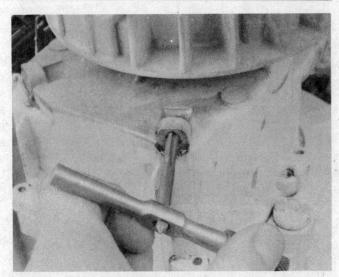

2.64   If you have one of the right size, run a tap into the hole after the bolt is out to clean up the threads and remove any rust or corrosion

If the thread isn't totally ruined, a tap or die can be used to clean it up so the fastener can be reused. If the nut or bolt is a standard size, or an extremely important fastener like a head bolt or flywheel nut, don't worry about salvaging it – buy and install a new one. Remember, if a bolt is stripped, the threads in the bolt hole may also be damaged. **Note:** *Always use thread cement on the threads of a restored nut or bolt when it's reinstalled and tighten it carefully to avoid further damage.*

If the thread in a bolt hole is completely stripped or seriously damaged, retapping may not work. In such cases a thread insert will be needed. The most commonly available inserts require drilling out the hole and cutting

Repairing stripped threads

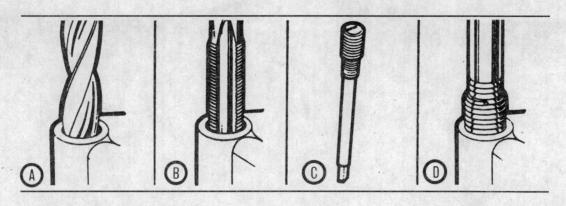

2.65   Installing a thread insert

A   *Drill out the hole to remove the old threads (this isn't required with all insert brands)*
B   *Use a tap to cut new threads in the hole (the tap is included with some thread repair kits)*
C   *Attach the insert to the installation tool (included with the kit)*
D   *Screw the insert into the newly-threaded hole (when it's flush with the top of the hole, break off the drive tang and remove the tool)*

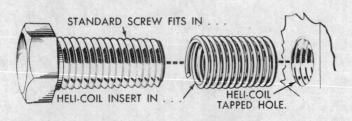

STANDARD SCREW FITS IN . . .

HELI-COIL INSERT IN . . .

HELI-COIL TAPPED HOLE.

2.66   The thread insert allows the original fastener to be used in the repaired hole

an oversize thread with a special tap. The resulting new thread is then reduced to the original size by installing a stainless steel wire insert in the threaded hole **(see illustration 2.65)**. This allows the original bolt or stud to be re-installed **(see illustration 2.66)**. Heli-Coil thread inserts are the most common and sets with the required tap, several inserts, an installation tool (mandrel) for common thread sizes and comprehensive instructions are available.

Thread inserts look like springs prior to installation and have a small drive tang at the lower end. The thread insert is attached to a special mandrel and the tang engages in a slot in the end of the tool. The insert is screwed into the hole until the upper end is flush with or slightly below the surface. Once in position, the drive tang is broken off, leaving the insert locked in place. If the drive tang doesn't break off when backing out the mandrel, use a pin punch or needle-nose pliers to snap it off.

This type of repair is a good way to reclaim badly worn or stripped threads in aluminum parts (very common in small engines). The new thread formed by the stainless steel insert is permanent and more durable than the original. In some cases, the original hole doesn't have to be enlarged prior to retapping, making the repair quick and simple to carry out. The only drawback for the home shop is the high cost of purchasing a range of taps and inserts. The taps needed for thread inserts are not standard sizes – they're made specially for use with each insert size. The inserts aren't expensive individually, but stocking up on them in each size that could be required on a small engine is probably too expensive for most home shops.

Small engine lubricants and chemicals

A number of lubricants and chemicals are required for small engine maintenance and repair. They include a wide variety of products ranging from cleaning solvents and degreasers to lubricants and penetrating oil. **Caution:** *Always follow the directions and heed the precautions and warnings printed on the containers of lubricants and chemicals designed for shop use.*

Ignition point/spark plug cleaner (see illustration 2.67) is a solvent used to clean oily film and dirt off points and oil deposits off spark plugs. It's oil free and leaves no residue. It can also be used to remove gum and varnish from carburetor jets and other orifices.

Carburetor cleaner is similar to contact point/spark plug cleaner but it has a much stronger solvent and may leave a slight oily reside. It isn't normally needed on small engine carburetors, but if deposits are heavy it will work faster and better than solvent.

Silicone-based lubricants are used to protect rubber parts such as hoses and grommets.

Multi-purpose grease (see illustration 2.68) is an all purpose lubricant used wherever grease is more practical than a liquid lubricant such as oil. Some multi-purpose grease is colored white and specially formulated to be more resistant to water than ordinary grease.

Motor oil, of course, is the lubricant specially formulated for use in an engine. It normally contains a wide variety of additives to prevent corrosion and reduce foaming and wear. Motor oil comes in various weights (viscosity ratings) of from 5 to 80. The recommended weight of the oil depends on the seasonal temperature and the demands on the engine. Light oil is used in cold climates and under light load conditions; heavy oil is used in hot climates and where high loads are encountered. Multi-viscosity oils are designed to have characteristics of both light and heavy oils and are available in a number of weights from 5W-20 to 20W-50. Be sure to follow the engine manufacturer's recommendations.

Gas additives perform several functions, depending on their chemical makeup. They usually contain solvents that help dissolve gum and varnish that build up on carburetor and intake parts. They also serve to break down carbon deposits that form on the inside surfaces of the combustion chamber. Some types contain upper cylinder lubricants for valves and piston rings. For small engine use, the most common additive is a gas stabilizer used when equipment is stored for long periods.

Degreasers are heavy duty solvents used to remove grease and grime that may accumulate on engines and machinery. They can be sprayed or brushed on and, depending on the type, are rinsed off with either water or solvent.

2.67 Contact point/spark plug cleaner

2.68 Multi-purpose grease

Haynes small engine repair manual

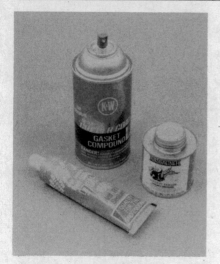

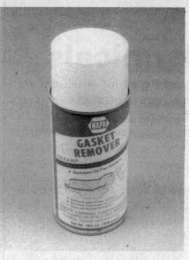

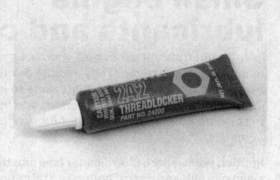

2.69   Sealants needed for small engine repair work

2.70   Aerosol gasket remover

2.71   Thread cement

2.72   WD-40 is a good moisture dispersant, solvent and lubricant

Solvents are used alone or in combination with degreasers to clean parts during repairs and overhauls. The home mechanic should use only solvents that are non-flammable and that don't produce irritating fumes.

Gasket sealants (see illustration 2.69) may be used in conjunction with gaskets, to improve their sealing capabilities, or alone, to seal metal-to-metal joints. Many gasket sealants can withstand extreme heat, some are impervious to gasoline and lubricants, while others are capable of filling and sealing cavities. Depending on the intended use, gasket sealants either dry hard or stay relatively soft and pliable. They're usually applied by hand, with a brush, or are sprayed on the gasket sealing surfaces.

Gasket/sealant removal solvents (see illustration 2.70) are available at auto parts stores and are helpful when removing gaskets that are baked on or stuck to engine components. They're usually powerful chemicals and should be used with care.

Thread cement (see illustration 2.71) is an adhesive compound that prevents threaded fasteners from loosening because of vibration. It's available in a variety of types for different applications.

Moisture dispersants (see illustration 2.72) are usually sprays that can be used to dry out ignition system components and wire connections. Some types also are very good solvents and lubricants for cables and other components.

3

Troubleshooting

How an engine works

All small, air-cooled, gasoline engines are internal-combustion engines much like the ones used in cars, trucks and motorcycles. The term "internal-combustion" is used because energy for turning the crankshaft is developed inside the engine.

This happens when the fuel/air mixture is burned inside a confined space called a combustion chamber (or cylinder). Because of the heat produced, the mixture expands, which then forces the piston to move. The piston is connected to the crankshaft, which changes linear motion into rotary motion. The crankshaft may be oriented vertically or horizontally, depending on the engine application. The crankshaft is situated at a right angle to the cylinder bore.

To supply power – motion – to the crankshaft, a series of events must occur. This series of events is called a combustion cycle. The events in the cycle are . . .

1 Intake of the fuel/air mixture into the cylinder
2 Compression of the fuel/air mixture
3 Ignition/expansion of the fuel/air mixture
4 Expulsion of the burned gases

The movement of the piston in one direction, either toward the crankshaft or away from it, is called a stroke. Some small engines complete a cycle during one revolution of the crankshaft (two strokes of the piston). Other types require two revolutions of the crankshaft (four strokes of the piston). In this manual, the shortened terms "two-stroke" and "four-stroke" are used in place of the technically correct terms "two-stroke cycle" and "four-stroke cycle." The major differences between four-stroke and two-stroke engines are:

The number of power strokes per crankshaft revolution

The method of getting the fuel/air mixture into the combustion chamber and the burned gases out

The number of moving parts in the engine

The method used to lubricate the internal engine components

Four-stroke engines

As mentioned above, a four-stroke engine completes one combustion cycle during two revolutions of the crankshaft, or four strokes of the piston. This is due to the design of the engine and the way the fuel/air mixture is introduced into the cylinder. A camshaft, which is driven off the crankshaft, opens valves that allow the fuel/air mixture in and exhaust gases out of the engine. The valves are closed by spring pressure. The four strokes of the piston have been labelled to describe what happens during each one (**see illustration 3.1**):

INTAKE STROKE – During the intake stroke, the piston moves down in the cylinder with the intake valve open. The fuel/air mixture is forced into the cylinder through the open intake valve. Near the end of the piston's movement, the intake valve closes, sealing off the combustion chamber.

COMPRESSION STROKE – The piston changes direction at the end of the intake stroke and begins to move up in the cylinder, which compresses and heats the fuel/air mixture.

POWER STROKE – As the piston reaches the end of the compression stroke, the ignition system fires the spark plug, which ignites the compressed fuel/air mixture in the combustion chamber. The piston changes direction again and moves down in the cylinder with great force produced by the burning/expanding gases. The connecting rod transfers the movement of the piston to the crankshaft, which changes the linear motion to rotary (turning) motion, which can be used to do work.

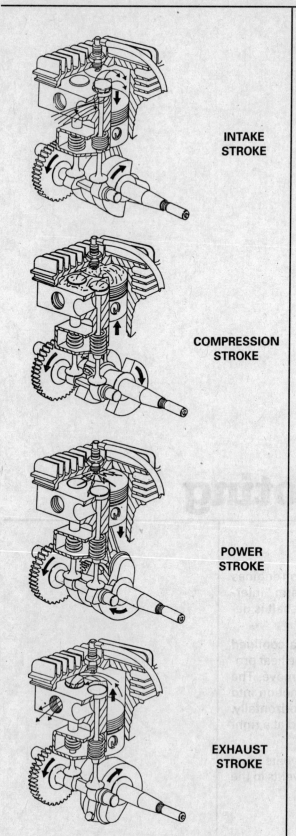

INTAKE
STROKE

COMPRESSION
STROKE

POWER
STROKE

EXHAUST
STROKE

3.1 The four stroke engine combustion cycle
Illustration courtesy of and with permission of Briggs and Stratton Corp.

EXHAUST STROKE – When the piston reaches the end of the power stroke, it changes direction again and the exhaust valve opens. As the piston moves up in the cylinder, the exhaust gases are pushed out through the exhaust valve. When the piston reaches the end of the exhaust stroke, the cycle starts all over again.

Two-stroke engines

Two stroke engines have a slightly different design that doesn't require valves. Instead, openings called ports are used to route the fuel/air mixture to the cylinder. Also, the crankcase is used as a temporary storage area as the fuel mixture is on its way to the cylinder, so it must be leakproof. The piston serves to open and close off the ports to seal off the combustion chamber.

A two-stroke engine is designed to complete the same cycle described for a four-stroke engine, but it does it during one revolution of the crankshaft. The INTAKE and COMPRESSION strokes actually occur simultaneously, during one stroke of the piston, and so do the POWER and EXHAUST STROKES (**see illustration 3.2**).

As the piston moves down in the cylinder, pushed by the burning/expanding gases, the fresh fuel/air charge in the crankcase is being pressurized slightly. Once the piston uncovers the exhaust port, the spent gases begin to exit the cylinder. Next, the piston uncovers the transfer ports and the fresh fuel/air charge begins to flow out of the crankcase, through the transfer ports and into the cylinder, helping to push out the exhaust gases. At the bottom of the stroke, the piston changes direction and begins to move up in the cylinder, sealing off the transfer and exhaust ports and compressing the fuel/air mixture in the cylinder. At the same time, the intake port (which may be sealed off by a one-way valve called a reed valve or by the piston skirt) opens and more fuel/air mixture is forced into the crankcase; this is because a slight vacuum is created as the piston moves up in the cylinder. At the top of the piston's stroke, the spark plug fires, which ignites the compressed fuel/air mixture in the combustion chamber. The piston changes direction again and moves down in the cylinder with great force produced by the burning/expanding gases. This overlapping cycle is repeated continuously as the engine is running.

Since a two-stroke engine uses the crankcase for storing a reserve charge of fuel/air mixture, the crankcase can't be used as an oil reservoir for lubricating the engine. Instead, lubrication is supplied by a specific quantity of oil that's mixed with the gas and circulated through the engine as it runs. Never put gasoline in a two-stroke engine without mixing oil with it – the engine will overheat because of improper lubrication. It won't run very long before the piston and bearings will overheat, score and seize!

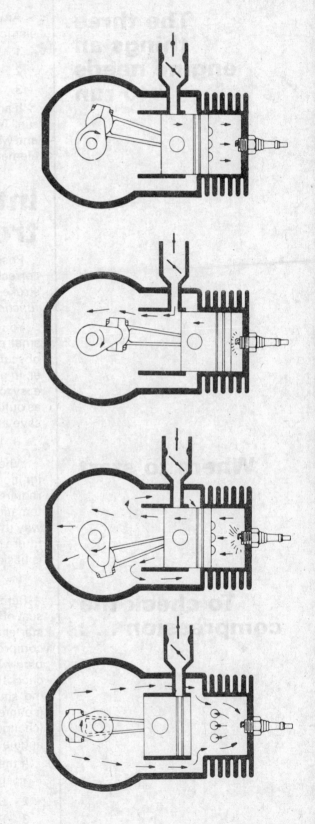

3.2   The two-stroke engine combustion cycle
Illustration courtesy of Tecumseh Products Co.

Haynes small engine repair manual

The three things an engine needs to run

Any engine, whether it's a two or four-stroke, must have three essential elements to run:

1 Fuel and air mixed together in the correct proportions
2 Compression of the fuel/air mixture
3 Ignition at the right time

If any one of these three elements is missing, the engine simply will not run. Troubleshooting is the process of determining which one is missing and why. Once you figure this out, repairs are done to restore the missing element.

Introduction to troubleshooting

Possible causes for various engine problems and recommendations for correcting them are covered in detail in separate sections for two and four-stroke engines in this chapter. **Note:** *What appears to be an engine malfunction may be a problem in the power equipment rather than the engine.*

You won't find any absolutely foolproof troubleshooting procedures for small engines that won't start and run properly. Some symptoms can be so obscure that it takes a professional mechanic to spot the problem. However, in general, malfunctioning engines have symptoms that are relatively easy to identify. By thoroughly checking the problem in an orderly manner, as outlined in this chapter, you usually will be able to find the problem and save a trip to the repair shop.

Where to start

When the cause of a malfunction isn't obvious, check the compression, ignition and carburetor, in that order, first (remember the three elements required for an engine to run?). This check, which must be done in a systematic manner, will only take a few minutes. It's the quickest and surest way to find out what the problem is. It will also reveal possible causes of future problems, which can be corrected at the same time. The procedure is basically the same for all engines.

To check the compression . . .

Remove the spark plug and ground the plug wire on the engine, then seal off the plug hole with your thumb **(see illustration 3.3)**. Operate the starter – if the compression pressure blows your thumb off the hole, the compression is adequate for the engine to run; be careful not to touch the plug wire as this is done – you'll get quite a jolt if you do! Another way to check the compression with the spark plug in place is to remove the cooling shroud/recoil starter mechanism and spin the flywheel in reverse (counterclockwise) **(see illustration 3.4)**. The flywheel should rebound (change directions) sharply; if it does, the compression is adequate for the engine to run.

If the compression is low, it may be due to:

1 Loose spark plug
2 Loose cylinder head bolts
3 Blown head gasket
4 Damaged valves/valve seats (four-stroke engine only)
5 Insufficient valve tappet clearance (four-stroke engine only)

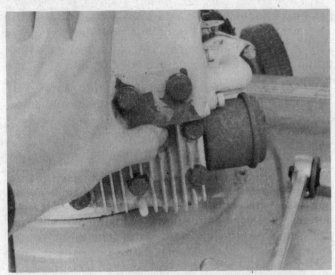

3.3   As a general rule, if the engine's compression will blow your thumb off the spark plug hole, it should be adequate for the engine to run

3.4   If the recoil starter/cooling shroud is off, spin the flywheel in a counterclockwise direction (with the spark plug in place) and see if it rebounds in response to engine compression

6   Warped cylinder head
7   Bent valve stem(s) (four-stroke engine only)
8   Worn cylinder bore and/or piston rings
9   Broken connecting rod or piston

Remove the spark plug and ground the threaded end on the engine (**see illustration 3.5**), then operate the starter. If bright blue, well-defined sparks occur at the plug electrodes, the ignition system is functioning properly. **Note:** *The sparks produced by electronic (CDI) ignition systems may not last very long, so be sure to pull vigorously on the recoil starter handle. It may also help to work in the shade so the sparks are easier to see.* If sparks aren't produced, or if they're intermittent, attach a spark tester to the plug wire

To check the ignition system . .

3.5   To check for spark, remove the plug and ground it on the engine with the wire attached, then operate the starter – if sparks occur at the plug, the ignition system is okay; if no sparks occur, the plug may be bad, so don't automatically condemn the ignition system (see illustration 3.6) and ground the tester on the engine, then operate the starter so the engine turns over rapidly. If bright blue, well-defined sparks are produced at the tester gap (3/16-inch wide), you can assume the ignition system is functioning properly – try a new spark plug and see if the engine will start and run.

3.6   A spark tester with the gap set at about 3/16-inch is the best tool to use for checking the ignition system – if it will produce a spark strong enough to jump the tester gap, it's adequate for the engine to run

If sparks do not occur, it may be due to:

1   A sheared flywheel key
2   Incorrect ignition point gap*
3   Dirty or burned ignition points*
4   Coil failure/electronic ignition failure
5   Incorrect armature air gap
6   Worn bearings and/or crankshaft on flywheel side only
7   Ignition point plunger stuck or worn**
8   Shorted ground wire (if equipped)
9   Shorted stop switch (if equipped)
10 Condenser failure*
11 Malfunctioning starter interlock system
12 Defective spark plug wire
13 Malfunctioning oil level switch

  * *Engines with ignition points only*
** *Briggs & Stratton engines with ignition points only*

If the engine runs but misses during operation, a quick check to determine if the ignition system is or is not at fault can be made by attaching a spark tester between the plug wire and the spark plug. An ignition system misfire will be apparent when watching the tester (it should spark continually). **Note:** *When conducting this test on Magnamatic equipped Briggs & Stratton engines, use a new spark plug with the gap set to 0.060-inch in place of the old plug.*

To check the carburetor . . .

Before proceeding, be sure the fuel tank is refilled with fresh, clean gasoline (or gasoline/oil mixed as required), the fuel shut-off valve is open (if equipped) and fuel flows freely through the fuel line. Check/adjust the mixture adjusting screw (if equipped) to make sure it's open and make sure the choke closes completely **(see illustration 3.7).**

3.7   The choke must be closed when starting the engine cold – if it isn't closing, free it up so it will (typical choke shown)

3.8   If the engine has good compression and spark, try priming it by carefully pouring gasoline directly into the plug hole with a small funnel – if the engine starts, you have a fuel delivery problem to find and fix

If the engine won't start, remove and check the spark plug – if it's wet or fouled, it may be due to:

1   Stuck choke
2   Overly-rich fuel mixture
3 · Water in fuel
4   Inlet needle valve stuck open (not all carburetors)
5   Clogged muffler
6   Plugged crankcase breather
7   Too much oil in crankcase
8   Worn piston rings

If the spark plug is dry, check for:

1   Leaking carburetor mounting gaskets
2   Gummy or dirty carburetor internal parts
3   Inlet needle valve stuck shut (not all carburetors)
4   Damaged or deteriorated rubber diaphragms in carburetor (not all carburetors)
5   Plugged fuel line or filter (not all engines)

A simple check to determine if fuel is getting to the combustion chamber through the carburetor is to remove the spark plug and pour a small amount of gasoline (about one teaspoonful) into the engine through the spark plug hole (this is called "priming" the engine) **(see illustration 3.8)**. Reinstall the plug. If the engine fires a few times and then stops, look for the same conditions described under *If the spark plug is dry . . .*

Troubleshooting a four-stroke engine

Most four-stroke engine problems will fall into one or more of the following categories:

1   Won't start
2   Hard to start/kicks back when starting
3   Stops suddenly
4   Lack of power/erratic operation
5   Excessive vibration
6   Noise
7   Engine smokes
8   Overheating
9   Excessive oil use

1 Won't start

Note: *When an engine won't start, it's usually because the controls are improperly set, the safety interlock devices are interrupting the ignition system or the ignition system is malfunctioning, although carburetor problems and low compression can also prevent an engine from starting (see the information under the heading Where to start? to rule out lack of compression as a cause).*

1   Make sure the controls are positioned properly.

Follow the control cable from the lever to the carburetor. The throttle should be all the way open and the choke should operate when the lever is set on START. As you move the control lever from START to FAST to STOP, the cable should be clamped so the throttle operates properly **(see illustration 3.9)**. The cable may be slipping in the clamp just enough to cause the throttle to malfunction and you might not see the slight movement.

Move the throttle to the open or START position with your fingers. You may have to move the control lever with your other hand to open the throttle.

If the engine now starts, let it run for several minutes, then pull the control lever back to STOP. If the engine slows down but doesn't stop, loosen the cable clamp with a screwdriver and pull the cable toward the control lever very slightly until the engine stops, then retighten the clamp. Start the engine again and run through the control positions. The engine should start, run slowly, run fast and stop when the lever is positioned next to the appropriate label on the control.

3.9 **Make sure the control cable (if used) is securely clamped to the engine so it doesn't slip when the control lever is moved (if the clamp is loose, tighten it and check the cable to see if it needs lubrication)**

2   Make sure the gas tank is at least half full of fresh fuel and that fuel is reaching the carburetor (the line between the tank and carburetor could be plugged, kinked or detached or the filter – if used – could be plugged).

3   Check the plug wire to make sure it's securely attached to the spark plug.

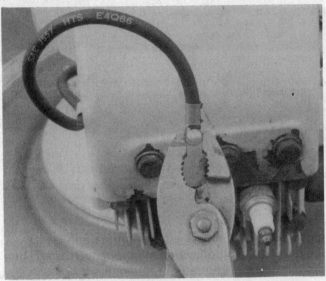

3.10   Spark plug wires are always coming loose – crimp the terminal with a pair of pliers so it fits snugly on the plug tip

3.11   If the gas tank cap vent is plugged, the engine will starve for fuel until you remove the cap to see if there's gas in the tank (which relieves the vacuum) – the engine will then start and run for a while before it stalls again

The terminal on the end of the spark plug wire can come loose and get corroded. Crimp the loop with a pair of pliers **(see illustration 3.10)** and remove corrosion with sandpaper, a wire brush or a round file.

4   Check the spark plug to make sure it's tight.

5   Check the spark plug ground strap to make sure it's not malfunctioning. Some engines have a metal strap that's used to short out the spark plug to stop the engine. If the engine has one, make sure it's not touching the plug.

6   If the engine has a fuel priming device, make sure it's working properly.

It should be pushed four or five times when the engine is cold to fill the carburetor. If the engine is hot, don't operate the primer – it may flood the carburetor. Instead, pull the starter handle several times with the control lever in the STOP position. This will help clear excess fuel out of the engine. Put the control lever on START and start the engine normally.

7   Make sure the grass catcher is properly installed.

Some lawnmowers have a safety switch for the grass catcher where it attaches to the mower housing. This device prevents the engine from starting until the grass catcher is properly installed. If the grass catcher isn't being used, make sure the chute is properly attached to the mower deck.

8   See if the gas tank cap vent is clogged.

If the gas tank vent is clogged, a vacuum will eventually form in the tank and prevent fuel from reaching the carburetor (the engine will act like it's out of gas).

Remove the cap and check the gasket in it. Sometimes the space between the gasket and cap gets clogged with debris, shutting off the air supply to the tank. Check the hole(s) in the cap to make sure it's open **(see illustration 3.11)**. If you're not sure if the vent is open or not, leave the cap

3.12 If the air filter is dirty or clogged with debris, remove and clean it or install a new one – foam types and pleated paper types are the most common

3.13 One way to check to make sure gas is getting to the carburetor is to remove the float bowl (if used) – it's usually held in place with a nut on the bottom, which is hard to get at and easily damaged

off and try to start the engine. If the engine runs, the cap vent is the problem. Either open the vent or install a new cap. DO NOT run the engine without a cap on the gas tank.

9   Check the air filter to see if it's clean and make sure the gasket between the filter and carburetor is in good shape (see illustration 3.12).

10   Check to see if the plug is firing (see *To check the ignition system . . .* in the section headed *Where to start?*).

You can clean spark plugs, but a new one should be installed – they're not expensive and you can usually be sure the new plug is good.

Every once in a while, a new plug will turn out to be faulty. If you install a new plug and the engine won't fire even though everything else seems to be okay, try another new plug or a spark tester.

11   Make sure the plug wire is in good condition.

Bend the wire by hand and look for cracks in the insulation. Also look for burned or melted insulation. If damage is noted, you may have to replace the ignition coil, since the wire usually is permanently attached to it.

12   See if the blade is loose – it must be tight on the shaft or adaptor.

13   If the equipment has a chain, drivebelt or belts, check to see if it's loose. A loose chain or belt, like a loose blade, can cause a backlash effect, which will work against engine cranking effort.

14   You may be trying to start the engine when it's under load. See if the equipment is disengaged when the engine is started, or, if engaged, doesn't create an unusual starting load.

15   Remove the float bowl (not all carburetors have one) and see if the carburetor is dirty or gummed up (see illustration 3.13). **Caution:** *Shut off the fuel valve or remove the tank before detaching the float bowl – if you don't, gas will run all over until the tank is empty!*

If there's dirt or sludge in the float bowl, the carburetor passages may be clogged. Remove the carburetor and clean it thoroughly. Some carburetors have a small spring-loaded valve on the bottom of the float bowl that's used to drain out sediment and water. Push up on it with a small screwdriver and let gas run out until it looks clean (you'll see little droplets if water comes out).

Note: Many Tecumseh/Craftsman engines are equipped with an "Auto-prime" float-type carburetor that has a fuel inlet which gets clogged easily by gasoline residue, particularly if the engine isn't run for a long time (suspect this in lawn mowers that are stored all winter without draining the gasoline out of the carburetor or adding a gas stabilizer to the tank).

Drain the fuel out of the tank or detach the tank from the engine and set it aside. Remove the float bowl and clean it out, then clear the fuel inlet with a very fine wire (see illustration 3.14). Reinstall the float bowl and tank, add gasoline and try to start the engine.

3.14 Craftsman engines with an "Auto-prime" carburetor often won't run because this fuel inlet gets clogged with dirt or sludge – clean it with a fine piece of wire and the engine should run fine

2 Hard to start/kicks back when starting

These problems are quite common and are usually caused by belts or chains that aren't disengaged when the engine is cranked or by a loose blade.

1   See if the blade is loose – it must be tight on the shaft or adaptor.

2   If the equipment has a chain, drivebelt or belts, check to see if it's loose. A loose chain or belt, like a loose blade, can cause a backlash effect, which will work against engine cranking effort.

3   You may be trying to start the engine when it's under load. See if the equipment is disengaged when the engine is started, or, if engaged, doesn't create an unusual starting load.

4   The recoil starter may not be operating properly.

3 Stops suddenly

1   Check the gas tank to make sure it hasn't run dry.

2   Check the flywheel key to see if it has sheared off and check the condenser to see if it has shorted out.

Sometimes when everything is running perfectly, the engine will stop suddenly and you won't be able to get it started again. If the problem isn't a dry gas tank, this problem can usually be traced to one of two things:

A sheared-off flywheel key

A defective condenser (engines with ignition points only)

3.15 If the flywheel key (arrow) is sheared, the ignition timing will be off and the engine won't run

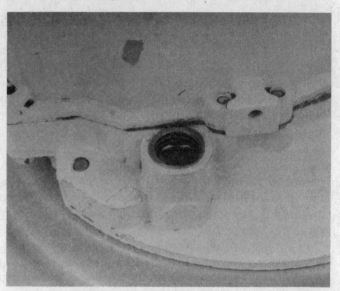

3.16 Even though you can see oil in the engine after the plug is removed, it must be at the very top of the hole or the crankcase will be dangerously low! – some engines have a dipstick with the safe level clearly marked on it

The flywheel key will shear if the equipment blade strikes an immovable object (this is to protect the crankshaft and other expensive engine components). It can happen without any indication to the equipment operator. The flywheel key is important for proper ignition timing – if it's damaged, the engine won't run.

The condenser (located under the flywheel) can stop working at any time without warning. Even brand new condensers can go bad, so don't be fooled into thinking the problem is something else if the engine has new, or nearly new, ignition parts. Instructions for getting to the condenser are included in Chapter 4 (under ignition point replacement).

You can also check the flywheel key at the same time you check the condenser. It's a rectangular piece of soft metal that fits into a slot in the flywheel and crankshaft taper to index the flywheel to the crankshaft **(see illustration 3.15)**. As mentioned above, the metal is soft for a reason – when the blade strikes something hard, the key shears and releases the force on the crankshaft. This prevents damage to the crankshaft, piston, valves, gears and other major (expensive) parts of the engine.

Replacement of the key is covered in each engine chapter (6, 7 or 8) (flywheel removal and installation).

3   Check the oil in the crankcase.

When you remove the oil check/fill cap, the engine may appear to be full but still need oil. Add more oil with a funnel until it runs out the hole **(see illustration 3.16)**. If the engine has a dipstick, the safe level will be clearly indicated.

Start the engine. If it's noisy, the lack of lubrication has probably damaged the engine. It may have to be overhauled or replaced.

4   Check the fuel lines and filter (if used) to make sure they're clear.

5   See if the muffler/exhaust pipe is clogged.

A plugged exhaust system can stop the engine and damage it. So can a defective muffler. Remove the muffler and see if the engine will start and run.

6   Check the plug wire to make sure it's securely attached to the spark plug.

The terminal on the end of the spark plug wire can come loose and get corroded. Crimp the loop with a pair of pliers **(see illustration 3.10)** and remove corrosion with sandpaper, a wire brush or a round file.

7   Check the cable and linkage between the handle controls, throttle and governor to see if they're binding or if anything has come loose. Lubricate the cable with WD-40 if necessary **(see illustration 3.17)**.

3.17   If the controls stick, lubricate the cable – from the top down, if possible – with WD-40 or a similar solvent/lubricant

4 Lack of power/erratic operation

These symptoms are usually caused by problems in the ignition system (especially on engines with ignition points) or the carburetor (particularly the idle adjustment).

1   Check the gas in the tank to make sure it's fresh and doesn't have any water in it. Drain the tank and refill it with new gas.

2   Check the flywheel key (see the section headed *Stops suddenly*).

3   Check the engine compression (see the section headed *Where to start?*).

4   Check the plug wire to make sure it's securely attached to the spark plug.

The terminal on the end of the spark plug wire can come loose and get corroded. Crimp the loop with a pair of pliers **(see illustration 3.10)** and remove corrosion with sandpaper, a wire brush or a round file.

5   Make sure the control lever is free and working properly (not stuck on any of the settings).

6   Make sure the air filter is clean **(see illustration 3.12)**.

7   Remove the spark plug and check the gap and the base of the plug for dirt. Clean the electrodes with a wire brush and use a fine file to square the side electrode tip so any worn edges are sharp **(see illustration 3.18)**. **Note:** *As a general rule, the spark plug gap can be set at 0.025-inch.*

8   Check the carburetor mixture screw to see if it's out of adjustment. **Note:** *Some carburetors don't have any mixture screws, while others have one for either high-speed adjustments or low speed adjustments, but not both. Still others have one screw to adjust the*

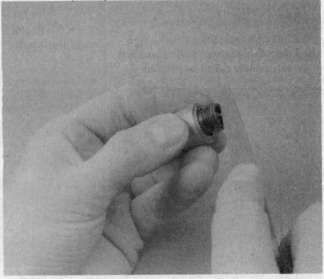

3.18   If the plug is covered with deposits, clean it with a wire brush, then file the electrode tips until they have sharp edges (this makes it easier for the ignition system to fire the plug when the engine is running)

3.19 Some carburetors have one or two adjusting screws for changing the fuel/air mixture – this one is typical of the types used on small engines

3.20 If the mixture screw tip is bent or worn, the correct adjustment will be difficult to maintain

fuel/air mixture at high speeds and another screw that controls the mixture at low speeds – if two screws are used, they must be adjusted separately.

The mixture screw is used to control the flow of fuel through the carburetor **(see illustration 3.19)**. If the screw is damaged or incorrectly adjusted, loss of power and erratic engine operation will result.

Remove the mixture screw and check the tip – if it looks bent or a groove has been worn in the tapered portion, install a new one **(see illustration 3.20)**. Do not attempt to straighten it. If the O-ring on the screw is damaged or deteriorated, replace it before attempting to adjust the mixture.

If the screw isn't bent or worn, reinstall it and turn it in until it stops – tighten it with your fingers only, don't force it. Back it out about 1-1/4 turns (counterclockwise) **(see illustration 3.21)**. Note: *The actual factory-recommended number of turns out is different for each carburetor type, but the figure given here is in the ballpark for most engines.*

Start the engine and turn the screw clockwise until the engine starts to slow down. This means the fuel mixture is too lean (not enough gas). Slowly turn the screw out (counterclockwise) until the engine begins to run smoothly. Keep going very slowly until the engine just begins to run rough again. Finally, turn the screw in again (clockwise) to a point about half-way between rough operation and smooth operation. This is the perfect setting.

If an idle (low-speed) mixture screw is used, adjust it in the same manner with the engine idling. After the low-speed mixture has been set, recheck the high-speed adjustment (if applicable) – it may be affected by the idle adjustment.

Some carburetors also have an idle speed adjusting screw that's used to open or close the throttle valve

3.21 When turning the mixture screw, make small changes only and wait to see the effect on the engine (don't confuse the mixture screw with the idle speed screw, which acts on the throttle linkage in some manner)

slightly to change the idle speed only, not the fuel/air mixture. Turning it will cause the engine to speed up or slow down.

9   Check to see if the engine is flooded.

Running equipment on hills and slopes can cause flooding. Flooding can also occur when the engine is cranked with the spark plug wire disconnected and when the mixture is too rich (when the carburetor mixture screw is out of adjustment).

Set the control lever to the STOP position. Pull the starter rope or crank the engine over several times. The closed throttle produces a high vacuum and opens the choke, which cleans excess fuel out of the engine. Start the engine.

If the engine continues to flood, adjust the mixture screws as outlined above. If this doesn't work, there is another alternative, but you must be very careful when doing it (there is a possibility of gasoline igniting in the carburetor).

Remove the air filter and hold the choke/throttle valves open with a small screwdriver (see illustration 3.22). Keep your face and hands away from the carburetor and crank the engine several times. The engine should start. When it starts, remove the screwdriver and reinstall the air filter.

When the engine is running, adjust the mixture screws as described above.

3.22   If the engine is flooded (the spark plug is wet with gasoline), hold the choke and throttle valves – if possible – wide open with a screwdriver while cranking the engine to clear out the excess gas

5   Excessive vibration

Engine vibration can be caused by a bent crankshaft, which results from hitting something with the blade. Many small engine repair shops can straighten a crankshaft without disassembling the engine. If the power take-off end of the crankshaft wobbles as it's turned by hand, remove the engine from the equipment and take it to a repair shop for crankshaft straightening.

1   Look for an out-of-balance blade. Mower blades can get twisted or badly nicked and may have poor lift. Sometimes sharpening the blade unevenly can throw it off. Resharpen the blade or install a new one.

2   Check to see if the blade is tight. Tighten the blade mounting bolt or bolts. Turn them counterclockwise.

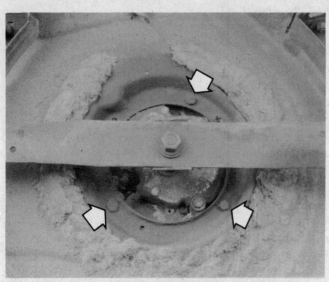

3.23 If the mounting bolts (arrows) are loose, the engine will vibrate and damage will result

3   Check the engine mounting bolts to see if they're tight. These bolts hold the engine to the equipment **(see illustration 3.23)**. You may have to hold the bolts on top while you tighten the nuts under the deck.

4   Check the deck for damage. If it's broken, cracked or badly rusted, the engine may get out of alignment and vibrate. If the deck is damaged, it must be repaired or replaced. Repairs usually involve welding (a job for a professional). If the deck must be replaced, get several estimates; a new mower may be cheaper.

5   Check the carburetor adjustment (see section 4 above.) A rough-running engine can cause vibration.

6 Noise

Excessive or unusual noise is almost always the result of a muffler that's rusted out, deformed or missing completely. A new muffler will remedy the problem.

1   Check the condition of the muffler. A deteriorated muffler must be replaced (see Chapter 5).

2   If the noise isn't caused by the exhaust system, but is in the engine itself, check the oil level immediately!

3   If you notice the engine is suddenly running quieter, check the muffler or exhaust system and remove matted grass clippings, dirt and other debris.

7 Engine smokes

This may be caused by a broken piston or ring or a damaged cylinder, although other causes are more likely.

1   Check the carburetor to see if it's adjusted properly (see Section 4 above).

Start the engine and allow it to idle (if possible), then open it up. If black smoke comes out of the exhaust, the mixture is probably too rich. Adjust the fuel mixture (if possible) (follow the procedure in Section 4).

2   If the smoke is blue and smells like burned oil, the trouble is probably with the rings, piston or cylinder bore (more than likely all three). The blue smoke may be accompanied by excessive internal engine noises – the engine may make a dull, knocking sound. It will have to be overhauled.

8 Overheating

This is usually a minor problem, but don't ignore it. Prolonged overheating can cause serious engine damage.

1   Check the oil level immediately. Add clean, fresh oil as needed. Make sure the oil used is the proper viscosity – if it's too thin or contaminated with fuel (from flooding the engine), lubrication will be inadequate.

2   Make sure the cooling fins aren't clogged with debris. Clean them with a putty knife and paint brush.

3   Make sure all shrouds and blower housings are correctly installed. If they aren't, air can't circulate properly through the cooling fins.

4   Check the carburetor to see if it's adjusted properly (see section 4 above).

5   See if the muffler is obstructed by dirt or debris.

6   Make sure the engine isn't overloaded. You may be running it too fast for too long (has the governor been tampered with?). Also, the engine may be overburdened with too much equipment. Stop the engine, let it cool and disengage the extra equipment.

7   Check the cylinder head for excessive carbon build-up (see Chapter 4 for instructions to remove the head and clean it).

8   Check the valve tappet clearances to see if they're too tight (see Chapter 4).

9   Make sure the correct spark plug is installed.

9 Excessive oil use

This problem can have several causes.

1   Check the oil level – if the engine is overfilled, excess oil will be blown out through the crankcase breather and get all over the engine.

2   Check the governor. The engine may be operating at speeds that are too high.

3   See if the oil level check/fill plug gasket is missing. The oil may be leaking out around the plug (it'll run down the engine if it is).

4   Check the crankcase breather assembly (see illustration 3.24). Clean or replace it as required. Make sure the oil drain back hole is open.

5   The rings or cylinder bore may be worn or damaged. To check this you'll have to disassemble the engine.

3.24   The crankcase breather assembly is used to vent the crankcase and keep oil from being expelled in the process

Troubleshooting a two-stroke engine

Most two-stroke engine problems will fall into one or more of the following categories:

1. Won't start/hard to start
2. Won't turn over
3. Stalls
4. Erratic operation
5. Lack of power
6. Excessive vibration
7. Overheating
8. Excessive smoke

1 Won't start/hard to start

Note: *When an engine won't start, it's usually because the controls are improperly set, the safety interlock devices are interrupting the ignition system or the ignition system is malfunctioning, although fuel problems and lack of compression can also prevent a two-stroke engine from starting (see the information under the heading Where to start? to rule out lack of compression as a cause).*

As mentioned in the section headed How an engine works, a two-stroke engine crankcase must be air-tight. If air leaks develop at seals or gaskets (or because of a porous casting), the engine may not want to start. Air leaks of this type are exasperating to locate, so if you eliminate all other possible reasons why the engine won't start or is very difficult to start, take it to a dealer with the special pressure-checking equipment required to isolate crankcase air leaks.

1 Make sure the controls are positioned properly.

Follow the control cable from the lever to the carburetor. The throttle should be all the way open and the choke should operate when the lever is set on START. As you move the control lever from START to FAST to STOP, the cable should be clamped so the throttle operates properly. The cable may be slipping in the clamp just enough to cause the throttle to malfunction and you might not see the slight movement.

Move the throttle to the open or START position with your fingers. You may have to move the control lever with your other hand to open the throttle.

If the engine now starts, let it run for several minutes, then pull the control lever back to STOP. If the engine slows down but doesn't stop, loosen the cable clamp with a screwdriver and pull the cable toward the control lever very slightly until the engine stops, then retighten the clamp. Start the engine again and run through the control positions. The engine should start, run slowly, run fast and stop when the lever is positioned next to the appropriate label on the control.

2 Make sure the gas tank is at least half full of fresh gasoline/oil mix (with the ratio of gas-to-oil correct) and that fuel is reaching the carburetor (the line between the tank and carburetor could be plugged, kinked or detached).

3   Check the plug wire to make sure it's securely attached to the spark plug.

The terminal on the end of the spark plug wire can come loose and get corroded. Crimp the loop with a pair of pliers (see illustration 3.10) and remove corrosion with sandpaper, a wire brush or a round file.

4   Check the spark plug ground strap to make sure it's not malfunctioning. Some engines have a metal strap that's used to short out the spark plug to stop the engine. If the engine has one, make sure it's not touching the plug (see illustration 3.25).

5   Make sure the grass catcher is properly installed.

Some lawnmowers have a safety switch for the grass catcher where it attaches to the mower housing. This device prevents the engine from starting until the grass catcher is properly installed. If the grass catcher isn't being used, make sure the chute is properly attached to the mower deck.

6   If the engine has a fuel priming device, make sure it's working properly.

It should be pushed four or five times when the engine is cold to fill the carburetor. If the engine is hot, don't operate the primer – it may flood the engine. Instead, pull the starter handle several times with the control lever in the STOP position. This will help clear excess fuel out of the engine. Put the control lever on START and start the engine normally.

7   See if the gas tank cap vent is clogged.

If the gas tank vent is clogged, a vacuum will eventually form in the tank and prevent fuel from reaching the carburetor (the engine will act like it's out of gas).

Remove the cap and check the gasket in it. Sometimes the space between the gasket and cap gets clogged with debris, shutting off the air supply to the tank. Check the hole(s) in the cap to make sure it's open (see illustration 3.11). If you're not sure if the vent is open or not, leave the cap off and try to start the engine. If the engine runs, the cap vent is the problem. Either open the vent or install a new cap. DO NOT run the engine without a cap on the gas tank.

8   Check the air filter to see if it's clean and make sure the gasket between the filter and carburetor is in good shape.

9   Remove the spark plug and check the gap and the base of the plug for dirt. Clean the electrodes with a wire brush and use a fine file to square the side electrode tip so any worn edges are sharp (see illustration 3.18). As a general rule, the spark plug gap can be set at 0.025-inch.

10   Check to see if the plug is firing (see *To check the ignition system* . . . in the section headed *Where to start?*).

If it's fouled, you can clean it, as mentioned above, but a new one should be installed – they're not expensive and you can usually be sure the new plug is good.

Every once in a while, a new plug will turn out to be faulty. If you install a new plug and the engine won't fire even though everything else seems to be okay, try another new plug or use a spark tester.

11   Make sure the plug wire is in good condition.

3.25   Make sure the ground strap used to stop the engine isn't touching the spark plug when trying to start the engine

Bend the wire by hand and look for cracks in the insulation. Also look for burned or melted insulation. If damage is noted, you may have to replace the ignition coil, since the wire usually is permanently attached to it.

12   Check the choke to make sure it's operating properly – if it doesn't close all the way, the engine may not start. If it doesn't open after the engine starts, flooding may occur.

13   See if the blade is loose – it must be tight on the shaft or adaptor.

2   Won't turn over

1   Check to see if something is blocking the blade.

2   See if the recoil starter is jammed (removal covered in Chapter 5).

3   Make sure dirt isn't jamming the flywheel and see if the key is sheared off. Refer to the information in Section 3 under the heading *Troubleshooting a four-stroke engine.*

4   The piston ring(s) may be broken and jammed in one of the ports. The engine will have to be disassembled to check it.

5   The connecting rod may be broken or seized. This will also require engine disassembly to know for sure.

3   Stalls

1   Make sure the gas tank is at least half full of fresh gas/oil mix (with the ratio of gas-to-oil correct) and that fuel is reaching the carburetor (the line between the tank and carburetor could be plugged, kinked or detached).

2   Check the air filter to make sure it isn't clogged.

3   See if the gas tank cap vent is clogged.

   If the gas tank vent is clogged, a vacuum will eventually form in the tank and prevent fuel from reaching the carburetor (the engine will act like it's out of gas).

   Remove the cap and check the gasket in it. Sometimes the space between the gasket and cap gets clogged with debris, shutting off the air supply to the tank. Check the hole(s) in the cap to make sure it's open **(see illustration 3.11)**. If you're not sure if the vent is open or not, leave the cap off and try to start the engine. If the engine runs, the cap vent is the problem. Either open the vent or install a new cap. DO NOT run the engine without a cap on the gas tank.

4   See if the carburetor is adjusted correctly. Turn the mixture screw out for a richer fuel mixture (follow the procedure in Section 4 under the heading *Troubleshooting a four-stroke engine*).

5   If the engine is equipped with ignition points, check them; they could be dirty, burned or out-of-adjustment (see Chapter 4).

4   Erratic operation

1   Make sure the gas tank is at least half full of fresh gas/oil mix (with the ratio of gas-to-oil correct) and that fuel is reaching the carburetor (the line between the tank and carburetor could be plugged, kinked or detached).

2   Check the carburetor to make sure it's adjusted properly. Refer to the information in Section 4 under the heading *Troubleshooting a four-stroke engine*.

3   Remove the spark plug and check the gap and the base of the plug for dirt. Clean the electrodes with a wire brush and use a fine file to square the side electrode tip so any worn edges are sharp **(see illustration 3.18)**. As a general rule, the spark plug gap can be set at 0.025-inch.

4   Check to see if the plug is firing (see *To check the ignition system . . .* in the section headed *Where to start?*).

If the plug is fouled, you can clean it, as mentioned above, but a new one should be installed – they're not expensive and you can usually be sure the new plug is good.

Every once in a while, a new plug will turn out to be faulty. If you install a new plug and the engine won't fire even though everything else seems to be okay, try another new plug or use a spark tester.

5   If the engine is equipped with ignition points, check them; they could be dirty, burned or out-of-adjustment (see Chapter 4).

6   Check the crankcase reed valve (mounted where the carburetor is attached to the crankcase) to see if it's stuck or clogged (not used on all engines).

7   If the crankcase isn't air-tight, the engine may run erratically (see the **Note** at the beginning of this section).

8   Check the wires for the engine stop switch. Loose connections in the wires can cause the engine to cut-out when the machine is being used.

5   Lack of power

1   Make sure the gas tank is at least half full of fresh gas/oil mix (with the ratio of gas-to-oil correct) and that fuel is reaching the carburetor (the line between the tank and carburetor could be plugged, kinked or detached).

2   Check the air filter to see if it's clogged.

3   Remove the spark plug and check the gap and the base of the plug for dirt. Clean the electrodes with a wire brush and use a fine file to square the side electrode tip so any worn edges are sharp **(see illustration 3.18)**. As a general rule, the spark plug gap can be set at 0.025-inch.

4   Check to see if the plug is firing (see *To check the ignition system . . .* in the section headed *Where to start?*).

If the plug is fouled, you can clean it, as mentioned above, but a new one should be installed – they're not expensive and you can usually be sure the new plug is good.

Every once in a while, a new plug will turn out to be faulty. If you install a new plug and the engine won't fire even though everything else seems to be okay, try another new plug or use a spark tester.

5   Check for carbon build-up in the exhaust port and muffler. You'll have to remove the muffler for this check (Chapter 5).

6   Check the carburetor to make sure it's adjusted properly. Refer to the information in Section 4 under the heading *Troubleshooting a four-stroke engine*.

7   Check the choke and throttle controls to make sure they aren't allowing the valves to move during engine operation.

3.26 If the cooling fins are clogged with grass and other debris, clean them with a paint brush or compressed air

3.27 The exhaust ports on a two-stroke engine can get clogged with carbon – use a hardwood stick to knock the carbon out to avoid damage to the piston and rings

8   Check the crankcase reed valve (mounted where the carburetor is attached to the crankcase) to see if it's stuck or clogged (not used on all engines).

9   If the crankcase isn't air-tight, the engine may lack power (see the **Note** at the beginning of this section).

10   If the piston rings are worn or the cylinder is damaged, power output can be reduced.

6   Excessive vibration

1   Check the blade to see if it's tight and in balance.

2   See if the engine mounting bolts are loose **(see illustration 3.23)**.

3   Other causes may include damaged crankshaft ball bearings, crankshaft or connecting rod.

7   Overheating

1   Make sure the gas/oil mixture ratio is correct – too little oil will result in poor lubrication and heat; too much oil can actually lean out the mixture.

2   Check the air filter to see if it's dirty.

3   Make sure the correct spark plug is installed.

4   Check the cooling fins to see if they're clogged **(see illustration 3.26)**. Remove debris from the fins with a brush or compressed air.

5   Check the exhaust ports to see if they're clogged with carbon **(see illustration 3.27)**. The muffler will have to be removed to get at the ports. If carbon is built-up, remove it with a hardwood stick.

6   See if the carburetor is dirty or out-of-adjustment. The mixture screw may be set too lean (turned in too far).

7   Check the nuts, bolts or screws holding the carburetor in place to see if they're tight **(see illustration 3.28).**

8   See if the flywheel nut is loose.

9   If the crankcase isn't air-tight, the engine may overheat (see the **Note** at the beginning of this section).

10   Don't overload the engine or run it too fast for too long.

8   Excessive smoke

1   Make sure the choke is off.

2   Make sure the gas/oil mixture ratio is correct – too much oil will result in excessive smoke.

3   See if the carburetor mixture screw is set too rich (too far out).

4   Check the exhaust ports to see if they're clogged with carbon **(see illustration 3.27).** The muffler will have to be removed to get at the ports. If carbon is built-up, remove it with a hardwood stick.

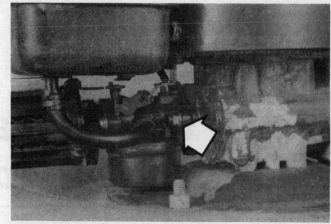

3.28   Two-stroke engines are especially sensitive to air leaks, so make sure the carburetor mounting nuts, bolts or screws are tightened evenly

4 Tune-up and routine maintenance

Introduction

This chapter covers the checks and procedures necessary for the tune-up and routine maintenance of typical small gas engines. It includes a checklist of service procedures designed to keep the engine in proper running condition and prevent possible problems. Separate sections contain detailed instructions for doing the jobs on the checklist, as well as additional maintenance information designed to increase the engine's reliability.

The sections detailing the maintenance and inspection procedures are written as step-by-step comprehensive guides to the actual performance of the work. References to additional information in other chapters is also included and shouldn't be overlooked.

The first step in this or any maintenance plan is to prepare yourself before the actual work begins. Read through the appropriate sections covering the procedures to be done before you begin. Gather up all necessary parts and tools. If it appears that you could have a problem during a particular job, don't hesitate to seek advice from a dealer, repair shop or experienced do-it-yourselfer.

Before attacking the engine with wrenches and screwdrivers, clean it with a degreaser to ensure that dirt doesn't contaminate the internal parts. This will also allow you to detect wear and damage that could otherwise easily go unnoticed.

Tune-up and maintenance checklist

Every time the engine is refueled

Check the oil level (four-stroke engines only)
Check control operation

Yearly maintenance

Note: *The following procedures should be done at least once a year under normal circumstances (approximately 25 hours of engine use per year) and more often if the engine is used extensively.*

- Service the air cleaner
- Clean the gas tank and line
- Clean the carburetor float bowl
- Change the oil (four-stroke engines only)
- Check the recoil starter
- Clean the cooling fins and shroud
- Check the compression
- Check the governor and linkage
- Replace or clean/adjust the ignition points*
- Check the coil and ignition wires
- Decarbonize the cylinder head
- Check the muffler
- Check the valve tappet clearances (four-stroke engines only)
- Install a new spark plug
- Check/adjust the controls
- Adjust the carburetor
- Check the engine mount bolts/nuts
  * Not all engines

1 Check the oil level (four-stroke engines only)

Each time you refill the gas tank, or every two or three hours of engine operation, check the crankcase oil level and add more oil as needed. Some manufacturers may recommend more or less frequent oil checks – follow the instructions in your owner's manual if they differ from the information here.

1 Locate the cap used to check the oil level and add oil to the engine – it may be a threaded or friction fit cap or plug. The cap may be marked "Engine oil" or "Oil fill" **(see illustration 4.1)**.

4.1 The engine oil check/fill plug should be clearly marked – clean it off before removing it

4.2   The oil level on engines that don't have a dipstick should be even with the top of the check/fill plug opening as shown here

2   Clean the plug and the area around it to prevent dirt from falling into the engine when the plug is removed.

3   Make sure the engine is level, then remove the oil check/fill cap or plug.

4   If the cap or plug doesn't have a dipstick attached to it, the oil level should be at the top of the opening **(see illustration 4.2)** or even with a mark or the top of a slot that indicates the FULL level.

5   If the cap or plug has a dipstick, wipe the oil off, then reinsert it into the engine and pull it out again. Follow the instructions on the dipstick – sometimes the plug must be threaded back in to get an accurate reading.

6   Note the oil level on the dipstick. It should be between the marks on the dipstick (usually ADD and FULL), not above the upper mark or below the lower mark.

7   Add oil to bring it up to the correct level. If it's time to change the oil, don't add any now – change the oil instead (see section 5).

2   Service the air cleaner

Most small engine air cleaners are either foam or pleated-paper types that should be checked/cleaned frequently to ensure proper engine operation. Some engines have a pleated-paper filter that's covered with a foam type filter. If the filter isn't serviced regularly, dirt will get into the engine or it'll build up on the filter and cause an excessively rich fuel mixture – either condition will shorten the engine's life.

1   Remove the filter from the engine. Some filters simply snap into place, while others are under a cover attached with screw(s) or wing nut(s) **(see illustrations 4.3 and 4.4)**.

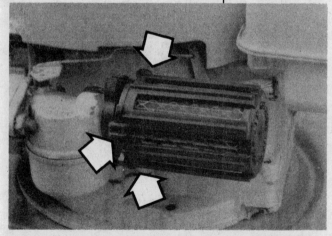

4.3   A typical pleated-paper air cleaner – this one is held in place with three plastic clips (arrows) that must be released to remove the element

4.4   This typical foam air cleaner is mounted in a housing – the cover is attached with one screw

2   If the filter is made of pleated-paper, tap it on a work-bench to dislodge the dirt or blow it out from the inside with LOW PRESSURE compressed air. If it's torn, bent, crushed, wet or damaged in any other way, install a new one. DO NOT wash a pleated-paper filter to clean it!

3   If the filter is foam, wash it in hot soapy water (**see illustration 4.5**) and wring it out, then let it dry thoroughly. Add about two teaspoons of engine oil to the filter and squeeze it several times to distribute the oil evenly (**see illustration 4.6**). This is very important – the oil is what catches the dirt in the filter. If the filter is torn or falling apart, install a new one.

4   Remove any dirt from the air cleaner housing and check the gasket between it and the carburetor. If the gasket is deteriorated or missing, dirt will get past the filter into the engine.

5   Reinstall the filter.

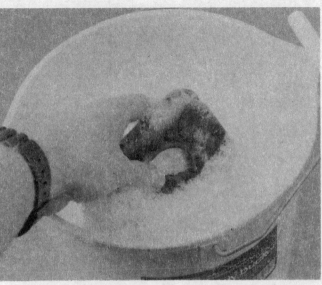

4.5   Most foam filters can be washed in soapy water and reused, although some of them are disposable and should be replaced with a new one

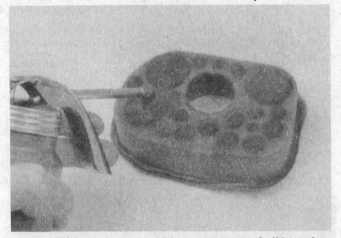

4.6   Work about two or three teaspoons of oil into the foam filter before reinstalling it in the housing

3 Clean the gas tank and line

Warning: *Gasoline is extremely flammable and highly explosive under certain conditions – safety precautions must be followed when working on any part of the fuel system! Don't smoke or allow open flames or unshielded light bulbs in or near the work area. Don't do this procedure in a garage with a natural gas appliance (such as a water heater or clothes dryer).*

The gas tank collects dust, grass clippings, dirt, water and other debris under normal circumstances and must be cleaned so the contaminants don't find their way into the carburetor. The tank may be mounted separately or attached directly to the carburetor. **Note:** *If the tank is attached to the carburetor, removing the screws may free it, but there's usually not enough room to maneuver it out of position unless the carburetor is removed first.*

1   Remove any covers or shrouds mounted over the gas tank, then remove the tank mounting screws (if used).

2   If a shut-off valve is installed, turn it off.

3   Detach the fuel line from the tank and plug the fitting with your finger so gas doesn't run all over (this isn't necessary if a shut-off valve is used).

4   Lift the tank off the engine.

5   Drain the fuel out of the tank into a gas can, then rinse the tank with solvent and dry it out with compressed air (if available) or let it sit out in the sun for several minutes. If it has a strainer at the outlet fitting, make sure it's clean.

6   Loosen the hose clamps, if used, and detach the fuel line from the carburetor fitting.

7   Make sure the line is clean and unobstructed. If it's cracked or otherwise deteriorated, install a new line and new clamps. **Note:** *If a filter is installed in the line or the tank outlet fitting, clean it or install a new one.*

8   Proceed to section 4 and clean the float bowl (if equipped), then reinstall the tank.

4   Clean the carburetor float bowl

Some carburetors have a float bowl (a reservoir for gasoline) that collects sediment and water which will clog the jets and cause the engine to run poorly or not at all. The float bowl should be drained/cleaned frequently.

1   Some carburetors have a drain plug or small spring-loaded valve on the bottom of the float bowl that's used to drain out sediment and water **(see illustration 4.7)**. Lay a rag under the carburetor, then push up on the valve with a small screwdriver or remove the plug and let gas run out until it looks clean (you'll see little droplets if water comes out).

2   On engines that don't have a drain valve, DO NOT remove the float bowl until the gas tank is drained, the fuel line is pinched off or the tank is removed, otherwise gas will run all over when the float bowl is detached.

3   You'll have to remove a bolt or fitting to detach the float bowl **(see illustration 4.8)**. Use a flare-nut wrench, if you have one, to avoid rounding off the bolt. On some engines you may have to remove the carburetor to get the bolt out so the float bowl will come off.

4.7   Some carburetors have a spring-loaded drain valve on the bottom of the float bowl (arrow) to get rid of sediment and water in the carburetor

4.8   The float bowl is usually attached to the carburetor with a bolt or other fitting at the bottom (and it's usually hard to get at)

4   Dump the gas out of the float bowl and clean it with a rag **(see illustration 4.9)**.

5   Check the condition of the gasket – if it's deteriorated or deformed, install a new one.

6   Reinstall the float bowl and tighten the bolt securely. Make sure the fiber washer is in place on the bolt (if used).

7   Reinstall the tank, remove the fuel line clamp or add gas to the tank, then start the engine and make sure it runs okay.

4.9   Wipe out the float bowl and check the gasket before reinstalling it

5   Change the oil (four-stroke engines only)

Oil is the lifeblood of an engine; check and change it often to ensure maximum performance and the longest engine life possible. If the equipment is operated in dusty conditions, change the oil more frequently than you normally would. **Note:** *Most small engine manufacturers recommend 30-weight oil – check your owner's manual for exact recommendations. Do not use multi-viscosity oil unless it's the only type available, then change it as soon as possible and install straight 30-weight.*

1   Start the engine and allow it to warm up (warm oil will drain easier and more contaminants will be removed with it).

2   Stop the engine – never attempt to drain the oil with the engine running!

3   Disconnect the spark plug wire from the spark plug and position it out of the way.

4   Locate the drain plug. Some are located on the outside edge of the bottom of the engine **(see illustration 4.10)**, while others (particularly on engines used on rotary mowers) are on the bottom of the engine

4.10   On some engines, the oil drain plug is on the side of the crankcase, . . .

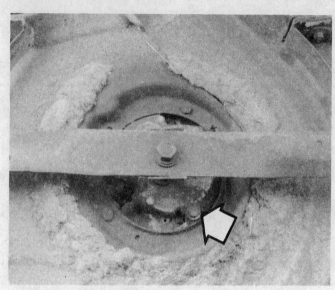

4.11 . . . while on others it's at the bottom – don't work under a mower deck unless the spark plug wire is disconnected!

(see illustration 4.11). **Note:** *Some engines don't have a drain plug – the oil is drained out through the filler hole by tilting the engine.*

5   Clean the plug and the area around it, then remove it from the engine and allow the oil to drain into a container. Don't rush this part of the procedure – let the oil drain until the engine is completely empty. Tip the engine so oil runs toward the opening if necessary.

6   Remove the oil check/fill plug also.

7   Clean the drain plug and reinstall it in the engine. If a gasket is used, be sure it's in place and undamaged. Tighten the plug securely.

8   Refill the crankcase with new, clean oil. Use a funnel to avoid spills, but be sure to wipe it out before pouring oil into it. Add oil until the level is at the top of the opening, then clean the plug and reinstall it. Wipe up any spilled oil.

9   Reconnect the spark plug wire and start the engine, then check for leaks and shut it off.

10   Recheck the oil level and add more oil if necessary, but don't overfill it.

11   Dispose of oily rags and the old oil properly.

6 Check the recoil starter

This is a simple check that can be done without removing anything from the engine. **Note:** *Disconnect the wire from the spark plug to prevent the engine from starting.*

1   Pull the starter rope out slowly.

2   If the starter is noisy, binding or rough, the return spring, pulley or rope may be jammed.

3   If the crankshaft doesn't turn as the rope is pulled out, the ratcheting drive mechanism isn't engaging.

4   After the rope is all the way out, check it for wear along its entire length.

5   Allow the rope to rewind, but don't release the handle so the rope flies back.

6   If the rope won't rewind, the pulley may be binding, the return spring may be broken, disengaged or insufficiently tensioned or the starter may be assembled incorrectly.

7 Clean the cooling fins and shroud

The shroud air intake and the engine cooling fins must be clean so air can circulate properly to prevent overheating and prolong the engine's life.

1   Refer to Chapter 5 and remove the shroud from the engine.

4.12   The shroud air intake is usually protected by a screen, which should be cleaned regularly

4.13   Use a paint brush or compressed air (if available) to remove grass, dirt and other debris from the engine cooling fins

2   Use a brush or compressed air to clean the shroud screen (**see illustration 4.12**).

3   Do the same for the fins on the cylinder and head (**see illustration 4.13**).

4   Proceed to Section 8.

8   Check the compression

Among other things, poor engine performance may be caused by leaking valves, incorrect valve tappet clearances, a leaking head gasket or worn piston, rings and/or cylinder. A compression check will help pinpoint these conditions.

The compression should be routinely checked once a year or every 50 hours of engine operation (more often if the engine is hard to start or power loss is evident). If the engine is run with low compression, fuel and oil consumption will increase and engine wear will be accelerated.

Honda is the only manufacturer of engines covered in this manual that recommends a gauge to check the compression – the other manufacturers don't publish compression pressure specifications, so a gauge can't be used to draw any conclusions about engine condition.

Honda OHV engines

Note: *The decompression device (if used) must be engaged during the following check.*

1   The only tools required are a compression gauge and a spark plug wrench. Depending on the results of the initial test, a squirt-type oil can may also be needed. A compression gauge that screws into the spark plug hole is preferred over the type that requires hand pressure to maintain the seal at the plug hole.

Haynes small engine repair manual

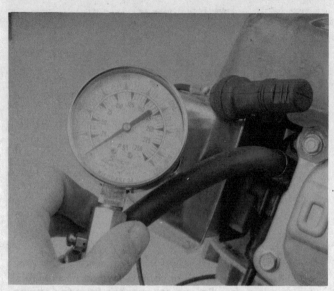

4.14 A compression gauge can be used on Honda engines because the manufacturer provides compression specs

2   Warm up the engine to normal operating temperature and remove any dirt around the spark plug with compressed air or a small brush, then remove the plug. Work carefully, don't strip the spark plug hole threads and don't burn your hands.

3   Ground the spark plug wire on the engine.

4   Install the compression gauge in the spark plug hole **(see illustration 4.14)**. Make sure the choke is open and hold or block the throttle wide open.

5   Crank the engine over a minimum of five to seven revolutions and note the initial movement of the compression gauge needle as well as the final total gauge reading; compare the results to the specifications in the Appendix at the end of the manual.

6   If the compression built up quickly and evenly to the specified amount, you can assume the engine upper end is in reasonably good mechanical condition. Worn or sticking piston rings and a worn cylinder will produce very little initial movement of the gauge needle, but compression will tend to build up gradually as the engine spins over. Valve and valve seat leakage, or head gasket leakage, is indicated by low initial compression which doesn't tend to build up.

7   Proceed to Step 11.

All other engines

8   Remove the spark plug and ground the plug wire on the engine, then seal off the plug hole with your thumb **(see illustration 3.3** in Chapter 3).

9   Operate the starter – if the compression pressure blows your thumb off the hole, the compression is adequate for the engine to run; be careful not to touch the plug wire as this is done – you'll get quite a jolt if you do!

10   Another way to check the compression with the spark plug in place is to remove the cooling shroud/recoil starter mechanism and spin the flywheel in reverse (counterclockwise) **(see illustration 3.4** in Chapter 3). It should return sharply; if it does, the compression is adequate for the engine to run.

All engines

11   To further confirm your findings, add about 1/2-ounce of engine oil to the cylinder by inserting the nozzle of a squirt-type oil can through the spark plug hole **(see illustration 4.15)**. The oil will tend to seal the piston rings if they're leaking. Repeat the test.

4.15   If the compression increases significantly after oil is squirted into the cylinder, the piston rings are bad and the engine should be disassembled for additional checks

12   If the compression increases significantly after the addition of oil, the piston rings and/or cylinder are definitely worn. If the compression doesn't increase, the pressure is leaking past the valves or the head gasket. Leakage past the valves may be caused by burned or cracked valve seats or faces, warped or bent valves or insufficient valve tappet clearances.

13   To summarize, if the compression is low, it may be due to:

Loose spark plug

Loose cylinder head bolts

Blown head gasket

Damaged valves/valve seats (four-stroke engine only)

Insufficient valve tappet clearance (four-stroke engine only)

Warped cylinder head

Bent valve stem(s) (four-stroke engine only)

Worn cylinder bore and/or piston rings

Broken connecting rod or piston

9   Check the governor and linkage

Two types of governors are in common use on small engines: The air-vane type and the mechanical (centrifugal) type. Routine checks of an air-vane governor require removal of the shroud (see Chapter 5). The mechanical governor is usually mounted inside the engine, but the linkage connected to the carburetor is visible on the outside of the engine. **Note:** *If the governor isn't hooked up or seems to be malfunctioning, it should be repaired and the engine operating speed adjusted by a dealer or repair shop with the necessary special tools.*

1   Clean grass clippings and other debris out of the governor linkage (**see illustration 4.16**).

2   See if the linkage moves freely.

3   The throttle on the carburetor should be wide-open with the engine stopped. If it isn't, the linkage may be binding or hooked up incorrectly.

4   Look for worn links and holes and disconnected springs.

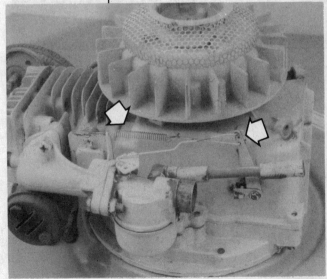

4.16   Typical governor linkage and springs – make sure nothing is disconnected and check for free movement

4.17   The air vane should be undamaged and move freely to operate the linkage correctly

5   If the engine has an air-vane governor, the vane should move freely and operate the linkage **(see illustration 4.17)**. If the vane is bent or distorted, the governor may not operate correctly.

6   If the engine has a mechanical governor, make sure the lever is securely attached to the shaft where it exits the crankcase.

10 Replace or clean/adjust the ignition points

The points should be checked and replaced or cleaned and adjusted at least once a year. On all engines covered in this manual, the ignition points are mounted under the flywheel, so it must come off first (see appropriate engine chapter). **Warning:** *Be sure to remove the spark plug from the engine before working on the ignition system!*

Separate step-by-step procedures for Briggs & Stratton **(see illustrations 4.18 through 4.30)** and Tecumseh/Craftsman engines **(see illustrations 4.31 through 4.43)** are included here – follow the appropriate photo sequence and be sure to read the caption accompanying each illustration.

Briggs & Stratton IGNITION POINT CHECK AND REPLACEMENT

Note: *Some Honda GV150 engines were also equipped with ignition points. The replacement procedure is very similar to the one for Tecumseh engines, but the factory specifies a special ignition timing check after the points are replaced. This is done by attaching an ohmmeter or continuity light to the ignition point wire and a good ground, turning the flywheel and watching the ohmmeter or continuity light to see if the points open when the 'F' mark on the flywheel is aligned with the index mark on the engine block (the ohmmeter will deflect or the light will go off when the points open). If adjustment is needed, remove the flywheel and open or close the point gap until the timing is correct.*

Since the flywheel is off to get at the points, be sure to check for oil leakage past the crankshaft seal under the flywheel. If the seal is leaking, oil more than likely will eventually foul the points and you'll have to remove the flywheel for additional repairs. Seal replacement is covered in Chapter 5.

4.18   Check the flywheel key (arrow) – if it's sheared off, install a new one; look for oil leaking past the crankshaft seal

4.19 Remove the screws and lift off the ignition point cover – check the contact points to see if they're burned, pitted, worn down or covered with oil; if they're in good condition, they can be dressed with a point file, cleaned and readjusted (illustrations 4.26 through 4.28), but once you've gone to the trouble of removing the flywheel, new points should be installed (they don't cost much)

4.20 Remove the screw and detach the condenser, then depress the small spring and release the primary wire from the terminal on the end of the condenser

4.21 Remove the screw and lift out the movable point, return spring and post

4.22 Pull out the plunger and check it for wear – if it's worn to less than 0.870-inch in length or damaged in any way, install a new one (take the old one with you to the dealer). **Note:** *If oil is leaking past the plunger and fouling the points, the plunger bore is probably worn. Take the engine to a dealer and have the bore checked (a special gauge is available for this purpose). If it's worn, the dealer will ream it out and install a bushing to restore the bore.*

4.23 Clean the ignition point cavity with contact cleaner and wipe it out with a rag – use the contact cleaner to remove oil and dirt from the new ignition point contact faces as well

4.24 Reinstall the plunger (with the grooved end out, against the movable point), the movable point, the return spring and the post – make sure the slot in the post engages the nub in the recess, the movable point arm is seated in the slot in the post and the ground wire is under the screw

4.25 Attach the wire to the new condenser (the new points should have a little plastic tool designed to compress the spring that holds the wire on the condenser) and carefully clamp the condenser to the engine – leave the screw loose enough to move the condenser back-and-forth

4.26 Slowly turn the crankshaft until the plunger/movable point is open as far as possible – you may have to try this several times until you get it just right

4.27 Insert a clean feeler gauge – 0.020-inch thick – between the contact points and move the condenser very carefully with a screwdriver until the gap between the points is the same thickness as the feeler gauge (be careful not to change the position of the movable point as this is done)

4.28   Turn the crankshaft and make sure the movable arm opens and closes

4.29   Reinstall the cover and tighten the screws – if the cover is distorted, replace it with a new one or oil and moisture will foul the points

4.30   Use RTV sealant to seal off the wires to prevent oil and moisture from getting to the points

Tecumseh/Craftsman
IGNITION POINT CHECK AND REPLACEMENT

4.31 Check the flywheel key (arrow) – if it's sheared off, install a new one – check the contact points to see if they're burned, pitted, worn down or covered with oil; if they're in good condition, they can be dressed with a point file, cleaned and readjusted (illustrations 4.40 through 4.42), but once you've gone to the trouble of removing the flywheel, new points should be installed (they don't cost much)

4.32 Release the retainer clip and lift off the point cover and gasket; look for oil leaking past the crankshaft seal

4.33 Remove the nut and detach the primary wires from the point terminal – when installing a new condenser, you'll have to cut the original wire at the terminal (the new one will have a terminal that fits over the post)

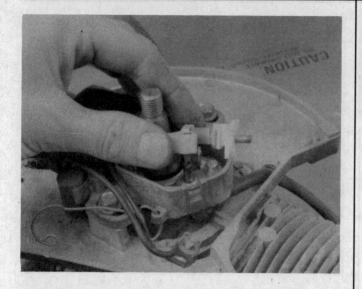

4.34 Slide the movable point up, off the post, and remove the spring and the terminal and insulator

4.35 Remove the screw and lift out the fixed point

4.36 Remove the mounting screw and detach the condenser, then install the new one in its place and route the wire over to the point terminal

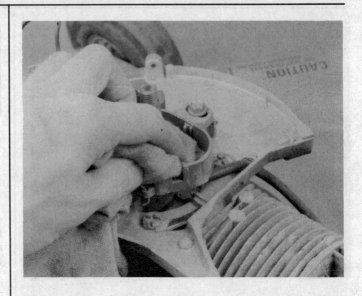

4.37   Clean the ignition point cavity with contact cleaner and wipe it out with a rag – use the contact cleaner to remove oil and dirt from the new ignition point contact faces as well

4.38   Install the new fixed point – leave the screw loose enough to allow movement of the plate

4.39   Slip the new movable point over the post and position the insulator in the cutout – slip the primary and condenser wires onto the terminal and install the nut

4.40 Turn the crankshaft very slowly until the cam opens the movable point as far as possible – if the cam was removed to replace the oil seal, make sure it's installed with the correct side out

4.41 Insert a clean feeler gauge – 0.020-inch thick – between the contact points and move the fixed point very carefully with a screwdriver until the gap between the points is the same thickness as the feeler gauge (be careful not to change the position of the movable point as this is done)

4.42 Turn the crankshaft and make sure the movable arm opens and closes

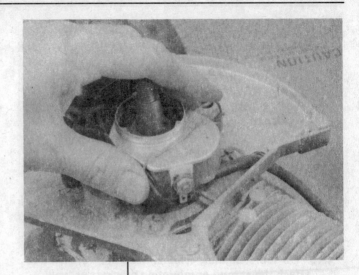

4.43 Install the gasket and point cover and snap the retainer clip into place

11 Check the coil and ignition wires

The ignition coil is usually mounted next to the flywheel, so the shroud will have to be removed to check the wires.

1 Check the spark plug wire for cracked and melted insulation and make sure it's securely attached to the ignition coil **(see illustration 4.44)**.

2 Make sure the terminal fits snugly on the spark plug end. crimp it with a pair of pliers if necessary.

3 Check the primary (small) wires as well. Look for loose and corroded connections and abraded or melted insulation. Now is also a good time to check the engine stop switch. Make sure the switch is actuated when the control lever is moved to STOP. If it isn't, adjust the cable **(see illustration 4.45)**.

4.44 Check the spark plug wire for cracked and melted insulation and make sure it's securely attached at the coil

4.45 This simple engine stop switch grounds the ignition system when the control lever is moved to STOP – if the arm doesn't contact the switch, adjust the cable until it does

4.46   On some engines, cylinder head bolts are used to attach the shroud or mounting brackets as well

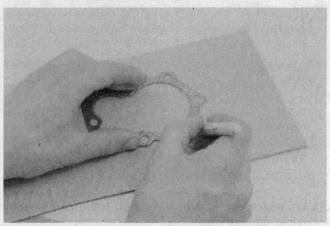

4.47   To avoid mixing up the head bolts (just in case they're different lengths), use the new gasket to transfer the hole pattern to a piece of cardboard, punch holes to accept the bolts and push each bolt through the matching hole in the cardboard as it's removed

12 Decarbonize the cylinder head

Now that unleaded gasoline is widely used, carbon build-up in the cylinder head is not the problem it used to be. However, it's still a good idea to remove the head during a Spring tune-up to scrape out the carbon and other deposits. Before beginning this procedure, buy a new head gasket for your engine. **Note:** *This procedure does not apply to OHV Honda engines.*

1   Begin by disconnecting the wire from the spark plug.

2   Next, remove the shroud and any covers that prevent direct access to the cylinder head and bolts. **Note:** *On many engines, some of the head bolts also are used to attach the shroud or carburetor mounting bracket to the engine* (**see illustration 4.46**). *If you're working on one, loosen all of the head bolts in 1/4-turn increments, following a criss-cross pattern, until the shroud mounting bolts can be removed by hand.*

3   Using the new head gasket, outline the head bolt pattern on a piece of cardboard (**see illustration 4.47**). Punch holes at the bolt locations.

4   If not already done, loosen the cylinder head bolts in 1/4-turn increments until they can be removed by hand. Follow a criss-cross pattern to avoid warping the head.

5   Store the bolts in the cardboard holder as they're removed – this will guarantee that they're reinstalled in their original locations, which is essential (different length bolts are used on some engines).

6   Detach the head from the engine. If it's stuck, tap it with a soft-face hammer to break the gasket seal – DO NOT pry it off with a screwdriver!

7   Remove and discard the gasket – use the new one when the cylinder head is reinstalled.

8   Turn the crankshaft until the piston is at the top of the cylinder, then use a scraper or putty knife and wire brush to remove all deposits from the

4.48   Use a putty knife to remove the deposits from the piston and valves – don't nick or gouge the block or piston (if the deposits are oily, the rings may be bad)

4.49   Turn the crankshaft to open each valve and check the seats and faces (arrows) for cracks and other damage

top of the piston and the area around the valves **(see illustration 4.48)**. Be careful not to nick the gasket mating surface.

9   Turn the crankshaft to open each valve and check them for burned and cracked faces and seats **(see illustration 4.49)**. If the valves are cracked, pitted or bent and the seats are in bad shape, major engine repairs are required.

10   Remove the deposits from the combustion chamber in the head **(see illustration 4.50)**.

11   The mating surfaces of the head and block must be perfectly clean when the head is reinstalled.

12   Use a gasket scraper or putty knife to remove all traces of carbon and old gasket material, then clean the mating surfaces with lacquer thinner or acetone. If there's oil on the mating surfaces when the head is installed, the gasket may not seal correctly and leaks could develop.

13   Check the block and head mating surfaces for nicks, deep scratches and other damage. If damage is slight, it can be removed with a file **(see illustration 4.51)**.

4.50   Scrape the deposits out of the head, then use a wire brush and solvent to finish cleaning it

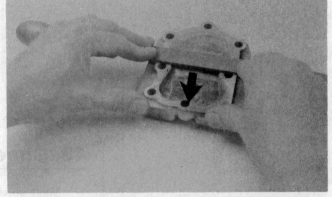

4.51   Use a single-cut file to flatten and restore the block and head mating surface – move the file sideways (arrow) and don't apply excessive pressure

4.52   If you have one of the correct size, use a tap to clean and restore the head bolt holes in the block

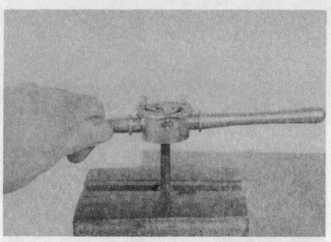

4.53   Mount each head bolt in a vise and restore the threads with a die of the correct size

14   Use a tap of the correct size – if you have one – to chase the threads in the head bolt holes **(see illustration 4.52)**, then clean the holes with compressed air (if available) – make sure that nothing remains in the holes. **Warning:** *Wear eye protection when using compressed air!*

15   If you have the correct size die, mount each bolt in a vise and run the die down the threads to remove corrosion and restore the threads **(see illustration 4.53)**. Dirt, corrosion, sealant and damaged threads will affect torque readings.

16   Reinstall the head using the new gasket. Do not use sealant on the gasket.

17   Once the head bolts are finger-tight, if you have a torque wrench, tighten them in 1/4-turn increments to the torque listed in the specifications in the Appendix at the back of the book. When tightening the bolts, follow a criss-cross pattern to avoid warping the head **(see illustration 4.54)**. **Note:** *Don't forget to install the shroud first if some of the bolts are used to hold it in place!*

18   If you don't have a torque wrench, tighten the bolts evenly and securely with a socket and ratchet or breaker bar.

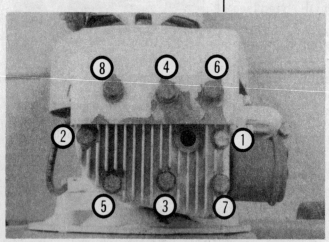

4.54   When tightening the head bolts, follow a criss-cross pattern – never tighten them in order around the edge of the head

13 Check the muffler

1   Make sure the muffler isn't restricted (if it's bent, dented, rusted or falling apart, install a new one).

2   Check the mounting bolts to make sure they're tight. A loose muffler can damage the engine.

3   If the muffler threads directly into the engine, make sure it's tight.

4   If the engine is a two-stroke, remove the muffler and check for carbon build-up in the exhaust ports (see illustration 4.55). Scrape the carbon out of the ports and reinstall the muffler.

4.55   The exhaust ports on a two-stroke engine can get clogged with carbon, which should be removed with a hardwood stick

14 Check the valve tappet clearance (four-stroke engines only)

Correct valve tappet clearance is essential for efficient fuel use, easy starting, maximum power output, prevention of overheating and smooth engine operation. It also ensures the valves will last as long as possible.

When the valve is closed, clearance should exist between the end of the stem and the tappet. The clearance is very small – measured in thousandths of an inch – but it's very important. The recommended clearances are listed in the specifications in Appendix A at the back of the book. Note that intake and exhaust valves often require different clearances. **Note:** *The engine must be cold when the clearances are checked.*

A feeler gauge with a blade thickness equal to the valve clearance(s) will be needed for this procedure.

On most engines, if the clearances are too small, the valves will have to be removed and the stem ends ground down carefully and lapped to provide more clearance (this is a major job, covered in the overhaul and repair procedures in the appropriate engine chapter). If the clearances are too great, new valves will have to be installed (again, a major repair procedure). **Note:** *Honda OHV engines have adjustable rocker arms for changing the valve clearances.*

1   Disconnect the wire from the spark plug and ground it on the engine.

All engines except Honda OHV

2   Remove the bolts and detach the tappet cover plate or the crankcase breather assembly (see illustration 4.56). **Note:** *On some engines the crankcase breather*

4.56   Remove the bolts and detach the tappet cover or crankcase breather from the engine

4.57   On some engines, the carburetor must be removed to get at the tappet chamber

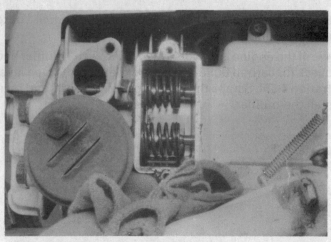

4.58   Make sure the valves are completely closed when checking the clearances

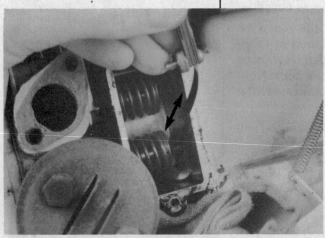

4.59   If the clearance is correct, the feeler gauge will fit between the valve stem and tappet with a slight drag

is behind the carburetor, so the carburetor will have to be removed first (**see illustration 4.57**).

3   Turn the crankshaft by hand and watch the valves to see if they stick in the guide(s).

4   Turn the crankshaft until the intake valve is wide open, then turn it an additional 360-degrees (one complete turn). This will ensure the valves are completely closed for the clearance check (**see illustration 4.58**).

5   Select a feeler gauge thickness equal to the specified valve clearance and slip it between the valve stem end and the tappet (**see illustration 4.59**).

6   If the feeler gauge can be moved back-and-forth with a slight drag, the clearance is correct. If it's loose, the clearance is excessive; if it's tight (watch the valve to see if it's forced open slightly), the clearance is inadequate.

7   If the clearance is incorrect, refer to the appropriate chapter for valve service procedures.

8   Reinstall the crankcase breather or tappet cover plate.

Honda OHV engines

9   Remove the bolts and detach the cylinder head cover from the engine. **Note:** *On some engines the shroud will have to be removed first to get the cylinder head cover off.*

10   Remove the spark plug and place your thumb over the plug hole, then slowly turn the crankshaft with the starter or blade until you feel pressure building up in the cylinder. Use a flashlight to look into the spark plug hole and see if the piston is at the top of it's stroke. Continue to turn the crankshaft until it is.

4.60 On Honda OHV engines, the valve clearance is checked between the valve stem and rocker arm

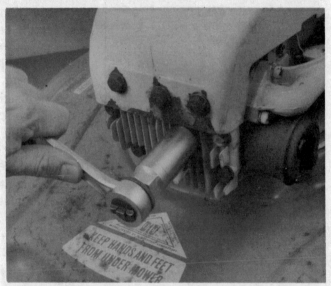

4.61 Use a spark plug socket to remove and install the plug

11   Select a feeler gauge thickness equal to the specified valve clearance and slip it between the valve stem end and the rocker arm **(see illustration 4.60)**.

12   If the feeler gauge can be moved back-and-forth with a slight drag, the clearance is correct. If it's loose, the clearance is excessive; if it's tight (watch the valve to see if it's forced open slightly), the clearance is inadequate.

13   To adjust the clearance, loosen the rocker arm locknut and turn the pivot in or out as required (turn it out to increase the clearance; turn it in to decrease the clearance).

14   Hold the pivot with a wrench and tighten the locknut securely, then re-check the clearance.

15 Install a new spark plug

A defective spark plug will increase fuel consumption, lead to formation of deposits in the cylinder head, cause hard starting, contribute to engine oil dilution (from contamination with raw gas) and cause the engine to misfire. The spark plug in a two-stroke engine is particularly prone to fouling and should be checked and cleaned frequently.

1   Detach the wire from the spark plug.

2   Remove the spark plug from the engine **(see illustration 4.61)**. Check the spark plug's condition, referring to the chart on the inside of the rear cover of this manual.

3   If the plug is coated with deposits, it can be cleaned with a wire brush **(see illustration 4.62)** and sprayed with plug/point cleaner (available in aerosol cans).

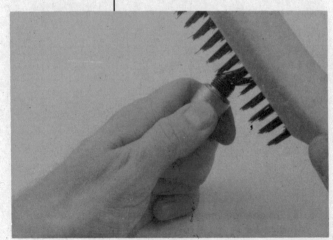

4.62 Use a wire brush and aerosol cleaner to remove deposits from the plug tip

4.63   The spark plug electrodes should be square and sharp – use a fine file to dress them

4   If the deposits are thick or hard, use a jack knife to remove them, then resort to the wire brush and aerosol cleaner.

5   If the electrodes are slightly rounded off, use a small file to square them up **(see illustration 4.63)**. The sharp edges will make it easier for the spark to occur.

6   If the electrodes are worn smooth or the porcelain insulator is cracked, install a new spark plug – the cost is minimal. Make sure the new plug has the same length threads and tip as the original.

7   Check the gap with a wire-type gauge **(see illustration 4.64)**. The correct gap is listed in the Appendix at the back of the book.

8   If adjustment is required, bend the side electrode only with the special notched adjuster on the gap gauge **(see illustration 4.65)**.

9   Check the threaded hole in the cylinder head. If the threads are damaged or stripped out, a special insert can be installed to salvage the head (see Chapter 2).

4.64   Spark plug manufacturers recommend using a wire-type gauge when checking the gap – if the wire doesn't slide between the electrodes with a slight drag, adjustment is required

10   Install the plug in the engine and tighten it finger-tight. A torque wrench should be used for final tightening of the spark plug to a specified torque value, but the torque figure isn't always readily available (it'll varydepending on the size of the plug, the type of seat and the material the head is made of). As a general rule, the plug should be tightened 1/2-to-3/4 turn after the gasket contacts the cylinder head.

11   Reconnect the spark plug wire. If it's loose on the plug, crimp the wire terminal loop with a pair of pliers **(see illustration 4.66)**.

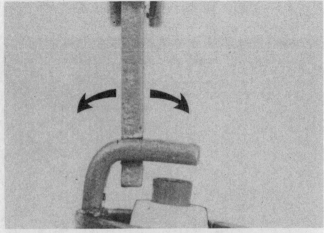

4.65   To change the gap, bend the side electrode only, as indicated by the arrows, and be very careful not to crack or chip the porcelain insulator surrounding the center electrode

4.66   Use a pair of pliers to crimp the plug wire terminal so it fits snugly on the plug

4.67 Lubricate the cable with WD-40 (apply the lubricant at the upper end of the cable)

4.68 The cable must be securely attached at the engine or the controls won't work properly

16 Check/adjust the controls

The engine controls normally consist of a single lever that operates a cable connected to the governor linkage and/or choke valve on the carburetor. Some types of power equipment also have safety-related controls that shut down the engine if the operator releases his grip on the equipment.

There are so many different control configurations in use on small engines that it would be impossible to cover the correct hook-up and adjustment of all of them, so the following information is general in nature.

1   Check the lever to make sure it operates smoothly and moves the cable. Lubricate the lever pivot and cable if necessary (**see illustration 4.67**).

2   The cable must be clamped in a stationary position at the engine. Tighten the clamp if necessary (**see illustration 4.68**).

3   When the lever is moved to the STOP position, the switch on the carburetor must operate and short out (ground) the ignition system (**see illustration 4.45**).

17 Adjust the carburetor

Carburetor adjustments are done by turning the high and/or low speed mixture screws. Some carburetors don't have any mixture screws, while others have one for either high-speed adjustments or low speed adjustments, but not both. Still others have one screw to adjust the fuel/air mixture at high speeds and another screw that controls the mixture at low speeds – the low speed screw is usually the one closest to the engine end of the carburetor. If two screws are used, they must be adjusted separately.

The mixture screws control the flow of fuel through the carburetor circuit(s) (**see illustration 4.69**). If the tip is damaged or the screw is incorrectly adjusted, loss of power and erratic engine operation will result.

4.69 Typical mixture adjusting screws

Haynes small engine repair manual

4.70   Check the mixture screw tip to make sure it isn't damaged

1   Remove the mixture screw and check the tip – if it looks bent or a groove has been worn in the tapered portion, install a new one **(see illustration 4.70)**. Do not attempt to straighten it. If the O-ring on the screw is damaged or deteriorated, replace it before attempting to adjust the mixture.

2   If the screw isn't bent or worn, reinstall it and turn it in until it stops – tighten it with your fingers only, don't force it.

3   Back it out about 1-1/4 turns (counterclockwise) **(see illustration 4.71)**. **Note:** *The actual recommended number of turns out is different for each carburetor type, but the figure given here is in the ballpark for most engines.*

4   Start the engine and turn the screw clockwise until the engine starts to slow down. This means the fuel mixture is too lean (not enough gas).

5   Slowly turn the screw out (counterclockwise) until the engine begins to run smoothly. Keep going very slowly until the engine just begins to run rough again. Also watch for black smoke from the exhaust.

6   Finally, turn the screw in again (clockwise) to a point about half-way between rough operation and smooth operation. This is the perfect setting.

7   If an idle (low-speed) mixture screw is used, adjust it in the same manner with the engine idling. **Note:** *Honda engines are equipped with a pilot air screw, rather than a low-speed mixture screw. Turning the pilot screw has the same effect (it changes the fuel/air mixture), but it's reversed. When the pilot screw is turned in, it causes a richer mixture; conversely, when it's backed out, the mixture becomes leaner.* After the low-speed mixture has been set, recheck the high-speed adjustment – it may be affected by the idle adjustment.

8   Some carburetors also have an idle speed adjusting screw that's used to open or close the throttle valve slightly to change the idle speed only, not the fuel/air mixture. Turning it will cause the engine to speed up or slow down. You can tell the idle speed screw from the mixture screw(s) because it acts on the throttle linkage and doesn't screw into the carburetor body.

4.71   Turn the mixture screw in small increments and wait for the engine to respond before continuing

18 Check the engine mount bolts/nuts

If the engine mounting bolts/nuts are loose, the engine will vibrate excessively and damage the equipment it's mounted on.

1   Disconnect the spark plug wire from the plug and ground it on the engine.

2   Use wrenches and sockets to tighten the mounting fasteners securely.

3   If the nuts/bolts are stripped, install new ones.

4   Reconnect the spark plug wire.

Preparing an engine for storage

Since power equipment is often designed for use only during certain times of the year (like lawn mowers and snow blowers, for example), small engines usually end up being stored for months at a time. As a result, needed repairs are neglected, corrosion takes place, gas left in the tank and carburetor gums up, moisture collects in ignition and fuel system components and the equipment is subjected to physical damage as it's moved to get at something stored behind it.

After a long dormant period, the equipment is hauled out, gas is added to the tank, the oil is checked (not always!) and the engine is fired up – but it won't start or it won't run very well. To avoid problems caused by seasonal storage, run down the following checklist of things to do and make sure the engine is properly prepared to survive a long period of non-use so it'll start and run well when you need it.

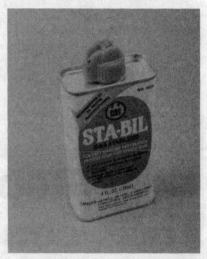

The most important thing when preparing an engine for storage is to drain the fuel system or add a gas stabilizing chemical to the tank

- Operate the engine until it runs out of gas, then drain the float bowl (if equipped)

- An alternative to running the engine out of gas is to add a gasoline stabilizer (available at auto parts stores and small engine dealers) to the tank – follow the instructions on the container

- Wipe off all dust and remove debris from engine parts

- Service the air cleaner (see section 2 in this chapter)

- Remove the spark plug and squirt some clean engine oil into the spark plug hole, then operate the starter to distribute the oil in the cylinder

- Clean and regap the spark plug, then reinstall it (see section 15 in this chapter)

- Store the equipment in a dry place and cover the engine with plastic – don't seal the plastic around the base of the engine or condensation may occur

Squirt oil into the spark plug hole to coat the piston, rings and cylinder and prevent rust

5 Repair procedures common to all engines

Engine removal and installation

Engine removal is usually done only if major repairs or an overhaul are required (or, obviously, if a new engine is being installed on the equipment). In most cases, minor repairs can be accomplished without removing the engine.

1 Detach the spark plug wire and ground it on the engine block.

2 Disconnect the control cables from the engine. **Note:** *On many newer pieces of equipment, a flywheel brake cable and wire harness may have to be detached as well as the throttle cable.*

3 Drain and/or remove the fuel tank so gas doesn't run all over if the equipment must be tipped to get at the blade or engine mount bolts.

4 Remove the blade and hub or drivebelt(s)/chain from the power take-off end of the crankshaft.

The bolt(s) holding a lawn mower blade in place are usually very tight and often corroded. Apply penetrating oil and let it soak in for several minutes, then use a six-point socket and breaker bar for added leverage. Wear a leather glove so the blade doesn't cut your hand or wedge a block of wood between the mower deck and blade so it doesn't turn. If all else fails, take the mower to a shop or gas station and have the bolt(s) removed with an air impact wrench.

5 Remove the mounting nuts/bolts and detach the engine from the equipment.

6 If major repairs are planned, use a degreaser to clean the engine before disassembling it.

7 Installation is the reverse of removal.

Muffler removal and installation

Some mufflers screw into the engine, while others are attached with bolts. Some are located above the mower deck; some (particularly on two-stroke engines) are located below it. **Note:** *If the muffler is in good condition, it can be cleaned by tapping it with a soft-face hammer and dumping out the carbon that's dislodged.*

Screw-in mufflers

1   To remove a screw-in type, first apply penetrating oil to the threads and let it sit for several minutes. You may have to tip the equipment to do this.

2   Try to remove the muffler with a pipe wrench by turning it counterclockwise **(see illustration 5.1)**. Some mufflers have a lock ring that must be loosened with a punch and hammer before turning the pipe. Others have a built-in hex to accept an open-end wrench (usually there's not enough room to use a pipe wrench with this type).

3   If it breaks off, try to remove the part left in the engine (if there's enough left to grasp with the wrench). If it won't come out, use a large screw extractor or cold chisel to remove it. The muffler material is fairly soft, so don't damage the threads in the engine.

4   Screw in the new muffler, but don't overtighten it. If a lock ring is used, tighten it with a hammer and punch.

5.1   Screw-in mufflers can be removed/installed with a pipe wrench – if the muffler has a built-in hex for an open-end wrench, be sure to take advantage of it (don't use a pipe wrench on the muffler body, only the pipe screwed into the engine)

Bolt-on mufflers

5   Apply penetrating oil to the bolt(s) and let it soak in for several minutes.

6   Remove the bolt(s) and detach the muffler (some mufflers also have a gasket).

7   If a bolt breaks off in the engine block (which they often do), you may be able to remove it with a screw extractor (read Chapter 2 before deciding to tackle this job). If it protrudes far enough, you may be able to grip it with a Vise-Grip pliers and unscrew it. Apply more penetrating oil before attempting this.

8   Install the new muffler (with a new gasket, if used) and tighten the bolt(s) securely.

5.2   Some recoil starters are attached to the shroud with screws, . . .

5.3   . . . while others are bolted to the engine and can be removed separately from the shroud

Shroud/recoil starter removal and installation

The recoil starter on most engines is an integral part of the shroud that's used to direct the cooling air around the cylinder and head. On some engines, the starter is attached to the shroud or engine with nuts or bolts and can be removed separately for repairs or replacement **(see illustrations 5.2 and 5.3)**.

1   Detach any control cables/wire harnesses clamped to the shroud.

2   If the gas tank is mounted on the shroud, remove it or detach the fuel line from the carburetor and plug it so gas doesn't run all over. **Note:** *Some engines are equipped with a shut-off valve on the tank – if your engine has one, turn it off and detach the line from the carburetor.*

3   Remove the nuts/bolts and lift the shroud off the engine **(see illustration 5.4)**.

4   Before installing the shroud, clean it to remove grass clippings and other debris. Also, make sure the bolt threads in the engine are clean and in good condition.

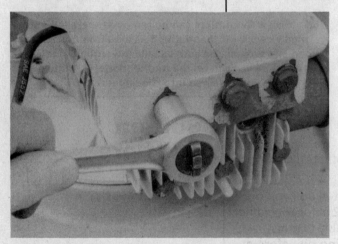

5.4   Three or four bolts or screws are usually used to hold the shroud to the engine – cylinder head bolts often are used to attach it at one end

Oil seal replacement

Two seals are normally used to keep oil inside the crankcase (four-stroke engines) or the gas/oil mixture inside the crankcase and air out (two-stroke engines) – one on the flywheel side and one on the drive or power take-off side of the crankshaft.

Repair procedures common to all engines

If an oil seal goes bad, oil will leak out all over the engine and/or performance will suffer (particularly on four-stroke engines with ignition points that can get fouled by the oil and all two-stroke engines). If the seals on a two-stroke engine are bad, hard starting, erratic operation and possible engine damage can occur due to a lean fuel/air mixture caused by extra air entering the crankcase through the leaking seal(s).

Seals can often be replaced without removing the crankshaft. If the seal on the power take-off end of the crankshaft is leaking, the blade or drive pulley/sprocket will have to be removed first. The flywheel will have to be removed first if the seal under it is leaking (refer to the appropriate engine chapter for the flywheel removal procedure).

Once the seal is exposed, proceed as follows:

1   Note how the seal is installed (what the side that faces out looks like and how far it's recessed into the bore), then remove it.

On most engines, the seal can be pried out with a screwdriver (see illustration 5.5). Be careful not to nick or otherwise damage the seal bore if this is done.

Some seals consist of three separate pieces – a lock ring, a retainer and the seal. **Note**: *Experience has shown that this type of seal is difficult to replace with the crankshaft installed. There's usually very little room to work, which makes the job very exasperating, and increases the chance the new seal may not be airtight, which defeats the whole purpose of doing the job. Additionally, the magneto will probably have to be removed to make room, so it may be easier in the long run to go ahead and disassemble the engine (remove the crankshaft) to replace the seal.*

Pry the lock ring out with a sharp tool like an awl, scribe or ice pick, then turn the engine upside-down and tap the end of the crankshaft to dislodge the retainer. Remove the seal with a scribe. If it won't come out, you may have to remove the crankshaft (which requires engine disassembly).

2   Clean the seal bore and the crankshaft. Remove any burrs that could damage the new seal from the crankshaft with a file or whetstone.

3   If necessary, wrap electrician's tape around the crankshaft to protect the new seal as it's installed. The keyway in the crankshaft is particularly apt to cut or otherwise damage the seal as it's slipped over it.

4   Apply a thin layer of multi-purpose grease to the outer edge of the new seal and lubricate the seal lip(s) with plenty of grease (see illustration 5.6).

5   Place the seal squarely in the bore with the open side facing into the engine.

5.5   Carefully pry out the oil seal with a screwdriver (top); grind a small groove in the side of the screwdriver tip so it'll grip the seal better (bottom)

5.6   Apply multi-purpose grease to the outer edge and the lip(s) of the new seal before installing it

5.7   A socket or piece of pipe makes a handy seal installation tool

5.8   Governor linkages are unique and somewhat complex, so make a sketch of how all the parts fit together before disconnecting anything

6   Carefully tap the seal into place with a large socket or section of pipe and a hammer until it's seated in the bore **(see illustration 5.7)**. The outer diameter of the socket or pipe should be the same size as the seal outer diameter.

7   If the seal consists of several pieces, install the retainer and lock ring and make sure the lock ring is seated in the groove.

Carburetor removal

Warning: *Gasoline is extremely flammable and highly explosive under certain conditions – safety precautions must be followed when working on the carburetor or gas tank! Don't smoke or allow open flames or un-shielded light bulbs in or near the work area. Don't do this procedure in a garage with a natural gas appliance (such as a water heater or clothes dryer) and have a fire extinguisher handy.*

1   If equipped, turn the fuel valve off.

2   Remove the air cleaner assembly.

3   Disconnect the governor spring(s) **(see illustration 5.8)**.

This is very important – most governor linkages have several holes for hooking things up and it can get very confusing. Don't rely on your memory or you may not be able to get everything hooked up correctly. Make a simple sketch to refer to later.

Sometimes it's easier to disconnect the governor spring(s) after the carburetor is detached from the engine.

4   Disconnect the throttle cable and kill switch wire (if equipped) from the carburetor. This isn't necessary on all engines – try to determine if the cable/wire will interfere with the actual carburetor removal before disconnecting them (sometimes they're attached to the governor linkage and don't have to be removed). Note that after the mounting bolts are re-

Repair procedures common to all engines

5.9   A governor link (arrow) typically must be
detached from the carburetor during removal

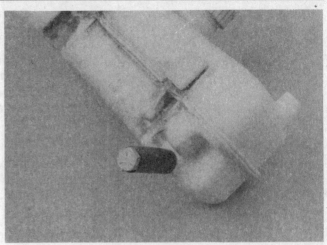

5.10   Plug the fuel line with a snug-fitting bolt or steel
rod so gas doesn't run all over

moved, the governor link (**see illustration 5.9**) willl have to be manipulated out of the throttle lever as the carburetor is detached.

5   Detach the fuel line from the carburetor or gas tank fitting and plug it (if a shut-off valve isn't used) (**see illustration 5.10**). Now is a good time to inspect the fuel line and install a new one if it's damaged or deteriorated. **Note:** *Some carburetors are mounted directly on the fuel tank and no fuel line is used.*

6   Remove the nuts/bolts and detach the carburetor (or fuel tank/carburetor assembly) from the engine, then disconnect any control linkage still attached to it. Watch for spacers on engines with the carburetor mounted on the tank – make sure they're returned to their original location(s) when the bolts are installed.

The carburetor may be attached directly to the engine or to an intake manifold (**see illustration 5.11**). If an intake manifold is used, it's usually easier to detach the manifold from the engine and separate the carburetor afterwards.

7   Remove the gasket and discard it – use a new one when the carburetor is reinstalled. Some engines also have an insulator and/or heat shield (and a second gasket) between the carburetor and engine. **Note:** *On Honda engines, the insulator must be reinstalled with the grooved side against the carburetor.*

8   Due to the many differences from manufacturer to manufacturer, carburetor disassembly and reassembly is covered in each engine chapter.

9   Reverse the removal procedure when installing the carburetor.

5.11   Most carburetors are attached to a manifold,
which is bolted to the engine – don't try to separate the
carb from the manifold until after they're detached
from the engine

Carburetor overhaul

Warning: *Gasoline is extremely flammable and highly explosive under certain conditions – safety precautions must be followed when working on the carburetor! Don't smoke or allow open flames or unshielded light bulbs in or near the work area. Don't do this procedure in a garage with a natural gas appliance (such as a water heater or clothes dryer) and have a fire extinguisher handy.*

Poor engine performance, hesitation, black smoke and little or no engine response to fuel/air mixture adjustments are all signs that major carburetor maintenance is required.

Keep in mind that many so-called carburetor problems are really not carburetor problems at all, but mechanical problems in the engine or ignition system faults. Establish for certain the carburetor needs servicing before assuming an overhaul is necessary. For example, fuel starvation is often mistaken for a carburetor problem. Make sure the fuel filter (if used), the fuel line and the gas tank cap vent hole aren't plugged before blaming the carburetor for this relatively common malfunction.

Most carburetor problems are caused by dirt particles, varnish and other deposits which build up in and block the fuel and air passages. Also, in time, gaskets and O-rings shrink and cause fuel and air leaks which lead to poor performance.

When the carburetor is overhauled, it's generally disassembled completely – disassembly is covered in the appropriate engine chapter – and the metal components are soaked in carburetor cleaner (which dissolves gasoline deposits, varnish, dirt and sludge). The parts are then rinsed thoroughly with solvent and dried with compressed air. The fuel and air passages are also blown out with compressed air to force out any dirt that may have been loosened but not removed by the carburetor cleaner. Once the cleaning process is complete, the carburetor is reassembled using new gaskets, O-rings, diaphragms and, generally, a new inlet needle and seat (not used in all carburetors).

Before taking the carburetor apart, make sure you have a rebuild kit (which will include all necessary gaskets and other parts), some carburetor cleaner, solvent, a supply of rags, some means of blowing out the carburetor passages and a clean place to work.

Some of the carburetor settings, such as the sizes of the jets and the internal passageways are predetermined by the manufacturer. Under normal circumstances, they won't have to be changed or modified and they should never be enlarged.

Before disassembling the carburetor, clean the outside with solvent and lay it on a clean sheet of paper or a shop towel.

After it's been completely disassembled, submerge the metal components in carburetor cleaner and allow them to soak for approximately 30 minutes. **Caution:** *Do not soak plastic or rubber parts in carburetor cleaner – they'll be damaged or dissolved. Also, don't allow excessive amounts of carburetor cleaner to get on your skin.*

After the carburetor has soaked long enough for the cleaner to loosen and dissolve the varnish and other deposits, rinse it thoroughly with solvent and blow it dry with compressed air. Also, blow out all the fuel and air passages in the carburetor body. **Note:** *Never clean the jets or passages with a piece of wire or drill bit – they could be enlarged, causing the fuel and air metering rates to be upset.*

Reassembly and carburetor adjustment is covered in the appropriate engine chapter.

Engine block cleaning

After the engine has been completely disassembled, clean the block as described here before conducting a thorough inspection to determine if it's reusable.

1   Using a gasket scraper, remove all traces of gasket material and old sealant from the block **(see illustration 5.12)**. Be very careful not to nick or gouge the gasket sealing surfaces.

2   Clean the block with solvent to remove dirt, sludge and oil, then dry it with compressed air (if available). Take your time and do a thorough job.

3   The threaded holes in the block must be clean to ensure accurate torque readings/prevent damaged threads during reassembly. Run the proper size tap into each of the holes to remove rust, corrosion, thread cement or sludge and restore damaged threads. If possible, use compressed air to clear the holes of debris produced by this operation. Now is a good time to clean the threads on the head bolts and the connecting rod cap bolts as well.

5.12   Use a scraper or putty knife to remove old gaskets from the engine components – if the gasket is stubborn, use a gasket removal solvent on it

Engine block inspection

1   Before the block is inspected, it should be cleaned as described above. Double-check to make sure the carbon or wear ridge at the top of the cylinder has been completely removed.

2   Visually check the block for cracks, rust and corrosion. Look for stripped threads in the threaded holes. It's also a good idea to have the block checked for hidden cracks by an automotive machine shop that has the special equipment to do this type of work. If defects are found, have the block repaired, if possible, or replaced.

3   Check the cylinder bore for scuffing and score marks.

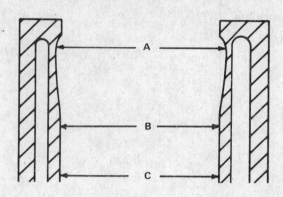

5.13   Measure the diameter of each cylinder just under the wear ridge (A), at the center (B) and at the bottom (C)

5.14   The ability to "feel" when the telescoping gauge is at the correct point will be developed over time, so work slowly and repeat the check until you're satisfied the bore measurement is accurate – the telescoping gauge is then measured with a micrometer to determine the actual bore size in inches

4   Measure the diameter of the cylinder bore.

This should be done at the top (just under the ridge area), center and bottom of the cylinder bore, parallel to the crankshaft (see illustrations 5.13 and 5.14).

Next, measure the cylinder diameter at the same three locations across the crankshaft. Compare the results to the specifications in the Appendix at the back of the manual.

If the cylinder is badly scuffed or scored, or if it's out-of-round or tapered beyond the limits given in the specifications, have the engine block rebored and honed at a small engine dealer or an automotive machine shop. If a rebore is done, an oversize piston and rings will be required.

5   If the cylinder is in reasonably good condition and not worn to the outside of the limits, and if the piston-to-cylinder clearance can be maintained properly, then it doesn't have to be resized. Honing is all that's necessary (see the next section).

Cylinder honing

Prior to engine reassembly, the cylinder bore should be honed so the new piston rings will seat correctly and provide the best possible combustion chamber seal. **Note:** *This procedure applies to engines with an iron bore only – aluminum cylinder bores do not require honing for the rings to seat. Also, most small engine manufacturers provide chrome ring sets (for both aluminum and iron-bore engines) that don't require cylinder honing before installation. If you don't have the tools or don't want to tackle the*

Repair procedures common to all engines

5.15   If this is the first time you've ever honed cylinders, you'll get better results with a "bottle brush" hone than you will with a traditional spring-loaded hone

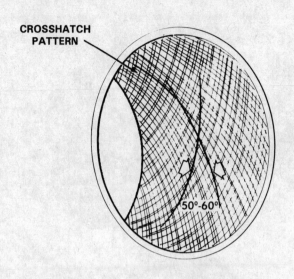

5.16   The cylinder hone should leave a smooth, crosshatch pattern with the lines intersecting at approximately a 60-degree angle

honing operation, most automotive machine shops and small engine dealers will do it for a reasonable fee.

Two types of cylinder hones are commonly available – the flex hone or "bottle brush" type and the more traditional surfacing hone with spring-loaded stones. Both will do the job, but for the less experienced mechanic the "bottle brush" hone will probably be easier to use.

You'll also need plenty of light oil or honing oil, some rags and an electric drill motor. Proceed as follows:

1   Mount the hone in the drill, compress the stones and slip it into the cylinder (see illustration 5.15). Be sure to wear safety goggles or a face shield!

2   Lubricate the cylinder with plenty of oil, turn on the drill and move the hone up-and-down at a pace that'll produce a fine crosshatch pattern on the cylinder walls.

Ideally, the crosshatch lines should intersect at approximately a 60-degree angle (see illustration 5.16). Be sure to use plenty of lubricant and don't take off any more material than absolutely necessary to produce the desired finish. Note: *Piston ring manufacturers may specify a smaller crosshatch angle than the traditional 60-degrees – read and follow any instructions included with the new rings.*

3   Don't withdraw the hone from the cylinder while it's running. Instead, shut off the drill and continue moving the hone up-and-down in the cylinder until it comes to a complete stop, then compress the stones and withdraw the hone. If you're using a "bottle brush" type hone, stop the drill, then turn the chuck in the normal direction of rotation while withdrawing the hone from the cylinder.

4   Wipe the oil out of the cylinder.

5.17   After honing the cylinder, run a file around the top edge of the bore to knock off the sharp edge so the rings don't catch when the piston is reinstalled – note the tape on the end of the file to prevent nicks in the cylinder wall

5   After the honing job is complete, chamfer the top edge of the cylinder bore with a small file so the rings won't catch when the piston is installed **(see illustration 5.17)**. Be very careful not to nick the cylinder wall with the end of the file!

6   The engine block must be washed again very thoroughly with warm, soapy water to remove all traces of abrasive grit produced during the honing operation. **Note:** *The bore can be considered clean when a white cloth – dampened with clean engine oil – used to wipe it down doesn't pick up any more honing residue, which will show up as gray areas on the cloth.*

7   After rinsing, dry the block and apply a coat of light oil to the cylinder to prevent the formation of rust. If the engine isn't going to be reassembled right away, store the block in a plastic trash bag to keep it clean and set it aside until reassembly.

Crankshaft and bearing inspection

Crankshaft

After the crankshaft has been removed from the engine, it should be cleaned thoroughly with solvent and dried with compressed air (if available). **Caution:** *Wear eye protection when using compressed air!* If the crankshaft has oil passages drilled in it, clean them out with a wire or stiff plastic bristle brush, then flush them with solvent.

1   Check the connecting rod journal for uneven wear, score marks, pits, cracks and flat spots. If the rod journal is damaged or worn, check the connecting rod bearing surface as well. If the crankshaft rides in plain bearings, check the main bearing journals and the thrust faces in the same manner (the thrust faces contact the bearings to restrict the end play of the crankshaft).

2   Rub a penny across each journal several times (if it rides in a plain bearing) **(see illustration 5.18)**. If a journal picks up copper from the penny, it's too rough.

5.18   Rubbing a penny lengthwise on the connecting rod journal will give you a quick idea of its condition – if copper rubs off the penny and adheres to the crankshaft, it's too rough and a new crankshaft should be installed

Repair procedures common to all engines

5.19 Check the gear teeth for wear and damage . . .

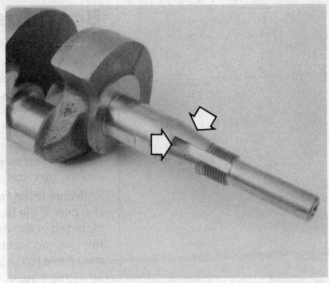

5.20 . . . and make sure the taper and keyway are in good shape

3   Check the gear teeth for cracks, chips and excessive wear (**see illustration 5.19**).

4   Check the threads on each end of the crankshaft – if they're worn or damaged, they may be salvageable with a die or thread file. Check the power take-off end to make sure it's not bent.

5   Check the crankshaft taper for rust and damage (**see illustration 5.20**). If damage is noted, check the matching taper in the flywheel.

6   Inspect each keyway for deformation – if the one in the taper is worn or spread open, the ignition timing will be off. A new crankshaft will be needed.

7   Check the rest of the crankshaft for cracks and other damage.

8   Using a micrometer, measure the diameter of the main and connecting rod journals (**see illustration 5.21**).

9   Compare the results to the specifications in the Appendix at the back of the manual.

By measuring the diameter at a number of points around each journal's circumference, you'll be able to determine whether or not the journal is out-of-round.

Take the measurement at each end of the rod journal, near the crank throws, to determine if the journal is tapered.

If the crankshaft journals are damaged, tapered, out-of-round or worn beyond the limits given in the specifications, a new crankshaft will be required.

10   Check the oil seal journals at each end of the crankshaft for wear and damage. If the seal has worn a groove in the journal, or if the journal is nicked or scratched, the new seal may leak when the engine is reassembled.

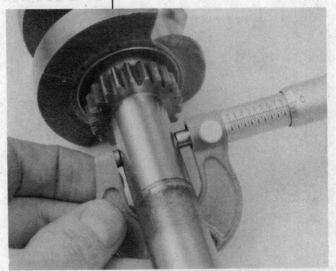

5.21 The connecting rod and main bearing journal diameters (if applicable) can be measured with a micrometer

Bearings

The bearings shouldn't be removed from the crankcase unless they're defective or they have to come out with the crankshaft.

11   Clean the bearings with solvent and allow them to air dry. **Caution:** *Do not use compressed air to spin ball bearings – spinning a dry bearing will cause rapid wear and damage.*

12   Check ball or roller bearings for wear, damage and play in the bore. **Note:** *If the engine is a two-stroke, check the connecting rod big end needle bearings and steel liners (if used) for wear, damage and distortion. Look for cracks, pits, flaked areas and flat spots on the needles.*

Rotate them by hand and feel for smooth operation with no axial or radial play. If the bearing is in the engine, make sure the outer race is securely fastened in the bore. If it's loose, the block may have to be peened to grip the bearing tighter or a liquid bearing mount (similar to thread cement) may have to be used.

13   Check plain bearings for wear, score marks and grooves or deep scratches. Be sure to check the thrust faces (they keep the crankshaft from moving end-to-end too much) as well.

The bearing face should be smooth and satiny, not brightly polished.

Use a telescoping gauge and a micrometer to measure the bearing inside diameter. Any bearing worn beyond the specified limits (see the Appendix in the back of the manual), must be replaced with a new one. If new plain bearings are needed, have them installed by a dealer so they can be reamed to size as well. **Note:** *On many engines, the crankshaft rides directly in the aluminum material used for the engine block. If the bearing surfaces are worn or damaged, a dealer can ream out the holes and install bushings.*

Camshaft and bearing inspection

After the camshaft has been removed from the engine, it should be cleaned thoroughly with solvent and dried with compressed air (if available). **Caution:** *Wear eye protection when using compressed air!*

1   Visually inspect the camshaft for wear and/or damage to the gear teeth, lobe surfaces and bearing journals. If the cam lobes are worn or damaged, check the matching tappets as well.

2   Measure the camshaft lobe heights **(see illustration 5.22)** and compare the results to the specifications listed in the Appendix.

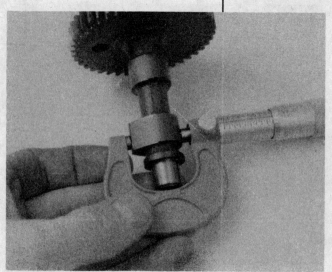

5.22   **If the cam lobe height is less than specified, engine performance will suffer – install a new camshaft**

3   Measure the camshaft bearing journal diameters **(see illustration 5.23)**.

4   If the journals or lobes are worn beyond the specified limits, replace the camshaft.

5   If an automatic spark advance mechanism is installed, check the weight for free movement and make sure the spring pulls it back. If it doesn't, and the weight isn't binding, install a new spring (if available separately).

6   If an automatic compression release mechanism is attached to the camshaft, check the components for binding and wear.

5.23   The camshaft bearing journal diameters can be measured with a micrometer to determine if excessive wear has occurred

Piston/connecting rod inspection

If the cylinder must be rebored, there's no reason to check the piston, since a new (larger) one will have to be installed anyway.

Before the inspection can be carried out, the piston/connecting rod assembly must be cleaned with solvent and the original piston rings removed from the piston. **Note:** *Always use new piston rings when the engine is reassembled – check with a dealer to ensure the correct ones are purchased and installed.*

1   Using a piston ring installation tool, if available, or your fingers, remove the rings from the piston **(see illustration 5.24)**. Be careful not to nick or gouge the piston in the process.

2   Scrape all traces of carbon off the top of the piston **(see illustration 5.25)**.

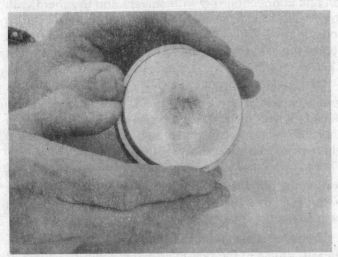

5.24   If you don't have the special tool, the rings can be removed from the piston with your fingers, but be careful not to break them (unless new ones are being installed)

5.25   Remove the carbon from the top of the piston with a scraper or wire brush, then use fine emery cloth or steel wool and solvent to finish the job

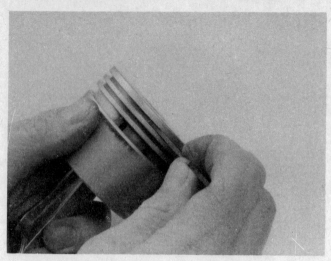

5.26   The piston ring grooves can be cleaned with a piece of broken piston ring

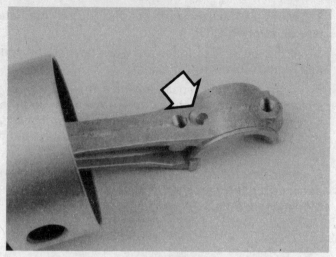

5.27   Make sure the oil hole in the connecting rod is clear

A hand-held wire brush or a piece of fine emery cloth can be used once the majority of deposits have been scraped away. Do not, under any circumstances, use a wire brush mounted in an electric drill to remove deposits from the piston – the piston material is soft and will be eroded by the wire brush.

3   Use a piece of broken piston ring to remove carbon deposits from the ring grooves (see illustration 5.26). Special tools are also available for this job.

Be very careful to remove only the carbon deposits. Don't remove any metal and don't nick or scratch the sides of the ring grooves.

4   Once the deposits have been removed, clean the piston and connecting rod with solvent and dry them with compressed air (if available). Make sure the oil return holes in the back side of the oil ring groove and the oil hole in the lower end of the rod are clear (see illustration 5.27).

5   If the piston and cylinder aren't damaged or worn excessively, and if the engine block isn't rebored or replaced, a new piston won't be necessary. New piston rings, as mentioned above, should normally be installed when an engine is rebuilt.

6   Carefully inspect the piston for cracks around the skirt, at the pin bosses and at the ring lands. **Note:** *If the piston is from a two-stroke engine, make sure the pins used to restrict rotation of the piston rings are secure.*

7   Look for scoring and scuffing on the thrust faces of the skirt, holes in the piston crown and burned areas at the edge of the crown.

8   Measure the piston ring side clearance by laying a new piston ring in each groove and slipping a feeler gauge in beside it (see illustration 5.28). Check the

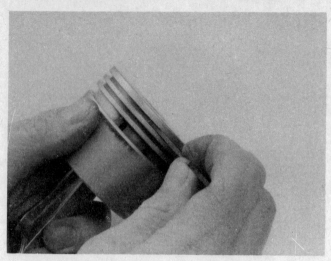

5.28   Check the ring side clearance with a feeler gauge at several points around the groove

clearance at three or four locations around each groove. Be sure to use the correct ring for each groove; they are different. If the side clearance is greater than specified (see the Appendix at the back of the manual), a new piston will have to be used.

9   Check the piston-to-bore clearance by measuring the bore (see *Engine block inspection*) and the piston diameter.

Measure the piston across the skirt, at a 90-degree angle to the piston pin, near the lower edge. Subtract the piston diameter from the bore diameter to obtain the clearance (if applicable – not all manufacturers provide specifications). If it's greater than specified, the cylinder will have to be rebored and a new piston and rings installed.

10   Check the piston-to-rod clearance by twisting the piston and rod in opposite directions. Any noticeable play indicates excessive wear, which must be corrected by installing a new piston, connecting rod or piston pin (or all three – see your dealer).

11   Check the connecting rod for cracks and other damage. Clean and inspect the bearing surface for score marks, gouges and deep scratches.

12   If the engine is a two-stroke, check the connecting rod big end needle/roller bearings and steel liners (if used) for wear, damage and distortion. Look for cracks, pits, flaked areas and flat spots on the needles/rollers.

Piston ring installation

1   Before installing the new piston rings, the ring end gaps must be checked. It's assumed the piston ring side clearance has been checked and verified correct (see *Piston/connecting rod inspection* above).

2   Insert the top (upper compression) ring into the cylinder and square it up with the cylinder wall by pushing it in with the top of the piston **(see illustration 5.29)**. The ring should be near the bottom of the cylinder, at the lower limit of ring travel.

3   Measure the end gap.

5.29   When checking piston ring end gap, the ring must be square in the cylinder bore – this is done by pushing it down with the top of a piston

5.30 Once the ring is at the lower limit of travel and square in the cylinder, measure the end gap with a feeler gauge

To do this, slip feeler gauges between the ends of the ring until a gauge equal to the gap width is found (**see illustration 5.30**). The feeler gauge should slide between the ring ends with a slight amount of drag.

Compare the measurement to the specifications in the Appendix at the back of the book. If the gap is larger or smaller than specified, double-check to make sure you have the correct rings before proceeding.

If the gap is too small, it must be enlarged or the ring ends may come in contact with each other during engine operation, which can cause serious damage. The gap can be increased by filing the ring ends very carefully with a fine file. Mount the file in a vise equipped with soft jaws, slip the ring over the file with the ends contacting the file face and slowly move the ring to remove material from the ends. When performing this operation, file only from the outside in.

4   Excess end gap isn't critical unless it's greater than 0.040-inch. Again, double-check to make sure you have the correct rings for the engine.

5   Repeat the procedure for each ring.

6   Once the ring end gaps have been checked/corrected, the rings can be installed on the piston. **Note:** *Follow the instructions with the new piston rings if they differ from the information here.*

7   Install the piston rings.

The oil control ring (lowest one on the piston – four-stroke engines only) is installed first. On most engines it's composed of three separate components. Slip the spacer/expander into the groove first. If an anti-rotation tang is used, make sure it's inserted into the drilled hole in the ring groove.

Next, install the lower side rail. Don't use a piston ring installation tool on the oil ring side rails – they may be damaged. Instead, place one end of the side rail into the groove between the spacer/expander and the ring land, hold it firmly in place and slide a finger around the piston while pushing the rail into the groove. Next, install the upper side rail in the same manner.

After the three oil ring components have been installed, check to make sure both the upper and lower side rails can be turned smoothly in the ring groove.

8   The lower compression ring is installed next (two-stroke engines only have compression rings).

It usually will be stamped with a mark which must face up, toward the top of the piston (**see illustration 5.31**). **Note:** *Always follow the instructions printed on the ring package or box – different manufacturers may require different approaches. Don't mix up the upper and lower compression rings, as they have different cross sections.*

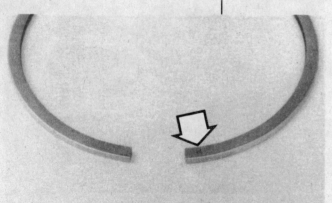

5.31 Piston rings are normally marked (arrow) to indicate the side that faces up, toward the top of the piston

Repair procedures common to all engines

Use a piston ring installation tool and make sure the identification mark is facing the top of the piston, then slip the ring into the middle groove (lower one on a two-stroke engine) on the piston (see illustration 5.32). Don't expand the ring any more than necessary to slide it over the piston.

9   Install the upper (top) compression ring in the same manner. Make sure the mark is facing up. Be careful not to confuse the upper and lower compression rings. **Note:** *On Honda engines, the top ring is usually chrome faced.*

10   Make sure the rings turn freely in the grooves (unless they're pinned in place).

11   Turn the rings so the gaps are staggered about 120-degrees (not lined up).

5.32   Install the compression rings with a ring expander – remember, the mark must face up!

Valve/tappet inspection and servicing

1   If you're working on an OHV Honda engine, inspect the head very carefully for cracks and other damage. If cracks are found, a new head is needed. On GX110/GX140 Honda engines, use a precision straightedge and feeler gauge(s) to check the head gasket surface for warpage. Lay the straightedge diagonally (corner-to-corner), intersecting the head bolt holes, and try to slip a 0.004-inch thick feeler gauge under it near each hole. Repeat the check with the straightedge positioned between each pair of holes along the sides of the head. If the feeler gauge will slip between the head surface and the straightedge, the head is warped. See your dealer about the possibility of resurfacing it.

2   Examine the valve seats (see illustration 5.33).

If they're pitted, cracked or burned, valve service that's beyond the scope of the home mechanic is required – take the engine or head to a dealer and have new valves and seats installed.

Inspection

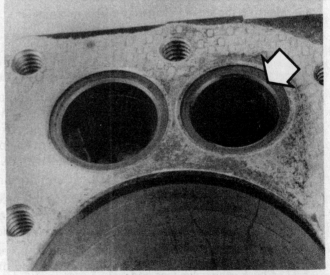

5.33   Check the valve seats (arrow) in the engine block or head – look for pits, cracks and burned areas

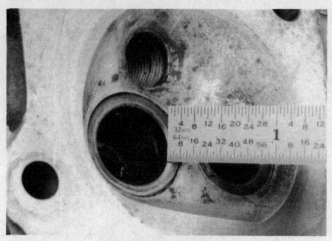

5.34   Use a ruler to measure the width of each valve seat

5.35   A small hole gauge can be used to determine the inside diameter of the valve guide

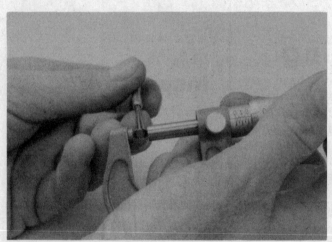

5.36   Measure the small hole gauge with a micrometer to obtain the actual size of the guide

5.37   Check each valve face and margin for wear and cracks

Measure each valve seat width and compare it to the specifications in the Appendix at the back of the manual (see illustration 5.34). If it's not within the specified range, or if it varies around its circumference, valve seat service is required.

3   Clean the valve guides to remove any carbon build-up, then measure the inside diameters of the guides (at both ends and the center of the guide).

This is done with a small hole gauge and a 0-to-1 inch micrometer (see illustrations 5.35 and 5.36). Record the measurements for future reference. These measurements, along with the valve stem diameter measurements, will enable you to compute the valve-to-guide clearance. This clearance, when compared to the specifications, will be one factor that will determine the extent of valve service work required. The guides are measured at the ends and at the center to determine if they're worn in a bell-mouth pattern (more wear at the ends). If they are, guide replacement or reconditioning is an absolute must.

Some manufacturers don't publish valve-to-guide clearance specifications. Instead, they distribute special plug gauges that are inserted into the guides to determine how much wear has occurred in the guide. If no specifications are listed for your particular engine, have the guides checked and serviced by a dealer.

4   Carefully inspect each valve.

Check the face (the area that mates with the seat) for cracks, pits and burned spots (see illustration 5.37). Check the valve stem and the keeper groove or hole for cracks (see illustration 5.38).

Rotate the valve and check for any obvious indication that it's bent. Check the end of the stem for pitting and excessive wear.

Repair procedures common to all engines

The presence of any of the above conditions indicates the need for valve replacement.

5   Measure the valve stem diameter (**see illustration 5.39**).

By subtracting the stem diameter from the valve guide diameter, the valve-to-guide clearance is obtained. If the valve-to-guide clearance is greater than specified, the guides will have to be replaced and new valves may have to be installed, depending on the condition of the old ones.

6   Check the end of each valve spring for wear and pitting.

Measure the free length and compare it to the specifications, if applicable (**see illustration 5.40**). Any springs that are shorter than specified have sagged and shouldn't be reused.

Stand the spring on a flat surface and check it for squareness (**see illustration 5.41**).

7   Check the spring retainers and/or keepers or pins for obvious wear and cracks. Questionable parts should not be reused – extensive damage will occur in the event of failure during engine operation.

8   Check the tappets for wear, score marks and galling (**see illustration 5.42**). Make sure they fit snugly in the holes and move freely without binding or catching.

5.38   Look for wear on the very end of the valve stem and make sure the keeper groove or pin hole isn't distorted in any way

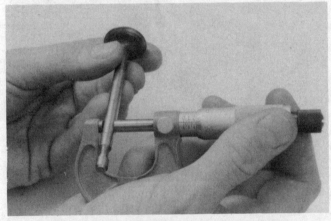

5.39   Measure the valve stem diameter with a micrometer

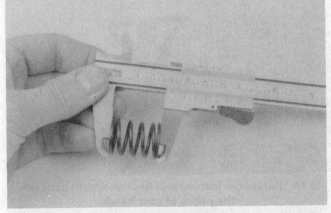

5.40   Measure the valve spring free length with a dial or vernier caliper

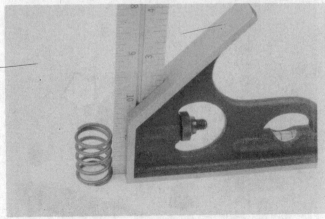

5.41   Check each valve spring for distortion with a square

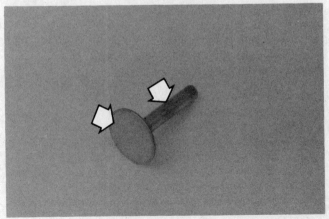

5.42   Check the tappet stems and ends (arrows) for wear and damage

Haynes small engine repair manual

Valve lapping

5.43   Apply the lapping compound very sparingly, in small dabs, to the valve face only

If the inspection indicates that no service work is required, the valve components can be reinstalled in the engine block or head (see the appropriate engine chapter).

Before reinstalling the valves, they should be lapped to ensure a positive seal between the faces and seats. This procedure requires fine valve lapping compound (available at auto parts stores) and a valve lapping tool (see Chapter 1).

9   Apply a small amount of fine lapping compound to the valve face (see illustration 5.43), then slip the valve into the guide. Note: *Make sure the valve is installed in the correct guide and be careful not to get any lapping compound on the valve stem.*

10   Attach the lapping tool to the valve and rotate the tool between the palms of your hands. Use a back-and-forth motion rather than a circular motion (see illustration 5.44). Lift the valve off the seat at regular intervals to distribute the lapping compound evenly (see illustration 5.45)

5.44   Rotate the lapping tool back-and-forth between the palms of your hands

5.45   Lift the tool and valve periodically to redistribute the lapping compound on the valve face and seat

5.46   After lapping, the valve face should have a uniform, unbroken contact pattern (arrow) . . .

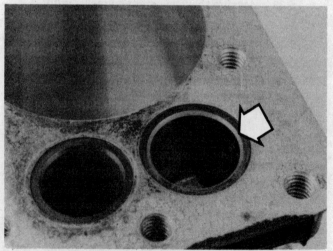

5.47   . . . and the seat should be the specified width (arrow), with a smooth, unbroken appearance

11   Continue the lapping procedure until the valve face and seat contact area is uniform in width and unbroken around the entire circumference of the valve face and seat **(see illustrations 5.46 and 5.47).**

12   Carefully remove the valve from the guide and wipe off all traces of lapping compound. Use solvent to clean the valve and wipe the seat area thoroughly with a solvent-soaked cloth. Repeat the procedure for the remaining valve.

13   Once both valves have been lapped, check for proper valve sealing by pouring a small amount of solvent into each of the ports with the valves in place and held tightly against the seats. If the solvent leaks past the valve(s) into the combustion chamber area, repeat the lapping procedure, then reinstall the valve(s) and repeat the check. Repeat the procedure until a satisfactory seal is obtained.

6 Briggs & Stratton engines

Engine identification numbers/models covered

The engine model designation system used by Briggs & Stratton consists of a five or six digit number, normally found on the shroud, with the term "model" immediately under it (see illustration 6.1). The model number can be used to determine the major features of the engine by comparing each digit to the accompanying chart (see illustration 6.2). The digits in the model number can be explained generally as follows:

The first one or two digits indicate the engine displacement in cubic inches. For example, a "5" would indicate a five cubic inch engine and an "11" would mean an eleven cubic inch engine.

Note: *The information in this repair manual applies only to engines with a displacement of 13 cubic inches or less! If the first two numbers are greater than 13 in a six-digit model number on your particular engine the information in this book will not apply.*

The next digit after the displacement (the second or third number) indicates the basic design series. It has to do with the cylinder type, ignition system and general engine configuration.

6.1 Typical Briggs & Stratton engine model number – if the first digit in a five-digit model number (circled) is 9 or less or the first two digits in a six-digit model number are 13 or less, the information in this manual applies to the engine

The second digit after the displacement indicates the crankshaft orientation (vertical or horizontal) and the type of carburetor and governor installed on the engine.

The third digit after the displacement indicates the type of bearings used in the engine. It also will tell you if the engine is equipped with a reduction gear or auxiliary drive.

The last digit in the model number indicates the type of starter used on the engine.

BRIGGS & STRATTON MODEL NUMBER KEY

Displacement (cubic inches)	First Digit After Disp. Basic Design Series	Second Digit After Disp. Crankshaft/ Carburetor/ Governor	Third Digit After Disp. Bearings/ Reduction gears/ Auxiliary drive	Fourth Digit After Disp. Starter type
6	0	0	0 = Plain bearing	0 = No starter
8	1	1 = Horizontal (Vacu-Jet)	1 = Flange mount plain bearing	1 = Rope starter
9	2			
10	3	2 = Horizontal (Pulsa-Jet)	2 = Ball bearing	2 = Rewind starter
13	4			
	5	3 = Horizontal (Flo-Jet; pneumatic governor)	3 = Flange mount ball bearing	3 = Electric (110-volt; gear drive)
	6			
	7	4 = Horizontal (Flo-Jet; mechanical governor)	4	4 = Electric starter/ generator (12-volt; belt drive)
	8			
	9			
		5 = Vertical (Vacu-Jet)	5 = Gear reduction (6 to 1)	5 = Electric starter only (12-volt; gear drive)
		6	6 = Gear reduction (6 to 1; reverse rotation)	6 = Wind-up starter
		7 = Vertical (Flo-Jet)	7	7 = Electric starter (12-volt; gear drive with alternator)
		8	8 = Auxiliary drive perpendicular to crankshaft	8 = Vertical-pull starter
		9 = Vertical (Pulsa-Jet)	9 = Auxiliary drive parallel to crankshaft	

6.2 Use this chart to decipher the model number on a Briggs & Stratton engine

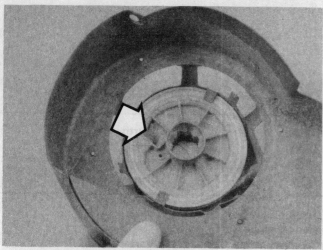

6.3   If the knot is visible, the rope can be replaced easily without disassembling the recoil starter

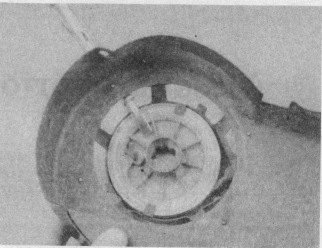

6.4   Use a Vise-Grip pliers or a C-clamp to restrain the pulley so it doesn't rewind

Horizontal-pull starter – rope replacement

Recoil starter service

If the rope breaks, the starter doesn't have to be disassembled to replace it, but it may be a good idea to take the opportunity to do a thorough cleaning job and check the spring and drive mechanism.

There are two approaches you may be faced with when replacing the rope on a recoil starter. The method you use will depend on the starter type.

1   Hold the shroud or recoil starter housing in a vise or clamp it to the workbench so it doesn't move around as you're working on the rope. Use soft jaws in the vise to prevent damage to the shroud or housing.

If you can't see the knot in the pulley end of the rope, the starter will have to be disassembled to install the new rope – the procedure is included later in this section. If the knot is visible **(see illustration 6.3)**, you should be able to replace the rope without disassembling the starter. Proceed as follows:

2   If it isn't broken, pull the rope all the way out.

3   Hold the pulley with Vise-Grip pliers or a C-clamp so the spring won't rewind and the pulley is held in position for installing the rope **(see illustration 6.4)**.

4   Cut the knot off and pull the rope out **(see illustration 6.5)**. Note the type of knot tied in the rope, then detach the handle – it can be used on the new rope.

5   If the old rope was broken, you'll have to wind up the recoil spring before installing the new rope.

6.5   Cut off the knot and pull the rope out

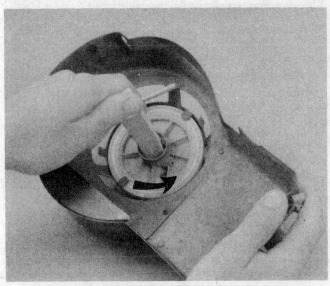

6.6 Turn the pulley to apply tension to the spring, then hold it in place while installing the rope

6.7 The rope is difficult to thread into the pulley, so attach it to a piece of wire and use the wire to pull it into place

Turn the pulley against spring tension until it stops completely (**see illustration 6.6**), then back it off one full turn. This will prevent the spring from being wound too far when the rope is pulled out (which can break it off).

6 Cut a piece of new rope the same length and diameter as the original.

Rope lengths may vary from three to four feet – if you don't have the exact replacement part, start with five feet of rope and cut it off if necessary when you see how it fills the pulley. The most common rope diameter is 5/32-inch. **Note:** *The rope should fill the pulley groove without binding.*

7 If the rope is made of nylon, melt the ends with a match to prevent fraying.

8 Turn the pulley so the opening for the rope is positioned as close to the opening in the housing as possible, then insert the rope into the housing opening and out through the pulley opening.

This can be tricky – if the rope won't cooperate, hook a piece of wire through the end of the rope and bend it over with a pliers, then thread the wire through the holes and use it to pull the rope into place (**see illustration 6.7**). **Note:** *The rope must pass inside a guide lug on the old style metal pulley.*

9 Tie a knot in the rope and pull the knot tight against the hole in the pulley. On some models, the knot can be manipulated/pulled down into a cavity in the pulley. Make sure the knot doesn't contact the pulley retaining tangs.

10 Release the Vise-Grips or C-clamp while holding the rope, then allow the rope to rewind onto the pulley until the groove is full.

11 Pull the rope out slightly and attach the handle (make sure it's secure or the rope will disappear into the starter and you'll have to start over).

12 Check the starter for proper operation.

6.8   Use a pliers to grasp the outer end of the recoil starter spring and pull it out

6.9   Bend up one of the tangs to remove the pulley – if it breaks off, use one of the spare tangs to hold the pulley in when it's reinstalled

Horizontal-pull starter – spring replacement

If the rope won't rewind and it isn't due to binding in the recoil starter, the spring may be broken.

1   Cut the knot at the pulley and remove the rope.

2   With the rope removed, grasp the outer end of the rewind spring with pliers (see illustration 6.8) and pull it out of the housing (if possible).

3   Bend one of the pulley retaining tangs up and lift out the pulley to disconnect the inner end of the spring (see illustration 6.9). The housing has two spare tangs in case they break off.

4   Clean the rewind housing, pulley and spring with solvent and dry them with compressed air (if available) or a cloth. Straighten the new spring so it doesn't tangle during installation.

5   Apply a light coat of oil to both sides of the spring.

6   If the pulley is made of steel, lubricate the end that contacts the housing and the spring face with grease.

7   Make sure the pulley, spring and housing are oriented correctly, then insert either end of the new spring through the housing opening and attach it to the pulley (see illustration 6.10).

8   Position the pulley in the housing and bend the tang down; if the tang breaks off, use the new ones to secure the pulley. The gap between the tang and pulley should be 1/16-inch (the pulley must be completely seated in the rewind housing when measuring the tang gap) (see illustration 6.11). **Note:** *Do not remove the nylon bumpers from the old style tangs when replacing a metal pulley with a nylon pulley. Replace the nylon bumpers if they're worn.*

6.10   Attach the new spring to the pulley

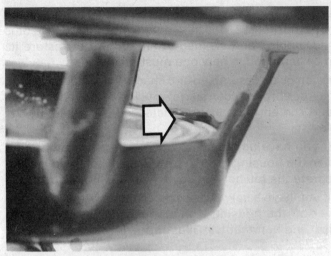

6.11 Check the pulley-to-tang gap so the pulley doesn't bind

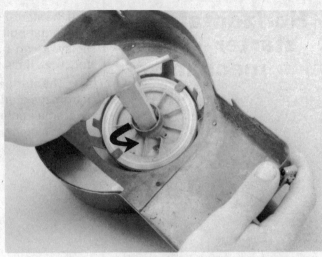

6.12 A 3/4-inch square piece of hardwood or metal can be used as a tool to wind up the spring

9   Carefully wind the spring up by turning the pulley counterclockwise until the outer end of the spring can be locked in the housing slot (**see illustrations 6.12 and 6.13**). **Note:** *A tool made from 3/4-inch square metal or hardwood stock will fit into the drive hole in the pulley and can be turned with a wrench.*

10   Keep turning the pulley until the spring is tight, then back it off one full turn or until the opening for the rope in the pulley and the opening in the housing are aligned (**see illustration 6.14**). Check again to make sure the outer end of the spring is locked in the small end of the tapered slot in the housing.

11   Use a C-clamp or Vise-Grip pliers to hold the pulley while the rope is installed.

12   Refer to the procedure above to install the rope. If the old one is worn or frayed, now is a good time to install a new one.

13   Check the starter for proper operation.

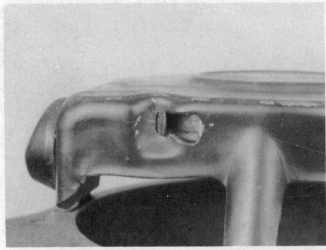

6.13 Make sure the outer end of the spring is securely locked in the narrow end of the housing slot

6.14 Wind up the spring until it's tight, then back it off one full turn or until the rope holes line up

Horizontal-pull starter – drive mechanism repair

If the starter drive mechanism (also called a starter clutch) used with the horizontal-pull starter binds, sticks, doesn't engage, doesn't release or is noisy, it can be disassembled and cleaned in an attempt to restore its function. If it's worn or damaged, a new one must be installed.

1   The starter drive can be disassembled and checked without removing it from the engine, but the shroud/recoil starter must be removed first. The two small screws and screen must also be detached. Disassemble the starter clutch as follows:

If you have an old style clutch, pry the retaining ring out of the housing groove with a small screwdriver and separate the ratchet and cover from the housing.

If you have a new style sealed clutch, carefully pry the cover off the housing with a small screwdriver or cold chisel and hammer (see illustration 6.15).

6.15   Use a small screwdriver or cold chisel and a hammer to pry the cover off the starter clutch

2   Clean the components with solvent and dry them with compressed air (if available) or a clean cloth. **Note:** *If you're working on a new style sealed clutch, clean the ratchet (the part that fits over the crankshaft) with a cloth only – don't submerge it in solvent.*

3   Check the balls for flat spots and the ratchet and housing for wear patterns caused by the balls (see illustration 6.16).

4   Check inside the ratchet bore for rust and damage that could cause it to bind on the crankshaft (see illustration 6.17). Check the crankshaft for nicks, burrs and a "mushroomed" end that could cause the drive mechanism to catch or bind.

5   If the clutch is a sealed type, make sure the seals are in place and in good condition (see illustration 6.18).

6.16   Check the balls for flat spots and look for wear in the housing recesses

6.17   Check the ratchet bore for rust and the end of the crankshaft for burrs and distortion that could cause the ratchet to bind on the shaft

6.18   Check the starter clutch seals – one is a rubber seal and one is a felt seal (arrows)

6 Reassemble and install the clutch. Note the following important points:

DO NOT lubricate the ball cavity area!

Starter clutch installation is part of Flywheel installation

When installing a sealed starter clutch, apply one drop of engine oil only to the end of the crankshaft

Tighten the starter clutch to the specified torque (Appendix A)

DO NOT run the engine without the screen screws installed!

Note: *A sealed clutch can be installed on older engines by modifying the recoil starter pulley and crankshaft. The old pulley can be made to fit the new clutch by cutting off the pulley hub until it's 1/2-inch tall. The crankshaft must be shortened 3/8-inch and the end chamfered with a file. A different screen (part no. 221661) is required with the new style starter clutch.*

Horizontal-pull, side-mount starter

Note: *When disassembling the side-mount starter, pay careful attention to how the parts fit together before removing them – make a sketch if necessary to simplify reassembly.*

1 Remove the starter mounting bolt and detach the starter. **Note:** *It may be necessary to remove or raise the fuel tank to get at the bolt and release the starter. Also, on some models, the starter rope is routed through a rope guide, so the handle may have to be removed as well.*

2 Pull the rope out as far as possible.

3 While holding the pulley and cover, cut or release the knot and remove the rope from the pulley. Slowly relieve the spring tension by releasing the cover or pulley.

4 Remove and save the decal.

5 Loosen the cover screw by turning it clockwise (it has left-hand threads). Remove the screw and washer.

6 Bend the anchor tang out and turn the cover counterclockwise to disengage the spring hook from the cover notch.

7 Lift the cover off the starter assembly. **Note:** *On early production starters, the tang was bent in to retain the spring hook.*

8 Using a pair of needle-nose pliers, grasp the spring across the coils as close to the hook on the outside edge of the pulley as you can and lift out the spring.

9 While still gripping the spring with pliers, slowly relieve the spring tension.

10 Remove the plastic washer, pulley and gear from the starter shaft. Remove the plastic and steel washers from the starter shaft as well.

11 Check the pulley for cracks, sharp edges and wear. Inspect the gear for broken and cracked teeth. Check the washers for cracks and sharp edges. Inspect the spring for kinks, cracks and nicks. Replace damaged parts with new ones.

12   Clamp the starter shaft in a vise with soft jaws or a shop rag (to protect the shaft).

13   Slide the plastic washer onto the shaft, followed by the steel washer.

14   Assemble the pulley and gear with the gear hub and brake spring facing out (toward the end of the helix).

15   Slide the gear and pulley assembly onto the shaft with the brake spring between the two tangs on the shaft.

16   The replacement spring is held in a retainer. To help during assembly, the outer spring hook should be against the end of the retainer – if it isn't, rotate the spring until it is.

17   Place the spring and retainer on the pulley with the hook over the spring notch in the pulley. Push the spring down into the pulley to release it from the retainer. **Note:** *If you're reusing the original spring, straighten it, then hook the outer end in the spring notch and wind the spring into the pulley.*

18   Apply grease to the pulley and spring, then lay the cover over the pulley and install the screw and washer. Turn the screw counterclockwise (remember, it's left-hand thread) until it's finger-tight.

19   Position the cover as follows:

If the starter handle is on top of the engine, turn the cover clockwise until the "O" or arrow on the cover is aligned with the starter shaft cam.

If the starter handle and rope are routed through a rope guide on the cylinder head, turn the cover clockwise until the "O" or arrow is 90-degrees away from the cam on the inner end of the starter shaft.

20   Hold the cover in the correct position and tighten the screw to 55 in-lbs.

21   Install the decal over the cover hole.

22   Hold the starter cover and turn the gear and pulley assembly clockwise until the spring is tight.

23   Turn the gear and pulley back about one turn until the rope knot pocket is in line with the cover opening.

24   Insert the end of the rope through the pulley and pull on it until the knot is seated in the rope pocket.

25   While holding the pulley and cover assembly, tie a slip knot in the rope and slowly let it rewind into the pulley.

26   Install the starter assembly on the engine with the "O" or arrow pointing at the rope eyelet. Tighten the starter mounting screw to 80 in-lbs.

27   Thread the rope through the eyelet(s) and handle insert. Tie a single overhand knot in the rope. The tail on the knot should be no more than 1/4-inch long.

28   Pull the knot into the insert and seat the insert in the handle.

29   Check the starter for proper operation.

6.19   The vertical-pull starter is held in place with
two bolts

6.20   Use a narrow screwdriver or scribe to pull out
the rope, . . .

1   The vertical-pull starter is attached to the engine with two bolts (**see illustration 6.19**). **Note:** *Before removing a vertical-pull starter with the rope coming out the rear, measure the length of rope from the starter housing to the starter handle at the equipment handlebar.*

2   Before servicing the starter, all tension must be removed from the spring.

Use a small screwdriver to pry the rope out of the starter, then pull it out approximately one foot. Turn the rope and pulley counterclockwise two or three turns. This will completely release the tension from the starter spring (**see illustrations 6.20 and 6.21**).

3   Note the warning on the plastic cover, then use a screwdriver to carefully pry it off (**see illustration 6.22**).

Vertical-pull starter

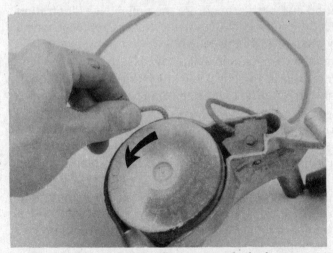

6.21   . . . then turn the pulley counterclockwise two or
three turns so the tension on the spring is relieved – be
very careful not to cut the rope on the sharp edge of
the housing as this is done!

6.22   Carefully pry off the cover with a screwdriver

6.23   Remove the small bolt and detach the spring anchor

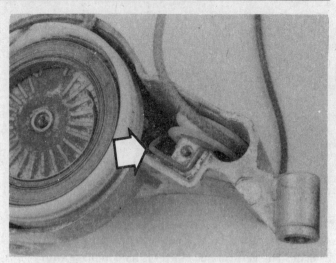

6.24   Remove the rope guide, then note how the link is positioned (arrow) before removing the starter assembly

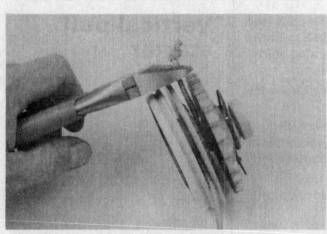

6.25   Pull out the rope and cut off the knot, then remove the rope from the pulley

Warning: *DO NOT pull on the rope with the pulley cover removed unless the spring is detached from the spring anchor!*

4   Remove the small bolt and detach the spring anchor **(see illustration 6.23)**.

5   Check the starter spring for kinks and damaged ends. If the spring must be replaced, carefully remove it from the housing at this time.

6   Remove the rope guide and note the position of the link before removing the assembly from the housing **(see illustration 6.24)**. The rope pulley and pin, if used, can be replaced if worn or damaged.

7   Use a pair of needle-nose pliers to remove the knotted end of the rope from the pulley **(see illustration 6.25)**. Cut off the knot (if the rope must be replaced with a new one) and pull the rope out.

8   If the pulley or gear is damaged, install a new assembly.

9   Clean all dirty or oily parts and check the link for proper operation. It should move the gear from one end of the helix to the other. If not, replace the link assembly.

10   Install a new spring by hooking the end in the pulley retainer slot and winding it up until the spring is coiled in the housing **(see illustration 6.26)**.

11   When installing a new rope, be sure it's the correct diameter and length.

Thread the rope through the handle and into the insert. Tie a small, tight knot **(see illustration 6.27)**. To keep it from loosening, heat the knot with a match until the rope begins to melt. Pull the knot into the insert pocket and snap the insert into the handle.

Note: *On the alternate style vertical-pull starter, measure from the handle end of the rope the distance measured before the starter was removed from the engine and tie a slip knot in the rope at this point. DO NOT install the handle and insert at this time!*

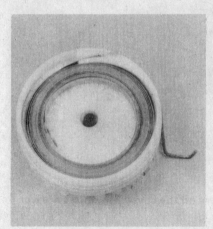

6.26   Install the spring and coil it up in the housing

6.27 Tie a small, tight knot in the handle end of the rope

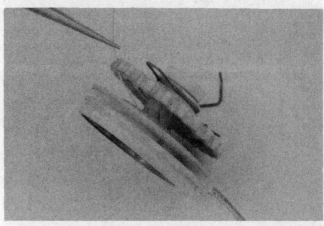

6.28 The rope is difficult to thread into the pulley, so attach it to a piece of wire and use the wire to pull it into place

12   Insert the rope through the housing opening, then route it through the pulley opening. This can be tricky – if the rope won't cooperate, hook a piece of wire through the end of the rope and bend it over with a pliers, then thread the wire through the holes and use it to pull the rope into place **(see illustration 6.28)**.

13   Tie a small knot in the end of the rope and make sure the tail is less than 3/16-inch long. Heat the knot with a match until the rope starts to melt, then pull it tight into the recess in the pulley. The rope must not interfere with gear motion.

14   Install the pulley assembly in the housing with the link in the pocket or hole **(see illustration 6.29)**.

15   Install the rope guide and tighten the screw securely.

16   Rotate the pulley in a counterclockwise direction until the rope is wound onto the pulley all the way.

17   Hook the free end of the spring to the spring anchor and install the bolt **(see illustration 6.30)**.

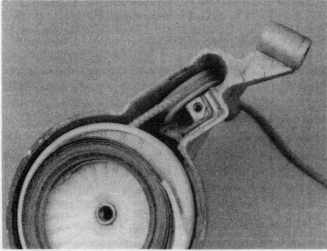

6.29 Make sure the link is positioned properly – the gears won't engage if it isn't

6.30 Install the spring anchor and tighten the bolt securely

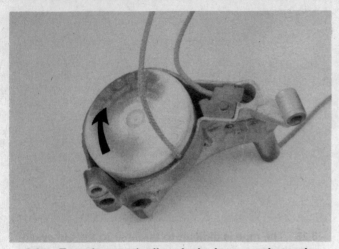

6.31 Turn the rope/pulley clockwise to apply tension to the spring so the rope will rewind – again, be careful not to cut the rope on the sharp edge of the housing!

18   If you have a torque wrench, tighten the bolt to 75 to 90 in-lbs.

19   Lubricate the spring with a small quantity of engine oil or lightweight grease.

20   Snap the cover into place.

21   Wind up the starter spring by pulling the rope out approximately one foot (see Step 2 in this section). Turn the rope and pulley two or three turns clockwise to obtain proper spring tension **(see illustration 6.31)**.

22   Install the starter and tighten the bolts, then check for proper operation.

After installing the alternate style starter on the engine, route the rope up to the equipment handlebar and install the starter handle and insert.

Carburetor disassembly and reassembly

Three carburetor types have been used on Briggs & Stratton engines. They include a conventional float-type, usually called "Flo-jet", which has a float, float bowl and inlet needle and seat. Another type, called "Pulsa-jet", is a non-float type carburetor equipped with a suction device that uses a diaphragm pump to draw fuel into the carburetor. The third type, called "Vacu-jet", is also a non-float carburetor that utilizes vacuum to draw fuel into the carburetor. **Note**: *It's not always easy to determine which type of non-float carburetor you have, since they're not marked, so be sure to take it with you when purchasing parts or a replacement carburetor.*

The following procedures describe how to disassemble and reassemble the carburetor so new parts can be installed. Read the sections in Chapter 5 on carburetor removal and overhaul before doing anything else.

In some cases it may be more economical (and much easier) to install a new carburetor rather than attempt to repair the original. Check with a dealer to see if parts are readily available and compare the cost of new parts to the price of a complete ready-to-install carburetor before deciding how to proceed.

Non-float carburetors (Pulsa-jet/Vacu-jet)

1   Remove the screws and detach the carburetor and diaphragm from the fuel tank **(see illustration 6.32)**. Lift straight up on the carburetor until the fuel tube(s) clear the tank.

2   Remove the rubber air cleaner gasket and the crankcase vent pipe elbow (if equipped).

3   Separate the diaphragm from the carburetor or fuel tank.

Some Pulsa-jet carburetors have a fuel pump diaphragm between the tank and carburetor. A coil spring and metal cup fit between the diaphragm and carburetor.

6.32   Remove the screws that attach the carburetor to the fuel tank

6.33   Pull out on the choke link to detach it from the choke valve shaft

On engines with a vacuum-operated automatic choke, remove the screw and cover from the carburetor, then detach the diaphragm link from the choke valve and separate the diaphragm from the carburetor body **(see illustration 6.33)**.

4   Clean the mounting surface on the tank, then check it for distortion with a straightedge and an accurate 0.002-inch thick feeler gauge.

Vacu-jet and Pulsa-jet tanks are checked in different locations **(see illustration 6.34)**. If the tank is distorted, a new one will be required. **Note:** *Pulsa-jet tanks (except those used with an All Temperature/Automatic Choke carburetor) can be repaired with a special kit that includes a Teflon washer and a roll pin – check with a Briggs & Stratton dealer.*

5   Check the throttle valve shaft for wear by moving it back-and-forth **(see illustration 6.35)**.

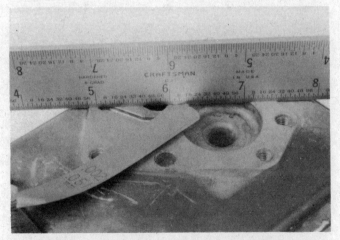

6.34   Use a straightedge and an accurate 0.002-inch feeler gauge to check the Vacu-jet tank surface for distortion at the point shown – if you have a Pulsa-jet carburetor, check for distortion at both sides of the deep well, right at the screw hole

6.35   Move the throttle shaft back-and-forth to feel for play indicating wear in the shaft bores

6.36 The throttle valve is attached to the shaft with a single screw – note how the valve is installed before removing the screw

6.37 Check the felt seal on the throttle shaft for damage and distortion

If you can feel side-to-side play, the shaft/bore is worn excessively, which will probably mean a new carburetor is required (check with a dealer to see if wear in the throttle shaft can be repaired on your particular carburetor).

6 Remove the throttle valve/shaft.

Cast one-piece aluminum throttle valves can be removed by backing off the idle speed adjusting screw until the throttle clears the lug on the carburetor body.

If the throttle valve is attached to the shaft with a screw, remove the screw, extract the valve and pull out the shaft **(see illustration 6.36)**.

7 Check the O-ring or felt seal on the throttle shaft **(see illustration 6.37)**.

8 Measure how far the fuel tube(s) protrude from the carburetor body **(see illustration 6.38)**, record the measurement, then remove them.

Nylon tubes used in metal carburetors are threaded into the body, have a hex-shaped end and can be removed with a 6-point socket and ratchet **(see illustration 6.39)**. Work carefully, DO NOT use a 12-point socket and don't break the tube off.

Nylon tubes used with "Minlon" plastic carburetors are a snap-fit in the body and can be removed by gripping them with a pliers – they usually require considerable force to pull out and push in.

The brass tubes used on Pulsa-jet carburetors are pressed into the carburetor and don't have to be removed – just carefully clamp the tube in a vise and drive off the nylon or brass strainer housing with a standard screwdriver and a hammer.

The brass tubes used on Vacu-jet carburetors are also pressed into place, but they can be removed. Gently clamp the tube in a vise, about 1/16-inch away from the carburetor body, then use two screwdrivers to pry up on the carburetor to separate it from the tube.

6.38 Measure how far the fuel tube protrudes from the carburetor body – the length must be maintained when the tube is reinstalled (this is especially critical on pressed-in brass tubes)

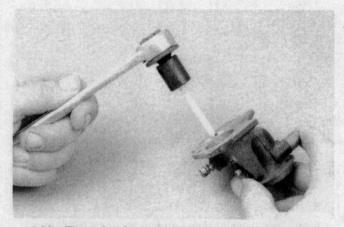

6.39 The nylon fuel tube can be unscrewed with a 6-point socket – work carefully to avoid breaking it off

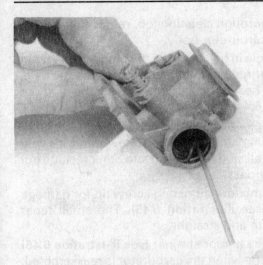

6.40   Remove the O-ring from the throttle bore and discard it

6.41   Remove the mixture adjusting screw, . . .

9   Remove the O-ring (if equipped) from the throttle bore and discard it **(see illustration 6.40)**. Use a new one when the carburetor is reassembled.

10   If a diaphragm-type pump is installed on the side of the carburetor, remove the screws and detach the cover and diaphragm from the carburetor body. A coil spring and metal cup fit between the carburetor body and the diaphragm.

11   Remove the mixture adjusting screw(s) (if equipped) **(see illustration 6.41)**.

Plastic ("Minlon") carburetors and some metal carburetors have a press-fit adjusting screw and seat assembly. To remove it, back out the screw four or five turns, then pull on it to extract the seat. Remove and discard the O-ring on the inner end of the seat.

12   Remove the mixture screw fitting(s) **(see illustration 6.42)**.

13   If the carburetor has removable mixture adjusting screw seats, they can be unscrewed as well **(see illustration 6.43)**.

6.42   . . . the screw fitting . . .

6.43   . . . and the adjusting screw seat (if possible)

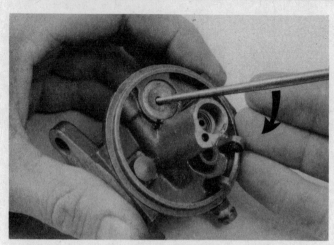

6.44   To remove a welch plug, drill a 1/8-inch hole in it and use an awl or other tool to pry it out – don't damage the bore in the process

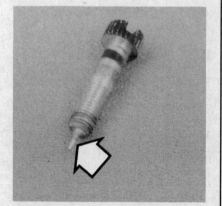

6.45   Check the mixture adjusting screw tip for damage and distortion – if it's blunted, bent or has a groove worn in it, install a new one

14   To do a thorough cleaning job, remove any welch plugs from the carburetor body.

Drill a small hole in the center of the plug and pry it out with a punch or thread a sheet metal screw into the hole, grasp the screw head with a pliers and pull the plug out **(see illustration 6.44)**.

15   Refer to Chapter 5 and follow the cleaning/inspection procedures outlined under *Carburetor overhaul*. It's very important to get all sludge, varnish and other residue out of the carburetor passages.

16   Check each mixture adjusting screw tip for damage and distortion **(see illustration 6.45)**. The small taper should be smooth and straight.

17   Clean the tube and/or strainer **(see illustration 6.46)** or install a new one when the carburetor is reassembled. **Caution:** *DO NOT soak nylon parts in carburetor cleaner for more than 30-minutes.*

Vacu-jet carburetors have a check ball in the fuel tube. Shake the tube to make sure the ball is free. When you suck on the carburetor end of the tube, air should pass through it; when you blow through the carburetor end, the tube should be restricted. If it fails any of the checks, install a new one.

18   On carburetors with an All Temperature/Automatic Choke (vacuum-operated), the choke spring length must be checked **(see illustration 6.47)**. If it isn't as specified, install a new spring.

Pulsa-jet carburetor spring length:
Minimum: 1-1/8 inches
Maximum: 1-7/32 inches

Vacu-jet carburetor spring length:
Minimum: 15/16-inch
Maximum: 1-inch

Model 110900/111900 engines only:
Minimum: 1-5/16 inches
Maximum: 1-3/8 inches

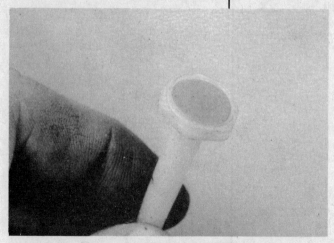

6.46   Clean or replace the fuel tube strainer

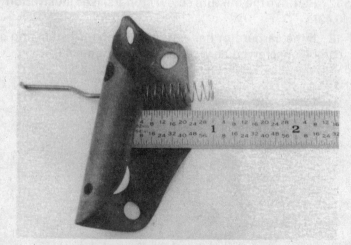

6.47   Check the choke spring length and compare it to the text

19 Once the carburetor parts have been cleaned thoroughly and inspected, reassemble it by reversing the above procedure. Note the following important points:

Be sure to use new O-rings, gaskets and rubber diaphragms.

Make sure the fuel tube length is the same as it was prior to removal from the carburetor. Brass tubes used with Vacu-jet carburetors should protrude 2-9/32 to 2-5/16 inches. It can be pressed into the carburetor body in the jaws of a vise – work carefully and don't damage the carburetor or tube.

When installing the fuel pump diaphragm, the metal cup, not the coil spring, must be against the diaphragm.

Tighten the fuel pump cover screws in small increments, following a criss-cross pattern, to avoid distorting the cover.

When installing new welch plugs, apply a small amount of non-hardening sealant (such as Permatex no. 2) to the outside edge and seat the plug in the bore with a 1/4-inch or larger diameter pin punch and a hammer. Be careful not to collapse the plug – flatten it just enough to secure it in the opening.

To install the press-fit mixture adjusting screw and seat assembly used in plastic (and some metal) carburetors, position a new O-ring on the inner shoulder of the seat, then thread the screw into place until the large washer just touches the outer end of the seat. Lubricate the O-ring with grease, align the flat on the seat with the flat in the carburetor bore and push the assembly into place until it bottoms.

Lubricate the O-ring in the throttle bore (if equipped) with a small amount of engine oil so it won't be damaged when the carburetor is installed (see illustration 6.48).

6.48 Apply a small amount of clean engine oil to the throttle bore O-ring before installing the carburetor

Float-type carburetors

1   Detach the float bowl from the carburetor body.

On some carburetors the float bowl is held in place with a bolt, while on others, it's held in place with the high speed mixture adjusting screw fitting (see illustrations 6.49 and 6.50).

6.49   The float bowl may be held in place with a bolt (arrow), . . .

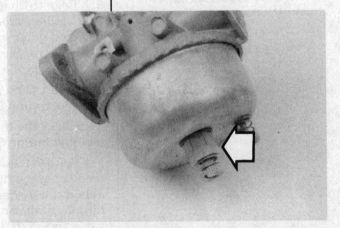

6.50   . . . or the high-speed mixture adjusting screw fitting (arrow)

6.51 Remove the pivot pin and lift straight up on the float to remove it, along with the inlet needle valve

On two-piece Flo-jet carburetors, the float bowl – which is actually the lower part of the carburetor housing – is attached to the upper carburetor housing with several screws. On these carburetors the fuel nozzle projects diagonally into a recess in the upper housing, so the high speed mixture adjusting screw, packing nut and fuel nozzle (visible after the screw and packing nut are removed) must be taken out before removing the screws and separating the two parts of the carburetor. **Caution:** *Be very careful not to damage the adjusting screw threads in the carburetor housing when removing the fuel nozzle from the bore.*

2   Push the float pivot pin out of the carburetor body (you may have to use a small punch to do this).

3   Remove the float assembly and the inlet needle valve **(see illustration 6.51)**. Note how the inlet needle valve is attached to the float – the spring retainer or hook, if used, must be positioned the same way during reassembly.

4   Remove the float bowl gasket.

5   While counting the number of turns, carefully screw the idle mixture adjusting screw in until it bottoms, then remove it along with the spring.

6   Remove the high speed screw and spring in the same manner (if not already done). Counting and recording the number of turns required to bottom the screws will enable you to return them to their original positions and minimize the amount of adjustment required after reassembly.

7   On one-piece Flo-jet carburetors, the main nozzle (jet) can be removed with a screwdriver.

8   To do a thorough cleaning job, remove any welch plugs from the carburetor body. **Note:** *Some two-piece Flo-jet carburetors have a large welch plug in the end of the throttle bore that should be removed only if the choke valve/shaft must be replaced with new parts.*

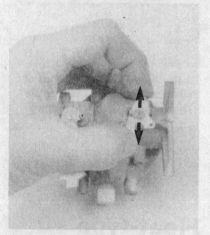

6.52 Move the throttle shaft back-and-forth to feel for play indicating wear in the shaft bores – the bushings used on some carburetors are replaceable

Drill a small hole in the center of the plug and pry it out with a punch or thread a sheet metal screw into the hole, grasp the screw head with a pliers and pull the plug out **(see illustration 6.44)**.

9   Refer to Chapter 5 and follow the cleaning/inspection procedures outlined under *Carburetor overhaul*. It's very important to get all sludge, varnish and other residue out of the carburetor passages. **Note:** *Don't soak plastic or rubber parts in carburetor cleaner. If the float is made of cork, don't puncture it or soak it in carburetor cleaner.*

10   Check each mixture adjusting screw tip for damage and distortion **(see illustration 6.45)**. The small taper should be smooth and straight.

11   Check the throttle valve shaft for wear by moving it back-and-forth **(see illustration 6.52)**.

If you can feel side-to-side play, the bore is worn excessively, which may mean a new carburetor is required (some Flo-jet carburetors have replaceable throttle shaft bushings – check with a dealer to see if wear in the throttle shaft can be repaired on your particular carburetor). The throttle valve and shaft don't have to be removed unless new parts are required.

12   Check the choke shaft for play in the same manner. Don't remove the choke shaft unless you have to install new parts to compensate for wear.

13 Check the inlet needle valve and seat.

Look for nicks and a pronounced groove or ridge on the tapered end of the valve **(see illustration 6.53)**. If there is one, a new needle and seat should be used when the carburetor is reassembled. **Note:** *Some inlet needle seats can be unscrewed, while others are a press-fit.*

To remove a pressed in seat, grip the hex-head of a self-tapping bolt in a vise and position the inlet seat bore over the threaded end of the bolt. Turn the carburetor body until the bolt cuts threads in the seat bore and draws the seat out. A tap can be used in place of the bolt.

If the seat is cylindrical, press it into place with the vise, using the old seat as a driver, until it's flush with the surface of the carburetor. Don't press it in below the surface of the carburetor body or the float level will be incorrect.

If the seat resembles a thick washer and has a circular groove in one side, install it so the inlet needle contacts the side opposite the groove.

14 Check the float pivot pin and bores for wear – if the pin is a sloppy fit in the bores, excessive amounts of fuel will enter the float bowl and flooding will occur.

15 Shake the float to see if there's gasoline in it. If there is, install a new one. Cork floats will absorb gasoline, but it's hard to tell if it has occurred.

16 Once the carburetor parts have been cleaned thoroughly and inspected, reassemble it by reversing the above procedure. Note the following important points:

Be sure to use new gaskets, seals and O-rings.

Whenever an O-ring or seal is installed, lubricate it with a small amount of grease or oil.

Don't overtighten any of the small fasteners or they may break off.

When installing new welch plugs, apply a small amount of non-hardening sealant (such as Permatex no. 2) to the outside edge and seat the plug in the bore with a 1/4-inch or larger diameter pin punch and a hammer. Be careful not to collapse the plug – flatten it just enough to secure it in the opening.

When the inlet needle valve assembly is installed, be sure the clip (if used) is attached to the float tab.

Invert the carburetor and check the float level – the float should be parallel to the carburetor body. On Walbro carburetors, the float is not adjustable. On one and two-piece Flo-jet carburetors, the small tang can be bent with needle-nose pliers until the float is positioned correctly (see illustration 6.54). DO NOT push down on the float to change the level!

When fastening the housings together on a two-piece Flo-jet carburetor, tighten the screws in small increments to avoid distorting anything. Also, make sure the upper end of the fuel nozzle enters the recess in the upper body.

Turn the mixture adjusting screw(s) in until they bottom and back each one out the number of turns required to restore them to their original positions.

6.53   Check the inlet needle valve for a groove or ridge in the tapered area (arrow)

6.54   Bend the tang to adjust the float level – DO NOT push down on the float to change the level

Carburetor adjustment

When making carburetor adjustments, the air cleaner must be in place and the fuel tank must be at least half full. **Note:** *When starting an engine equipped with a Pulsa-jet carburetor for the first time after an overhaul, fill the fuel tank completely to avoid having to prime the fuel pump.*

6.55   The fuel/air mixture adjusting screw can be turned with a screwdriver (Vacu-jet carburetor shown)

Pulsa-jet/Vacu-jet carburetors with butterfly choke valve

1   Turn the FUEL/AIR MIXTURE adjusting screw clockwise until it seats lightly, then back it out 1-1/2 turns (**see illustration 6.55**).

2   Start the engine and allow it to reach operating temperature before making the final adjustments.

3   Place the throttle control lever in the FAST position, then slowly turn the mixture adjusting screw in until the engine begins to miss (run roughly).

4   Turn the mixture adjusting screw out 3/8-turn.

5   Turn the throttle counterclockwise and hold it against the idle stop, then turn the IDLE SPEED adjusting screw to obtain 1750 rpm's.

6   Release the throttle – the engine should accelerate without hesitating or sputtering. If it doesn't, turn the FUEL/AIR MIXTURE adjusting screw out slightly to richen the fuel/air mixture.

Pulsa-jet fixed jet carburetor

1   Follow the procedure in Steps 2 and 3 under *Pulsa-jet/Vacu-jet* above.

2   Place the throttle control lever in the SLOW position, then slowly turn the FUEL/AIR MIXTURE adjusting screw in until the engine slows down (overly lean mixture).

3   Slowly turn the mixture screw out until the engine begins to run roughly (overly rich mixture).

4   Adjust the screw until it's halfway between too lean and too rich and the engine runs smoothly.

5   Follow the procedure in Steps 5 and 6 under *Pulsa-jet/Vacu-jet* above.

Pulsa-jet/Vacu-jet carburetors with sliding cylindrical choke valve

1   Turn the FUEL/AIR MIXTURE adjusting screw clockwise until it seats lightly, then back it out 1 turn.

2   Start the engine and allow it to reach operating temperature before making the final adjustments.

3   Place the throttle control lever in the FAST position, then slowly turn the mixture adjusting screw in until the engine begins to miss (overly lean mixture).

4   Slowly turn the screw out until the engine begins to run unevenly (overly rich mixture).

5   Adjust the screw until it's halfway between too lean and too rich and the engine runs smoothly.

6   Turn the throttle counterclockwise and hold it against the idle stop, then turn the IDLE SPEED adjusting screw to obtain 1750 rpm's.

7   Release the throttle – the engine should accelerate without hesitating or sputtering. If it doesn't, turn the mixture adjusting screw out slightly.

Briggs & Stratton/Walbro float-type carburetors

1   Turn the IDLE MIXTURE adjusting screw clockwise until it seats lightly, then back it out 1 turn.

2   If the carburetor has a HIGH-SPEED MIXTURE adjusting screw, back it out 1-1/4 turns from the seated position.

3   Start the engine and allow it to reach operating temperature.

4   Place the throttle control lever in the SLOW position, then turn the IDLE SPEED adjusting screw until 1750 rpm is obtained.

5   Slowly turn the IDLE MIXTURE adjusting screw in until the engine begins to slow down.

6   Slowly turn the screw out until the engine begins to slow down.

7   Adjust the screw until it's halfway between the two points and the engine runs smoothly.

8   If the carburetor has a high-speed mixture screw, place the throttle control lever in the FAST position, then adjust the HIGH-SPEED MIXTURE screw as described in Steps 5 through 7.

9   Move the control lever from SLOW to FAST – the engine should accelerate without hesitating or sputtering. If it doesn't, turn the IDLE MIXTURE adjusting screw out 1/8-turn.

One-piece Flo-jet carburetor

1   Turn the IDLE MIXTURE adjusting screw clockwise until it seats lightly, then back it out 1-1/2 turns.

2   Back the HIGH-SPEED MIXTURE adjusting screw out 2-1/2 turns from the seated position on the small Flo-jet and 1-1/2 turns on the large Flo-jet.

3   Start the engine and allow it to reach operating temperature.

4   Place the speed control lever in the FAST position, then turn the HIGH-SPEED MIXTURE adjusting screw in until the engine begins to slow down.

5   Slowly turn the screw out until the engine begins to run unevenly.

6   Adjust the screw until it's halfway between the two points and the engine runs smoothly.

7   Adjust the IDLE MIXTURE screw as described in Steps 4 through 6.

8   Turn the throttle counterclockwise and hold it against the stop, then turn the IDLE SPEED adjusting screw until 1750 rpm (aluminum engines) or 1200 rpm (cast-iron engines) is obtained.

9   Slowly turn the IDLE MIXTURE adjusting screw in until the engine begins to slow down.

10   Slowly turn the screw out until the engine begins to run unevenly.

11   Adjust the screw until it's halfway between the two points and the engine runs smoothly.

12   Move the speed control lever from SLOW to FAST – the engine should accelerate without hesitating or sputtering. If it doesn't, turn the adjusting screws out in small increments.

Two-piece Flo-jet carburetor

1   Turn the IDLE MIXTURE adjusting screw clockwise until it seats lightly, then back it out 3/4-turn.

2   Back the HIGH-SPEED MIXTURE adjusting screw out 1-1/2 turns from the seated position.

3   Follow the procedure in Steps 3 through 12 under *One-piece Flo-jet carburetor* above.

Engine disassembly

The engine components should be removed in the following general order:

Engine cover (if used)
Cooling shroud/recoil starter
Carburetor/fuel tank
Muffler
Cylinder head
Small shroud around cylinder fins (if used)
Flywheel
Flywheel brake components (if equipped)
Ignition components
Intake manifold
Crankcase breather
Oil sump, crankcase cover or bearing support(s)
Oil slinger/governor
Crankshaft
Camshaft
Tappets
Piston/connecting rod assembly
Valves

For shroud/recoil starter, carburetor, muffler and cylinder head removal, refer to Chapters 4 and 5 as necessary. The remaining components can be removed to complete engine disassembly by following the photo sequence shown here. Be sure to read the information in each caption. **Note:** *If the engine is cast-iron or has a cast-iron sleeve, use a ridge reamer to remove the carbon/wear ridge from the top of the cylinder bore after the cylinder head is off. Follow the manufacturer's instructions included with the tool. If the engine is made of aluminum, the ridge does not have to be removed.*

6.56 Remove the small bolts (arrows) and lift off the debris screen (if equipped)

6.57 Hold the flywheel with the special tool and remove the starter clutch (as shown here) or the large nut and washer – if you don't have the special tool, be very careful not to damage the flywheel

6.58 In most cases, a special puller (available from the engine manufacturer) will be needed for removing the flywheel – in this example, the puller body is slipped over the end of the crankshaft, the bolts are threaded into the flywheel holes (they may have to cut their own threads if the flywheel has never been removed before), the lower nuts are tightened against the flywheel and the upper nuts are tightened in 1/4-turn increments until the flywheel pops off the shaft taper

Note: *If a flywheel brake is used, remove the brake and related components.*

6.59   Remove the flywheel key (arrow) – if it's sheared off, install a new one

6.60   Refer to Chapter 4 and remove the ignition points and plunger (if equipped), then note how the wires to the coil are routed (it's a very good idea to draw a simple sketch). Remove the bolts (arrows) and detach the coil/spark plug wire assembly.

Note: *On engines with a pneumatic governor, the vane assembly is held in place by one of the coil mounting bolts.*

6.61   If it's still in place, remove the bolts and separate the intake manifold/tube from the engine – remove the gasket and discard it

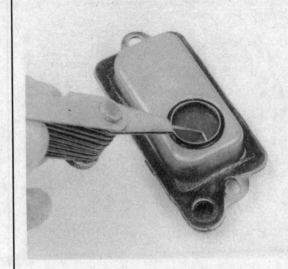

6.62 Remove the mounting bolts and detach the crankcase breather assembly and gasket from the engine. Clean it with solvent, then try to slip a 0.045-inch wire-type spark plug gauge into the space between the fiber disc valve and the breather body (at several points) as shown here. DO NOT apply any force to the valve as this check is done. If the gauge fits into the space, install a new breather assembly when the engine is reassembled.

6.63 Use emery cloth to remove any rust and burrs from the drive end of the crankshaft so the bearing in the oil sump, crankcase cover or bearing support can slide over it

Note: *If the engine has an auxiliary power take-off (PTO), one of the oil sump mounting bolts may be hidden under the PTO cover (all series except 120000). To get at it, remove the cover, lift out the shaft stop and slide the gear and shaft to the side to expose the bolt.*

6.64 Loosen the oil sump-to-engine block bolts in 1/4-turn increments to avoid warping the sump, then remove them — some engines have a crankcase cover and others have a cover and bearing support (one on each side of the engine) instead of an oil sump (cast-iron series); they're attached to the engine block with several bolts and removal is similar.

6.65 Tap the sump/crankcase cover/bearing support with a soft-face hammer to break the gasket seal, then separate it from the engine block and crankshaft – if it hangs up on the crankshaft, continue to tap on it with the hammer, but be very careful not to crack or distort it if it's made of aluminum. If thrust washers are installed on the crankshaft or camshaft, slide them off and set them aside.

6.66 On aluminum block engines, lift the oil slinger/governor assembly off the end of the camshaft. Some engines have a spring washer that fits over the camshaft – it must be removed first.

6.67 On aluminum block engines, turn the crankshaft until the marks on the timing gears are aligned, then lift out the camshaft.

Note: *On ball-bearing equipped engines, the camshaft and crankshaft must be removed as an assembly, (with the timing marks aligned) which means the piston/connecting rod must be removed first (**see illustrations 6.69, 6.70 and 6.71**).*

*On cast-iron engines with plain bearings and series 9 engines with ball-bearings, the crankshaft can be maneuvered out (**see illustrations 6.69, 6.70 and 6.71**) with the camshaft in place. After the crankshaft is out, support the camshaft while carefully driving out the support shaft from the drive side. After the support shaft has been removed, the camshaft can be withdrawn from the crankcase.*

On cast-iron engines with ball-bearings (except series 9), support the camshaft while carefully driving out the support shaft from the drive side. After the support shaft has been removed, the camshaft can be positioned so the gear is in the large recess in the crankcase, which will provide room for the crankshaft to be withdrawn from the magneto side of the engine.

6.68 After the camshaft is removed, pull out the tappets and store them in marked containers so they can be returned to their original locations

6.69 Mark the side of the connecting rod and cap that faces out and note how the oil dipper (if used) is installed – the parts must be reassembled in the exact same relationship to the crankshaft

6.70 Flatten the locking tabs on the connecting rod bolts with a punch and hammer, . . .

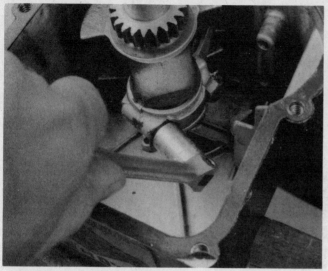

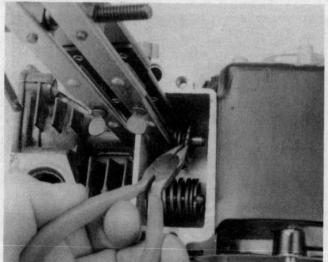

6.71 ... then loosen the bolts in 1/4-turn increments until they can be removed by hand. Separate the cap from the connecting rod, move the end of the rod away from the crankshaft journal and push the piston/rod assembly out through the top of the bore. The crankshaft can now be pulled out of the crankcase.

Note: *Three methods have been used to hold valve spring retainers in place: Pins, slotted retainers (one per valve) and split-type keepers (two per valve). If the engine you're working on has pins or keepers, insert the valve spring compressor jaw between the retainer and the valve chamber wall. If it has slotted retainers, insert the compressor jaw between the spring and retainer and position the remaining jaw on the outside of the valve chamber as shown here.*

6.72 Compress the intake valve spring with the special tool and remove the pin, keepers or retainer, then withdraw the valve through the top of the engine. Pull out the spring (and retainer if necessary), then repeat the procedure for the exhaust valve.

Note: *At this point, the power take-off and/or crankcase-mounted mechanical governor components can be removed (if equipped).*

The PTO gear is attached to the shaft with a roll pin, which can be driven out with a punch and hammer. On series 120000 engines, remove the Allen-head plug from the sump so the roll pin can be driven through the threaded hole. Lift out the shaft stop and pull out the shaft, then remove the gear. Check the gears and shaft for wear and damage. Install new parts if necessary – replace the shaft oil seal even if the original shaft is reinstalled.

The PTO drive gear and clutch (if used) are replaced as part of the camshaft assembly on early models. Later models have replaceable clutch parts – check with a dealer. The PTO control lever shaft is secured in the crankcase with an E-ring. If the lever is loose on the shaft or the shaft is loose in the bore, install a new one. Use a new O-ring when installing the shaft and lubricate it with clean oil or grease.

On some engines, the mechanical governor housing is bolted to the engine; on others, the mechanical governor is integrated into the oil slinger assembly that slips over the end of the camshaft. The lever is attached to the governor shaft with a roll pin or clamped to it with a bolt or bolt/nut. If the governor components are worn or damaged, install a new assembly and have the shaft bushing replaced by a dealer service department.

Inspection of components

After the engine has been completely disassembled, refer to Chapter 5 for the cleaning, component inspection and valve lapping procedures. **Note:** *Special test equipment is needed to check the ignition coil/electronic ignition module. If you suspect the coil/module is causing ignition problems, have it checked by a dealer service department.*

Once you've inspected and serviced everything and purchased any necessary new parts, which should always include new gaskets and seals, reassembly can begin.

Begin by reinstalling the PTO and mechanical governor components (if used) in the crankcase, then proceed as follows:

Engine reassembly

6.73 Coat the intake valve stem with clean engine oil, moly-base grease or engine assembly lube, then reinstall it in the block. Make sure it's returned to its original location.

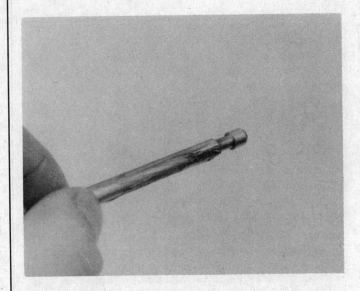

6.74 Compress the spring with the retainer in place (the small cutout [arrow] in the edge of the slotted retainer should face out to facilitate retainer installation), then pull the valve out enough to position the spring. Push the valve back in and install the pin/keepers or slotted retainer. Release the compressor and make sure the retainer is securely locked on the end of the valve. Repeat the procedure for the exhaust valve.

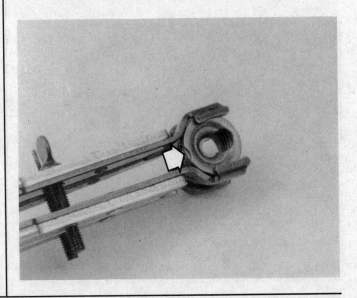

Haynes small engine repair manual

Note: *On ball-bearing equipped aluminum block engines, the crankshaft and camshaft must be installed as an assembly. Align the timing marks on the camshaft gear and crankshaft – this is very important! The crankshaft timing mark is on the counterweight.*

6.75 Lubricate the crankshaft magneto side oil seal lip, the plain bearing (if applicable) and the connecting rod journal with clean engine oil, moly-base grease or engine assembly lube, then reposition the crankshaft in the crankcase. If a ball-bearing is used on the magneto side, lubricate it with clean engine oil.

On cast-iron engines with plain bearings and series 9 engines with ball-bearings, install the camshaft and support shaft before the crankshaft.

On cast-iron engines with ball-bearings (except series 9), position the camshaft gear in the crankcase recess, install the crankshaft, then install the camshaft/support shaft.

In any case, the tappets must be installed first (see illustration 6.82). Be sure to lubricate the camshaft lobes and journals/shaft bore and *check the timing marks on the camshaft and crankshaft to make sure they're aligned properly.* Apply sealant to the cam support shaft hole plug and press or drive it into the opening in the flywheel side of the crankcase. Camshaft end play must be as specified (it should be okay unless the flywheel side cam bearing was replaced or a new camshaft was installed.)

6.76 Before installing the piston/connecting rod assembly, the cylinder bore must be perfectly clean and the top edge of the bore must be chamfered slightly so the rings don't catch on it. Position the piston ring end gaps about 120-degrees apart. Lubricate the piston and rings with clean engine oil, then attach a ring compressor to the piston. Leave the skirt protruding about 1/4-inch. Tighten the compressor until the piston cannot be turned, then loosen it until the piston turns in the compressor with resistance.

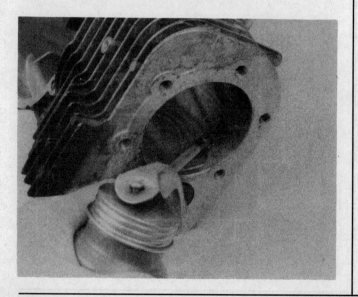

6.77 Rotate the crankshaft until the connecting rod journal is at TDC (Top Dead Center – top of the stroke) and apply engine oil to the cylinder walls. If the piston has a notch in the top, it must face the magneto side of the engine. Make sure the mark you made on the rod will be facing out when the rod/piston assembly is in place. Gently insert the piston/connecting rod assembly into the cylinder and rest the bottom edge of the ring compressor on the engine block. Tap the top edge of the ring compressor to make sure it's contacting the block around its entire circumference.

6.78 Carefully tap on the top of the piston with the end of a wooden or plastic hammer handle while guiding the end of the connecting rod into place on the crankshaft journal. The piston rings may try to pop out just before entering the bore, so keep some pressure on the ring compressor. Work slowly – if any resistance is felt as the piston enters the cylinder, stop immediately. Find out what's hanging up and fix it before proceeding. Do not, for any reason, force the piston into the cylinder – you'll break a ring and/or the piston.

6.79 Install the connecting rod cap, a NEW lock plate, the oil dipper (if used) and the bolts. Make sure the marks you made on the rod and cap are aligned and facing the direction they were originally and the oil dipper is oriented correctly.

Note: *Some replacement connecting rods are packaged with a thick washer under each bolt head – remove and discard them. If a lock plate is installed, one, two or no thin washers may be used. If no oil dipper is used, use two thin washers. If the oil dipper is held by one bolt, use one thin washer under the bolt not holding the dipper. If the dipper is attached by two bolts, don't use any washers.*

6.80 Tighten the bolts to 100 in-lbs. Work up to the final torque in three steps. Temporarily install the camshaft (if not already in place) and turn the crankshaft through two complete revolutions to make sure the rod doesn't hit the cylinder or camshaft. If it does, the piston/connecting rod or camshaft is installed incorrectly.

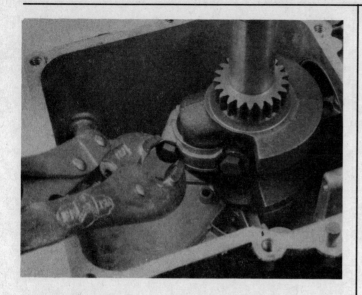

6.81   If nothing binds or contacts anything else, bend up the locking tabs to keep the connecting rod bolts from loosening

6.82   Apply clean engine oil, moly-base grease or engine assembly lube to the tappets, then reinstall them – make sure they're returned to their original locations

6.83   If it's not already in place, install the camshaft. Apply clean engine oil, moly-base grease or engine assembly lube to the lobes and bearing journals and align the timing marks on the gears – this is very important! The marks are usually dimples/lines (or a combination of the two) near the outer edge of the gears.

6.84 Install the oil slinger/governor assembly on the end of the camshaft (aluminum block engines). Some engines also have a spring washer that must be slipped over the end of the camshaft after the oil slinger is in place.

6.85 Lubricate the crankshaft main bearing journal . . .

6.86 . . . and the lip on the oil seal in the sump (or crankcase cover/bearing support) with clean engine oil, moly-base grease or engine assembly lube

6.87 Make sure the dowel pins are in place, then position a new gasket on the crankcase (the dowel pins will hold it in place). A very thin coat of non-hardening sealant can be used if desired. Carefully lower the oil sump (or crankcase cover/bearing support) into place over the end of the crankshaft until it seats on the crankcase. If a removable bearing support is used on the flywheel side of the engine, it must be installed now as well.

6.88 Install the bolts and tighten them to the specified torque. Follow a criss-cross pattern and work up to the final torque in three equal steps to avoid warping the oil sump.

6.89 The crankshaft end play must be checked and adjusted as follows:

On aluminum engines, it must be 0.002 to 0.008-inch with a 0.015-inch thick gasket (standard).

Note: *If the engine is a 92500 or 92900 series, with a 5 as the second-to-last digit of the number, a 100700 series or a 120000 series, it should be 0.002 to 0.030-inch.*

If the end play is less than specified, use additional gaskets in various combinations to correct it (they're available in 0.005, 0.009 and 0.015-inch thicknesses). If the end play is greater than specified, a thrust washer is available for installation over the drive end of the crankshaft to reduce play (additional or different thickness gaskets may be needed along with the thrust washer).

Note: *The thrust washer cannot be used on engines with two ball-bearings – replace worn parts instead.*

On cast-iron engines (series N, 5, 6 and 8), the crankshaft end play must be 0.002 to 0.008-inch with a 0.015-inch thick gasket (standard) under the bearing support plate. If the end play is less than specified, use additional gaskets in various combinations to obtain the correct end play (they are available in various thicknesses).

On Series 9 engines, it must be 0.002 to 0.008-inch with a 0.020-inch thick gasket (standard) under the magneto side bearing support. If the end play is less than 0.002-inch, use additional gaskets in various combinations to obtain the correct end play (they are available in 0.005, 0.009 and 0.020-inch thicknesses). If the end play is greater than specified, use one 0.005 or 0.009-inch thick gasket to obtain the correct play. If the play is excessive with one 0.005-inch thick gasket, a thrust washer is available for installation over the drive end of the crankshaft to reduce play (additional or different thickness gaskets may be needed along with the thrust washer).

Note: *The thrust washer cannot be used on engines with two ball-bearings – replace worn parts instead.*

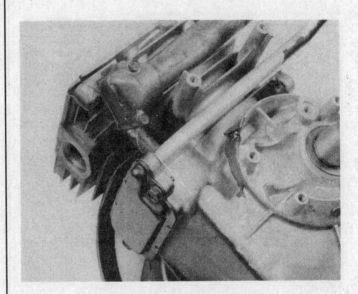

6.90 Install the crankcase breather and intake manifold. Use new gaskets and tighten the bolts securely.

6.91 Install the ignition coil/spark plug wire assembly and pneumatic governor vane (if applicable), but don't tighten the bolts completely – just snug them up. The ignition coil bolt holes are slotted; move the coil as far away from the flywheel as possible before snugging up the bolts. Be sure to reroute the wires from the ignition coil properly.

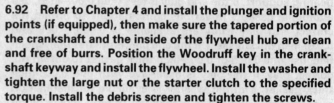

6.92 Refer to Chapter 4 and install the plunger and ignition points (if equipped), then make sure the tapered portion of the crankshaft and the inside of the flywheel hub are clean and free of burrs. Position the Woodruff key in the crankshaft keyway and install the flywheel. Install the washer and tighten the large nut or the starter clutch to the specified torque. Install the debris screen and tighten the screws.

6.93 Turn the flywheel so the magnets are facing away from the coil assembly, then insert a feeler gauge equal to the thickness of the air gap listed in the specifications (Appendix A at the back of the manual) between the flywheel and the legs of the coil armature. Turn the flywheel until the magnets are aligned with the armature legs, then loosen the coil mounting screws so the magnets will draw the armature against the flywheel. Tighten the coil mounting screws securely, then turn the flywheel to release the feeler gauge.

Note: *If a flywheel brake is used, reinstall it now.*

To install the remaining components, refer to Chapters 4 and 5 as necessary. **Caution:** *Be sure to fill the crankcase to the correct level with the specified oil before attempting to start the engine.*

7 Tecumseh/Craftsman engines

Engine identification numbers/models covered

The engine designation system used by Tecumseh consists of a model and serial number, normally found on the shroud. It may also be located on a tag attached to the crankcase. The number can be used to determine the major features of the engine by comparing each digit to the key (**see illustration 7.1**). The letters/digits in the model number can be explained generally as follows:

The first letter or group of letters in a model number indicates the basic engine type:

V	=	*Vertical shaft*
LAV	=	*Lightweight Aluminum Vertical*
VM	=	*Vertical Medium Frame*
TVM	=	*Tecumseh Vertical (medium frame)*
VH	=	*Vertical Heavy Duty (cast-iron)*
TVS	=	*Tecumseh Vertical Styled*
TNT	=	*Toro N' Tecumseh*
ECV	=	*Exclusive Craftsman Vertical*
H	=	*Horizontal Shaft*
HS	=	*Horizontal Small Frame*
HM	=	*Horizontal Medium Frame*
HHM	=	*Horizontal Heavy Duty (cast-iron) Medium Frame*
HH	=	*Horizontal Heavy Duty (cast-iron)*
ECH	=	*Exclusive Craftsman Horizontal*

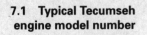

7.1 Typical Tecumseh engine model number

MODEL / SPEC NO.

TVS 90 – 430 56A

ENGINE TYPE

DISPLACEMENT
(9.0 cubic inches)

SPEC. NO.
(for buying parts)

SERIAL NO.

SER 8310C

SHIFT AND LINE

CALENDAR DAY
(310 th day)

YEAR OF MFG.

The number group following the letter(s) indicates the engine displacement in cubic inches or the horsepower rating.

Note: *The information in this repair manual applies only to engines up to and including 5 horsepower or a displacement of 12 cubic inches or less!*

The next group of numbers is the specification number. The last three digits of the specification number indicate variations to the basic engine design.

Following the specification number is the serial number, which indicates the date of production of the engine.

The model number on Craftsman engines is slightly different, but it's located in the same place. The number can be cross-referenced in Appendix A at the back of the manual to determine the engine size and applicable specifications.

Recoil starter service

If the rope breaks, the starter doesn't have to be disassembled to replace it, but it may be a good idea to take the opportunity to do a thorough cleaning job and check the spring and dog mechanism.

There are two approaches you may be faced with when replacing the rope on a recoil starter. The method you use will depend on the starter type.

1   Hold the shroud or recoil starter housing in a vise or clamp it to the workbench so it doesn't move around as you're working on the rope. Use soft jaws in the vise to prevent damage to the shroud or housing.

If you can't see the knot in the pulley end of the rope, the starter will have to be disassembled to install the new rope – the procedure is included later in this section. If the knot is visible (**see illustration 7.2**), you can replace the rope without disassembling the starter. Proceed as follows:

2   If it isn't broken, pull the rope all the way out.

3   Hold the pulley with Vise-Grip pliers or a C-clamp so the spring won't unwind and the pulley is held in position for installing the rope (**see illustration 7.3**).

Horizontal-pull starter – rope replacement

7.2   If the knot is visible, the rope can be replaced easily without disassembling the recoil starter

7.3   Use a Vise-Grip pliers or a C-clamp to restrain the pulley so it doesn't rewind

7.4 Cut off the knot and pull the rope out

7.5 Turn the pulley to apply tension to the spring,
then hold it in place while installing the rope

4   Pull the knot out of the cavity with a pair of needle-nose pliers, then cut the knot off and pull the rope out **(see illustration 7.4)**. Note the type of knot used in the rope, then detach the handle – it can be used on the new rope.

5   If the old rope was broken, you'll have to wind up the recoil spring before installing the new rope. Release the clamp, then turn the pulley against spring tension until it stops completely **(see illustration 7.5)**. Back it off one full turn. This will prevent the spring from being wound too far when the rope is pulled out (which can break it off). Restrain the pulley with the clamp.

6   Cut a piece of new rope the same length and diameter as the original. Standard rope size (diameter) is 4-1/2 or 5 and standard length is 54-inches, although some are longer – if in doubt, make it the same length as the old rope or start with 54-inches and cut off any excess when you see how it fills the pulley. **Note:** *The rope should fill the pulley groove without binding.*

7   If the rope is made of nylon, cauterize (melt) the ends with a match to prevent fraying.

8   Turn the pulley so the opening for the rope is positioned as close to the opening in the housing as possible, then insert the rope into the housing opening and out through the pulley opening. This can be tricky – if the rope won't cooperate, hook a piece of wire through the end of the rope and bend it over with a pliers, then thread the wire through the holes and use it to pull the rope into place **(see illustration 7.6)**.

9   Tie a knot in the rope and manipulate it down into the cavity in the pulley.

10   Release the Vise-Grips or C-clamp while holding the rope, then allow the rope to rewind onto the pulley until the groove is full.

11   Attach the handle to the rope (make sure it's secure or the rope will disappear into the starter and you'll have to start over).

12   Check the starter for proper operation.

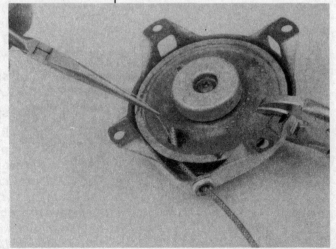

7.6 The rope can be difficult to thread into the pulley, so attach it to a piece of wire and use the wire to pull it into place

7.7   Remove the screw and detach the retainer cup, . . .

7.8   . . . then lift out the starter dog and brake spring (arrows)

Horizontal-pull starter – spring replacement

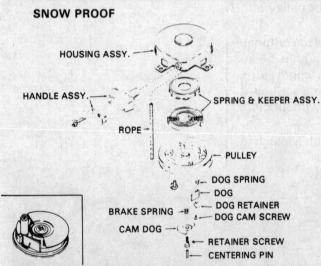

SNOW PROOF

HOUSING ASSY.

HANDLE ASSY.

SPRING & KEEPER ASSY.

ROPE

PULLEY

DOG SPRING

DOG

DOG RETAINER

DOG CAM SCREW

BRAKE SPRING

CAM DOG

RETAINER SCREW

CENTERING PIN

7.9   Snow proof starter components – exploded view

Illustration courtesy of and with permission of Tecumseh Products Co.

If the rope won't rewind and it isn't due to binding in the recoil starter, the spring may be broken.

1   Cut the knot at the pulley and remove the rope.

2   Remove the retainer screw, the retainer cup (cam dog on snow proof type starter), the starter dog and spring and the brake spring **(see illustrations 7.7, 7.8 and 7.9)**. **Note:** *The snow proof starter has a dog retainer as well.* Be sure to note how the parts fit together – lay them out in the correct order to avoid confusion during reassembly.

3   Lift out the pulley.

4   Turn the spring and keeper assembly to remove them.

5   Clean the parts with solvent and dry them with compressed air, if available, or a clean cloth. Replace all worn and damaged parts with new ones.

6   Position the new rewind spring and keeper assembly in the pulley and turn it to lock it in place **(see illustration 7.10)**. The spring should have a light coat of grease on it.

7   Position the pulley in the starter housing and make sure it's connected to the spring **(see illustration 7.11)**.

8   Install the brake spring, starter dog and dog return spring.

9   Replace the retainer cup (cam dog and dog retainer on snow proof starter) and install the screw. Tighten it to 65 to 75 in-lbs. **Note:** *Older models used a 10-32 retainer screw. The larger size (12-28) replacement screw (part no. 590409A) can be used by drilling a 13/64-inch hole in the starter housing. Starters with the add-on alternator must have the tubular rivet in the center of the starter replaced every time the starter is worked on and the rivet is removed. The rivet must be pressed in to a depth of 1/4-inch from the top of the starter body.*

10   To put tension on the recoil spring, wind the pulley counterclockwise until it's tight, then allow it to unwind until the hole in the pulley lines up

7.10   This is what the spring looks like when correctly installed

7.11   Make sure the spring is secured to the pulley

with the eyelet in the housing. Install the rope and handle as described above, then check the starter for proper operation.

11   Some models have a centering pin to align the starter in the starter cup. Bottom the pin in the center of the retaining screw hole. Install the nylon bushing on the pin and position the bushing in the depression in the crankshaft. Gently push the starter down and install the mounting screws.

Vertical-pull starter – horizontal engagement

1   Remove the handle and relieve the spring tension (if necessary) by allowing the rope to slip past the rope clip.

2   Remove the two small screws and detach the spring cover (**see illustration 7.12**).

3   Carefully remove the spring (**see illustration 7.13**).

Disassembly

7.12   Remove the screws and detach the cover (vertical-pull starter)

7.13   Grasp the spring securely when removing it to avoid having it get away from you

7.14   Remove the screw and detach the center hub

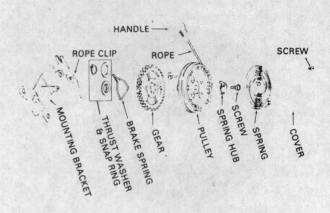

7.15   Detach the snap-ring and thrust washer to disassemble the gear and pulley

Illustration courtesy of and with permission of Tecumseh Products Co.

4   Remove the screw and detach the center hub **(see illustration 7.14)**.

5   Detach the gear and pulley assembly. Disassemble the components by removing the snap-ring and washer **(see illustration 7.15)**.

6   The rope can now be removed from the pulley.

Reassembly

7   Attach the new rope. Use number 4-1/2 or 5 braided rope. Cauterize (melt) the ends by burning them with a match and wiping them with a cloth while hot. Standard rope length is 61-inches, although some applications require a longer rope. Check the old one if in doubt and make it the same length.

8   Assemble the gear and pulley and install the washer and snap-ring. **Caution:** *The brake spring must fit snugly in the gear groove. DO NOT lubricate the brake spring or the spiral on the pulley.*

9   Lubricate the center shaft with a small amount of grease.

10   Place the gear and pulley in position and make sure the brake spring loop is positioned over the metal tab on the bracket. The rope clip must fit tightly on the bracket. The raised spot fits into the hole in the bracket **(see illustration 7.16)**.

11   Install the center hub and screw. Tighten the screw to 44 to 55 in-lbs. If the screw is loose, it'll prevent the rope from retracting.

12   Install the spring (new springs are confined in a retainer). Lay the spring and retainer over the receptacle and push the spring out of the retainer into position – make sure the ends are positioned correctly.

13   Install the cover and screws.

14   Wind the rope onto the pulley by slipping it past the rope clip. When the rope is completely wound onto the pulley, turn the pulley two more turns to put ten-

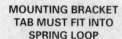

MOUNTING BRACKET TAB MUST FIT INTO SPRING LOOP

BRAKE

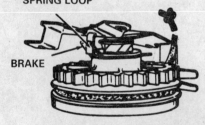

RECEPTACLE FOR RAISED SPOT

ROPE CLIP

RAISED SPOT

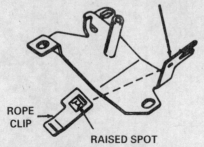

7.16   Make sure the spring loop is positioned over the metal tab on the bracket

Illustration courtesy of and with permission of Tecumseh Products Co.

sion on the spring. Tie a knot in the end of the rope so it doesn't rewind completely into the pulley.

15   When installing the starter on the engine, adjust it so the head of the tooth is no closer than 1/16-inch to the base of the flywheel gear tooth.

16   Thread the rope through the guide and install the handle, then check the starter for proper operation.

Vertical-pull starter – vertical engagement

1   Pull the rope out far enough to lock it in the V-shaped cutout in the bracket.

2   If you have to remove the handle, pry out the staple with a small screwdriver.

3   Place the starter bracket on top of a deep socket large enough to receive the head of the center pin, then drive out the pin.

4   Rotate the spring capsule strut until it's aligned with the legs of the brake spring. Insert a pin or nail no longer than 3/4-inch through the hole in the strut so it catches in the gear teeth (see illustration 7.17). This will keep the capsule in a wound position.

5   Slip the sheave out of the bracket. **Caution:** *Do not attempt to remove the spring capsule from the sheave assembly unless it's completely unwound.*

6   Squeeze and hold the spring capsule firmly against the gear sheave with your thumb at the outer edge of the capsule.

7   Carefully remove the retainer pin from the strut and slowly relieve your grip on the assembly so the spring capsule rotates in a controlled manner to unwind completely.

8   Take the spring capsule off the gear sheave. If the rope is being removed, pry the staple up with a small screwdriver.

Note: *Do not lubricate any of the starter parts. The starter uses number 4-1/2 braided rope. Standard rope length with the handle mounted on the shroud is 65-inches. If the handle is mounted in any other position, measure from the shroud to the handle and add the additional length. Cauterize (melt) the rope ends by burning them with a match and wiping them with a cloth while hot.*

9   Insert the rope end through the hole of the gear sheave opposite the staple platform and tie a left-hand knot. Pull the knot back into the cavity, making sure the rope end doesn't protrude from the cavity.

10   Wind the rope onto the sheave clockwise, as seen from the gear side of the gear sheave.

11   Reinstall the brake spring – be careful not to spread it more than necessary.

Disassembly

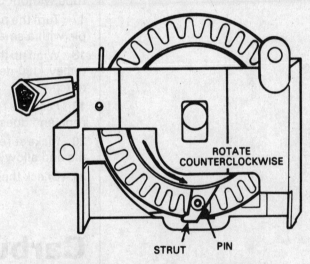

7.17   Use a nail (or other pin) to hold the spring capsule in a wound-up position

Illustration courtesy of and with permission of Tecumseh Products Co.

Reassembly

12 Install the spring capsule. Make sure the starter spring end hooks on the gear hub.

13 Wind the spring up four full turns and position the strut between the two brake spring legs. Insert the pin into the strut.

14 If the starter is equipped with a locking pawl or delay pawl and spring, make sure they're in place, then grasp the gear and spring capsule assembly and slide it into the bracket, making sure the legs of the brake spring are positioned in the slots of the bracket.

15 Feed the rope end under the rope guide and hook it into the V-notch. Remove the pin – the strut will rotate clockwise against the bracket.

16 Insert the new center pin by carefully pressing or driving it firmly into place.

Rope replacement

On starters with V-notches in the bracket, it's possible to change the rope without disassembling the starter.

17 Turn the pulley until the staple lines up with the notch. Pry out the staple with a small screwdriver and remove the old rope.

18 Wind up the spring until it's tight, then let it unwind until the hole in the pulley (180-degrees from the original staple mount) lines up with the notch.

19 Feed the rope through the hole and tie a left-hand knot. Make sure the rope end doesn't protrude from the knot cavity.

20 Make sure the rope is routed through the shroud, then attach the handle and allow the pulley to slowly rewind the rope.

21 Check the starter for proper operation.

Carburetor disassembly and reassembly

The following procedures describe how to disassemble and reassemble the carburetor so new parts can be installed. Read the sections in Chapter 5 on carburetor removal and overhaul before doing anything else.

In some cases it may be more economical (and much easier) to install a new carburetor rather than attempt to repair the original. Check with a dealer to see if parts are readily available and compare the cost of new parts to the price of a complete ready-to-install (standard service) carburetor before deciding how to proceed. The carburetor model number and date code are stamped on the edge of the mounting flange.

1 While counting the number of turns, carefully screw the idle mixture adjusting screw in until it bottoms, then remove it along with the spring (see illustration 7.18).

7.18 Remove the idle mixture adjusting screw, . . .

7.19 . . . and the high-speed mixture adjusting screw (if equipped)

7.20 The float bowl may be held in place with a bolt . . .

2   Remove the high speed (main) adjustment screw and spring from the fitting in the same manner (if not already done) **(see illustration 7.19)**. Counting and recording the number of turns required to bottom the screws will enable you to return them to their original positions and minimize the amount of adjustment required after reassembly.

3   Detach the float bowl from the carburetor body.

On some carburetors the float bowl is held in place with a bolt, while on others, it's held in place with the high speed mixture adjusting screw fitting **(see illustrations 7.20 and 7.21)**. Be sure to note the locations of any gaskets/washers used.

4   If you're working on a Walbro carburetor, note how the float spring is positioned before removing the float – it may be a good idea to draw a simple sketch to refer to during reassembly. Push the float pivot pin out of the carburetor body (you may have to use a small punch to do this) **(see illustration 7.22)**.

7.21 . . . or the high-speed mixture adjusting screw fitting

5   Remove the float assembly and the inlet needle valve. Note how the inlet needle valve is attached to the float – the retainer clip, if used, must be positioned the same way during reassembly.

6   Remove the float bowl gasket.

7   To do a thorough cleaning job, remove any welch plugs from the carburetor body. **Note:** *Do not remove any brass cup or ball plugs (if used). One may be located near the inlet needle seat cavity to seal off the idle air bleed. Another one may be located in the base, where the float bowl mounting bolt or high speed adjustment screw fitting seals the idle fuel passage. A third plug may be located on the side of the main nozzle casting, sealing the idle fuel passage.*

7.22 Remove the pivot pin and lift straight up on the float to remove it, along with the inlet needle valve

7.23   To remove a welch plug, drill a 1/8-inch hole in it and use an awl or other tool to pry it out – don't damage the bore in the process

Drill a small hole in the center of the welch plug and pry it out with a punch or thread a sheet metal screw into the hole, grasp the screw head with a pliers and pull the plug out **(see illustration 7.23)**.

8   If the carburetor has a primer bulb, it can be removed with a pliers. Grasp it securely and twist and pull to detach it from the carburetor body. The retainer can be pried out with a screwdriver. If the original primer is removed, discard it and install a new one when reassembling the carburetor. A 3/4-inch deep socket can be used to seat the new bulb/retainer in the cavity.

9   Refer to Chapter 5 and follow the cleaning/inspection procedures outlined under Carburetor overhaul. **Note:** *Don't soak plastic or rubber parts in carburetor cleaner. If the float is made of cork, don't puncture it or soak it in carburetor cleaner.*

10   Check each mixture adjusting screw tip for damage and distortion **(see illustration 7.24)**. The small taper should be smooth and straight.

11   Check the throttle plate shaft for wear by moving it back-and-forth **(see illustration 7.25)**.

12   Check the throttle plate fit in the carburetor bore.

If there's play in the shaft, the bore is worn excessively, which may mean a new carburetor is required (on some carburetors, replacing the throttle plate shaft or plate, or both, may cure the problem – check with a dealer). The throttle plate and shaft don't have to be removed unless new parts are required. If they are removed, make sure the line or number on the plate is facing out and the line is in the 12 o'clock position when reinstalled **(see illustration 7.26)**. If the throttle binds after the parts are reinstalled, loosen the screw and reposition the plate on the shaft. If dust seals are used, they should be positioned next to the carburetor body.

13   Check the choke shaft for play in the same manner and examine the linkage holes to see if they're worn. Don't remove the choke shaft unless you have to install new parts to compensate for wear. Note how the choke plate is installed before removing it – the flat side must face down, toward the float bowl. They will operate in either direction, so make sure it's reassembled correctly. If dust seals are used, they should be positioned next to the carburetor body.

14   Check the inlet needle valve and seat.

Look for nicks and a pronounced groove or ridge on the tapered end of the valve **(see illustration 7.27)**. If there is one, a new needle and seat should be used when the carburetor is reassembled. They are normally installed as a matched set. **Note:** *Some inlet needle seats can be unscrewed, while others are a viton plastic insert that can be pulled out with a piece of hooked wire or forced out with a short blast of compressed air.*

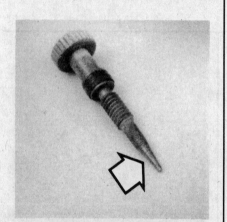

7.24   Check the mixture adjusting screw tip for damage and distortion – if it's blunted, bent or has a groove worn in it, install a new one

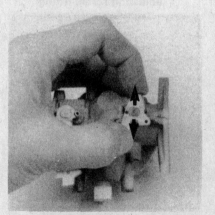

7.25   Check for wear in the throttle shaft or bores by moving it back-and-forth

7.26 The line on the throttle valve plate (arrow) must be in the 12 o'clock position when it's reinstalled

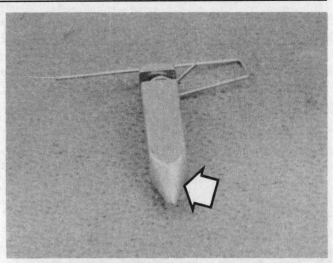

7.27 Check the inlet needle valve for a groove or ridge in the tapered area (arrow)

Install the new viton seat so the inlet needle contacts the side opposite the groove (grooved side in, smooth side facing out). Lubricate it with a small amount of clean engine oil and use a pin punch the same diameter as the seat to install it in the bore **(see illustrations 7.28 and 7.29)**.

If a threaded seat is used, be sure to install a new gasket as well.

15   Check the float pivot pin and the bores in the carburetor casting, the float hinge bearing surfaces and the inlet needle tab for wear – if wear has occurred, excessive amounts of fuel will enter the float bowl and flooding will result.

16   Shake the float to see if there's gasoline in it. If there is, install a new one.

17   Check the fuel inlet fitting to see if it's clean and unobstructed. If it's damaged or plugged, a new one can be installed. Twist and pull on the old one to remove it. When installing the new one, insert it into the opening in the carburetor body, then apply Locktite to the exposed part of the shank. Push it in until the shoulder on the fitting contacts the carburetor. Make sure the fitting points in the same direction as the original.

18   Once the carburetor parts have been cleaned thoroughly and inspected, reassemble it by reversing the above procedure. Note the following important points:

Make sure all fuel and air passages in the carburetor body, main nozzle, inlet needle seat and float bowl mounting bolt are clean and clear.

Be sure to use new gaskets, seals and O-rings.

Whenever an O-ring or seal is installed, lubricate it with a small amount of grease or oil.

Don't overtighten small fasteners or they may break off.

7.28 The viton inlet needle valve seat must be installed with the grooved side in

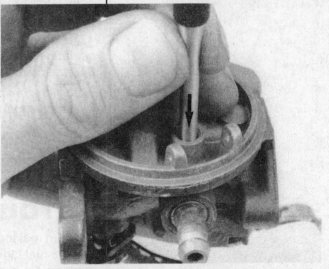

7.29 Use a pin punch to push the viton seat in until it's bottomed in the bore

When installing new welch plugs, apply a small amount of non-hardening sealant (such as Permatex no. 2) to the outside edge and seat the plug in the bore with a 1/4-inch or larger diameter pin punch and a hammer. Be careful not to collapse the plug – flatten it just enough to secure it in the opening.

When the inlet needle valve assembly is installed, be sure the retaining clip is attached to the float tab.

On Walbro carburetors only, when attaching the float to the carburetor, position the spring between the float hinges with the long spring end pointing toward the choke end of the carburetor. Wind the spring back to put tension on it, then set the float in place, release the tension and install the pin.

Invert the carburetor and check the float level:

On Walbro carburetors, the gap between the float and the carburetor body on the side directly opposite the pivot pin should be 0.110 to 0.130-inch – a 1/8-inch diameter drill bit can be used as a gauge (**see illustration 7.30**). The float should move freely from this point to a point where the brass plug in the carburetor main nozzle casting is visible. If the entire plug is not visible, pull down GENTLY on the float until it is. This will bend the limiting tab to allow extra float travel, which will prevent fuel starvation.

7.30   A 1/8-inch drill bit can be used as a gauge to check the float level on Walbro carburetors

All Tecumseh carburetors require a special gauge (part no. 670253A) to check the float level – the float should NOT be parallel to the carburetor body. If a fiber washer is used between the float bowl and carburetor main nozzle casting, be sure it's in place when the check is made. The gauge is positioned 90-degrees to the hinge pin, resting on the main nozzle casting, and is pulled slowly across the casting until the first step contacts the float. The side of the float directly opposite the pivot pin must fit under the first step of the gauge and can fit under the second step if there is no gap between them. Adjustment is accomplished by carefully bending the tab on the float.

Install the float bowl with the flat surface on the same side of the carburetor as the fuel inlet fitting and make sure it's parallel to the float hinge pin.

Install the idle speed adjustment screw with the carburetor in an upright position (not upside-down or sideways). This will prevent damage to carburetors with a metering rod in the idle circuit.

Turn the mixture adjusting screw(s) in until they bottom and back each one out the number of turns required to restore them to their original positions.

Carburetor adjustment

When making carburetor adjustments, the air cleaner must be in place and the fuel tank should be at least half full. Some carburetors have fixed main or idle jets (or both). If the jet is fixed, no mixture screw is installed and no adjustment is required.

1   To adjust the idle speed, back out the IDLE SPEED adjusting screw (which contacts the throttle), then turn it in until it just contacts the throttle lever.

2   From this position, turn the screw in one full turn. Final idle speed must be set with a tachometer (take the equipment to a dealer or borrow a tachometer). **Caution:** *DO NOT exceed equipment manufacturer's recommended governed speed. Excessive rpm's can cause a lean fuel/air mixture, which may lead to overheating and engine failure.*

Engine models V, H80, VM and HM80 with a Walbro carburetor

3   If not already done, turn the idle and high speed FUEL/AIR MIXTURE adjusting screws clockwise until they seat lightly, then back them out. The idle mixture screw should be opened 1-3/4 turns. The high-speed mixture screw should be opened two turns **(see illustrations 7.18 and 7.19).**

4   Start the engine and allow it to reach operating temperature before making the final adjustments.

5   Place the throttle control lever in the SLOW or IDLE position, then turn the IDLE MIXTURE adjusting screw in, in 1/8-turn increments, until the engine begins to miss/run erratically.

6   Slowly turn the screw out 1/4-to-3/8 turn from that position.

7   The high-speed mixture must be set with the engine under load (cutting grass, blowing snow, etc.).

8   Open the high-speed mixture adjusting screw in 1/8-turn increments until the engine runs smoothly under load.

9   If the engine smokes excessively, try turning the screw in, in very small increments, until the smoke is diminished.

10   Return the engine to idle. If it doesn't idle smoothly, turn the IDLE MIXTURE adjusting screw slightly in either direction until it does.

All other engines

11   If not already done, turn the idle and high speed FUEL/AIR MIXTURE adjusting screws clockwise until they seat lightly, then back them out as indicated below:

Walbro carburetors only (all engines)
Idle mixture screw: 1-turn
High-speed mixture screw: 1-turn

All other carburetors
Idle mixture screw: 1-turn
High-speed mixture screw: 1-1/4 turns

12   Start the engine and allow it to reach operating temperature before making the adjustments. **Note:** *If the engine is a two-stroke and it falters or dies after the choke lever is moved to the OFF position, turn the mixture adjusting screw another 1/4-turn open (counterclockwise) and restart the engine.*

13   Place the throttle control lever in the FAST position.

14   With the engine running at maximum speed, slowly turn the HIGH-SPEED MIXTURE screw out until the engine begins to run unevenly (overly rich mixture).

15   Turn the screw slowly in the opposite direction until the engine begins to run roughly or cut out (overly lean mixture.

16 · Adjust the screw until it's halfway between too lean and too rich and the engine runs smoothly.

17   Place the throttle control lever in the SLOW or IDLE position and re-peat the procedure for the IDLE MIXTURE adjusting screw.

All carburetors

18   Move the speed control lever from SLOW to FAST – the engine should accelerate without hesitating or sputtering.

19   If the engine dies, it's too lean – turn the adjusting screws out in small increments.

20   If the engine sputters and runs rough before picking up the load, it's too rich – turn the adjusting screws in slightly.

21   If the adjustments are "touchy", check the float level and make sure it isn't sticking.

Four-stroke engine disassembly

The engine components should be removed in the following general order:

Engine cover (if used)
Fuel tank
Cooling shroud/recoil starter
Carburetor/intake manifold
Muffler
Cylinder head
Flywheel
Flywheel brake components (if equipped)
Ignition components
Crankcase breather assembly
Oil sump/crankcase cover
Crankshaft
Camshaft
Tappets
Piston/connecting rod assembly
Valves
Governor components

For fuel tank, shroud/recoil starter, carburetor/intake manifold, muffler and cylinder head removal, refer to Chapters 4 and 5 as necessary. The re-maining components can be removed to complete engine disassembly by following the photo sequence shown here. Be sure to read the information in each caption. **Note:** *Use a ridge reamer to remove the carbon/wear ridge from the top of the cylinder bore after the cylinder head is off. Follow the manufacturer's instructions included with the tool.*

7.31 Hold the flywheel and remove the large nut and washer. After the nut is removed, the starter cup and debris screen can be detached.

7.32 In most cases, the flywheel can be removed with a knock-off tool and hammer, as shown here. If the flywheel has tapped holes, or cored holes (untapped), a special puller (available from the engine manufacturer) will be needed for removing the flywheel. In this example, the knock-off tool is slipped or threaded onto the end of the crankshaft and a large screwdriver is used to carefully apply upward pressure to the flywheel as the knock-off tool is struck with a hammer. DO NOT hammer on the end of the crankshaft and DO NOT use a jaw-type puller that applies force to the outer edge of the flywheel! As the tool is hit with the hammer, the flywheel should pop off the shaft taper.

Note: *If a flywheel brake is used, remove the brake and related components.*

7.33 Place the flywheel upside-down on a wooden surface and check the magnets by holding a screwdriver at the extreme end of the handle while moving the tip toward one of the magnets – when the screwdriver tip is about 3/4-inch from the magnet, it should be attracted to it. If it doesn't, the magnets may have lost their strength and ignition system performance may not be up to par. Remove the flywheel key – if it's sheared off, install a new one.

Haynes small engine repair manual

7.34   Refer to Chapter 4 and remove the ignition points and related parts (if equipped), then note which side of the point cam is facing out and slide it up, off the end of the crankshaft (it should be marked TOP)

7.35   Note how the wires to the coil are routed (it's a very good idea to draw a simple sketch). Mark the coil bracket and engine bosses with a scribe or center punch, . . .

7.36   . . . then remove the bolts (arrows) and detach the coil/spark plug wire assembly (note that this engine has the coil mounted under the flywheel; some engines are equipped with an ignition coil mounted outside the flywheel – the removal procedures are basically the same for both types).

7.37 If it's still in place, remove the bolts and separate the intake manifold from the engine – remove the gasket and discard it. Remove the mounting bolts and detach the crankcase breather assembly (shown here) and gasket from the engine.

7.38 Use emery cloth to remove rust and burrs from the drive end of the crankshaft so the bearing in the oil sump or cover can slide over it

Note: *On horizontal crankshaft engines with ball bearings, the drive side oil seal must be removed first to get at the snap-ring on the crankshaft. Remove the snap-ring before attempting to pull off the crankcase cover.*

7.39 Loosen the oil sump-to-engine block bolts in 1/4-turn increments to avoid warping the sump, then remove them – some engines have a crankcase cover instead of an oil sump (horizontal crankshaft engines); they're attached to the engine block with several bolts and removal is similar.

Note: *On engines with a Power Take-off (PTO), you must turn the crankshaft as the oil sump/crankcase cover is removed to allow the PTO gear to roll off the crankshaft worm gear – DO NOT force it!*

7.40 Tap the sump/cover with a soft-face hammer to break the gasket seal, then separate it from the engine block and crankshaft – if it hangs up on the crankshaft, continue to tap on it with the hammer, but be very careful not to crack or distort it (especially if it's made of aluminum). If thrust washers are installed on the crankshaft or camshaft, slide them off and set them aside.

7.41 Vertical crankshaft engines are equipped with a plunger-type oil pump (arrow) that's driven by an eccentric on the camshaft – it can be lifted out before the camshaft is removed

7.42 Turn the crankshaft until the marks on the timing gears are aligned, then lift out the camshaft

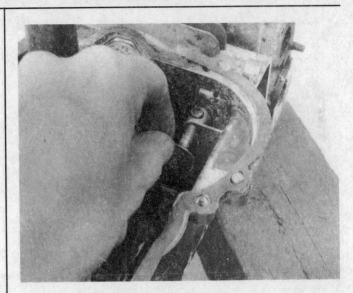

7.43 After the camshaft is removed, pull out the tappets and store them in marked containers so they can be returned to their original locations

7.44 Look for match marks on the connecting rod and cap – if you can't see any, mark the side of the connecting rod and cap that faces out and note how the oil dipper (if used) is installed (the parts must be reassembled in the exact same relationship to the crankshaft)

7.45 Turn the crankshaft so the rod journal is at the bottom of its stroke (Bottom Dead Center). Flatten the locking tabs (if used) on the connecting rod bolts with a punch and hammer, . . .

7.46 . . . then loosen the bolts or nuts in 1/4-turn increments until they can be removed by hand. Separate the cap (and washers, if used) from the connecting rod, move the end of the rod away from the crankshaft journal and push the piston/rod assembly out through the top of the bore. The crankshaft can now be lifted out.

7.47 Two methods have been used to hold valve spring retainers in place: Pins and slotted retainers (one per valve). Compress the intake valve spring and remove the pin or retainer, then withdraw the valve through the top of the engine. Pull out the spring, then repeat the procedure for the exhaust valve. Some engines have a retainer at the base of the spring as well.

7.48 Do not separate the lever from the governor shaft unless new parts are needed – the lever mount will be damaged during removal

7.49 The governor assembly can be withdrawn from the gear shaft after the retaining rings are removed (one on each side of the spool). Note how the parts fit together to simplify reassembly (a simple sketch would be helpful).

Check the governor parts for wear and damage. If the gear shaft must be replaced, measure how far it protrudes before removing it and don't damage the crankcase boss. Clamp the shaft in a vise and tap the crankcase boss with a soft-face hammer to extract the shaft from the hole.

Caution: *DO NOT twist the shaft with a Vise-Grip pliers or the mounting hole will be enlarged and the new shaft won't fit into it securely.*

When installing the new shaft, coat the serrated end with stud and bearing mount liquid after the shaft has been started in the hole with a soft-face hammer. Use a vise or press to finish installing the shaft and make sure it protrudes the same amount as the original (or the distance specified on the instruction sheet included with the new part). Wipe any excess stud and bearing mount liquid off the shaft and mounting boss flange.

Note: *At this point, the power take-off components can be removed (if equipped). Be sure to note how the parts fit together – a simple sketch may prove helpful during reassembly. Check the gears and shaft for wear and damage. Install new parts if necessary – replace the shaft oil seal even if the original shaft is reinstalled.*

Inspection of components

After the engine has been completely disassembled, refer to Chapter 5 for the cleaning, component inspection and valve lapping procedures. **Note:** *Special test equipment is needed to check the ignition coil/electronic ignition module. If you suspect the coil/module is causing ignition problems, have it checked by a dealer service department.*

Once you've inspected and serviced everything and purchased any necessary new parts, which should always include new gaskets and seals, reassembly can begin.

Begin by reinstalling the PTO components (if used) in the crankcase, then proceed as follows:

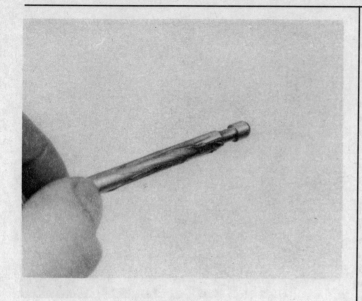

Four-stroke engine reassembly

7.50 Coat the intake valve stem with clean engine oil, moly-base grease or engine assembly lube, then reinstall it in the block. Make sure it's returned to its original location.

Note: *If a seal is used on the intake valve, always install a new one when the engine is reassembled.*

7.51 Compress the spring with both retainers in place, then pull the valve out enough to position the spring and install the pin or secure the slotted retainer. Release the compressor and make sure the retainer is securely locked on the end of the valve. Repeat the procedure for the exhaust valve.

7.52 Install the washer and gear assembly and make sure the retaining ring is secured in the shaft groove, . . .

7.53 . . . then install the spool and the outer retaining ring

7.54 Lubricate the crankshaft magneto side oil seal lip, the plain bearing (if applicable) and the connecting rod journal with clean engine oil, moly-base grease or engine assembly lube, then reposition the crankshaft in the crankcase. If a ball-bearing is used on the magneto side, lubricate it with clean engine oil.

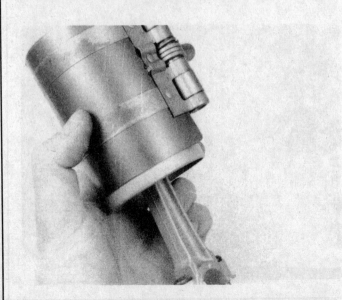

7.55 Before installing the piston/connecting rod assembly, the cylinder must be perfectly clean and the top edge of the bore must be chamfered slightly so the rings don't catch on it. Stagger the piston ring end gaps and make sure they're positioned opposite the valve seats when the piston is installed. Lubricate the piston and rings with clean engine oil, then attach a ring compressor to the piston. Leave the skirt protruding about 1/4-inch. Tighten the compressor until the piston cannot be turned, then loosen it until the piston turns in the compressor with resistance.

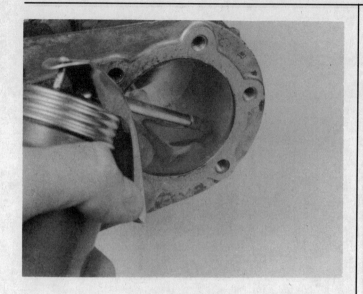

7.56 Rotate the crankshaft until the connecting rod journal is at TDC (Top Dead Center – top of the stroke) and apply a coat of engine oil to the cylinder walls. If the piston has an arrow in the top, it must face the valve seat side of the engine (if possible) or to the right when looking at the engine with the connecting rod pointing down. Make sure the match marks on the rod and cap will be facing out when the rod/piston assembly is in place. Gently insert the piston/connecting rod assembly into the cylinder and rest the bottom edge of the ring compressor on the engine block. Tap the top edge of the ring compressor to make sure it's contacting the block around its entire circumference.

7.57 Carefully tap on the top of the piston with the end of a wooden or plastic hammer handle while guiding the end of the connecting rod into place on the crankshaft journal. The piston rings may try to pop out just before entering the bore, so keep some pressure on the ring compressor. Work slowly – if any resistance is felt as the piston enters the cylinder, stop immediately. Find out what's hanging up and fix it before proceeding. Do not, for any reason, force the piston into the cylinder – you'll break a ring and/or the piston.

7.58 Install the connecting rod cap, a NEW lock plate, the oil dipper (if used) and the bolts or washers and nuts. Make sure the marks you made on the rod and cap (or the manufacturer's marks) are aligned and facing out and the oil dipper is oriented correctly.

7.59 Tighten the bolts or nuts to the specified torque (see Appendix A). Note that Durlock bolts (used without locking tabs) and regular bolts have different torques. Work up to the final torque in three steps. Temporarily install the camshaft and turn the crankshaft through two complete revolutions to make sure the rod doesn't hit the cylinder or camshaft. If it does, the piston/connecting rod is installed incorrectly.

7.60 Apply clean engine oil, moly-base grease or engine assembly lube to the tappets, then reinstall them – make sure they're returned to their original locations

7.61 If it's not already in place, install the camshaft. Apply clean engine oil, moly-base grease or engine assembly lube to the lobes and bearing journals and align the timing marks on the gears – this is very important! The marks are usually dimples/lines or bevelled teeth (or a combination of them) near the outer edge of the gears. On many engines, the camshaft gear mark must be aligned with the keyway for the crankshaft gear – no mark is included on the crankshaft gear itself.

7.62   Install the plunger-type oil pump (if used) after lubricating it with clean engine oil. Be absolutely certain the chamfered side of the pump body faces the camshaft and the plunger ball is seated in the recess in the oil sump after the sump is in place.

7.63   Lubricate the crankshaft main bearing journal . . .

7.64   . . . and the lip on the oil seal in the sump (or crankcase cover) with clean engine oil, moly-base grease or engine assembly lube

7.65 Make sure the dowel pins are in place, then position a new gasket on the crankcase (the dowel pins will hold it in place). Carefully lower the oil sump (or crankcase cover) into place over the end of the crankshaft until it seats on the crankcase. DO NOT damage the oil seal lip or leaks will result! The governor shaft must match up with the spool end and the oil pump shaft ball end must be engaged in the recess.

7.66 Apply thread cement to the bolt threads, then install and tighten them to the specified torque. Follow a criss-cross pattern and work up to the final torque in three equal steps to avoid warping the oil sump/cover.

7.67 The crankshaft end play must be checked with a dial indicator. If it's excessive, check with a dealer regarding the best way to correct it.

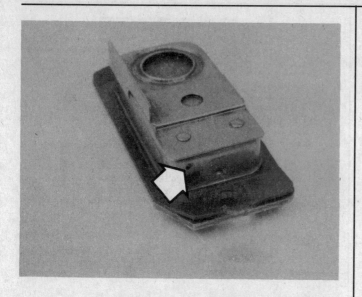

7.68 Install the crankcase breather (with the small hole [arrow] down, as shown here) and intake manifold (unless the carburetor and manifold were removed as an assembly). Use new gaskets and tighten the bolts securely.

7.69 Install the ignition coil/spark plug wire assembly and align the marks on the coil bracket and crankcase bosses, then tighten the coil mounting bolts securely.

Note: If the coil is mounted on the outside of the flywheel, don't tighten the bolts completely – just snug them up. The bolt holes are slotted; move the coil as far away from the flywheel as possible before snugging up the bolts. Be sure to reroute the wires from the ignition coil properly.

7.70 Refer to Chapter 4 and install the ignition points (if equipped) with the TOP side of the point cam facing up, then make sure the tapered portion of the crankshaft and the inside of the flywheel hub are clean and free of burrs. Position the Woodruff key in the crankshaft keyway and install the flywheel. Install the starter cup, washer and nut. Tighten the nut to the specified torque.

Note: If the ignition coil is mounted outside the flywheel, turn the flywheel so the magnets are facing away from the coil assembly, then insert a feeler gauge equal to the thickness of the air gap listed in the specifications (Appendix A at the back of the manual) between the flywheel and the legs of the coil armature. Turn the flywheel until the magnets are aligned with the armature legs, then loosen the coil mounting bolts so the magnets will draw the armature against the flywheel. Tighten the coil mounting bolts securely, then turn the flywheel to release the feeler gauge.

If a flywheel brake is used, install it now. To install the remaining components, refer to Chapters 4 and 5 as necessary. **Caution:** *Be sure to fill the crankcase to the correct level with the specified oil before attempting to start the engine.*

Two-stroke engine disassembly

The engine components should be removed in the following general order:

Engine cover (if used)
Fuel tank
Cooling shroud/recoil starter
Carburetor
Muffler
Flywheel
Ignition components
Cylinder head
Piston/connecting rod/bearing assembly
Crankshaft/bearing plate

For fuel tank, shroud/recoil starter, carburetor and muffler removal, refer to Chapters 4 and 5 as necessary. The remaining components can be removed to complete engine disassembly by following the photo sequence shown here. Be sure to read the information in each caption.

7.71   Hold the flywheel and remove the large nut and washer. After the nut is removed, the starter cup and debris screen can be detached.

7.72   In most cases, the flywheel can be removed with a knock-off tool and hammer, as shown here. If the flywheel has tapped holes, or cored holes (untapped), a special puller (available from the engine manufacturer) will be needed for removing the flywheel. In this example, the knock-off tool is slipped or threaded onto the end of the crankshaft and a large screwdriver is used to carefully apply upward pressure to the flywheel as the knock-off tool is struck with a hammer. DO NOT hammer on the end of the crankshaft and DO NOT use a jaw-type puller that applies force to the outer edge of the flywheel! As the tool is hit with the hammer, the flywheel should pop off the shaft taper.

Haynes small engine repair manual

7.73 Place the flywheel upside-down on a wooden surface and check the magnets by holding a screwdriver at the extreme end of the handle while moving the tip toward one of the magnets – when the screwdriver tip is about 3/4-inch from the magnet, it should be attracted to it. If it doesn't, the magnets may have lost their strength and ignition system performance may not be up to par. Remove the flywheel key – if it's sheared off, install a new one

7.74 Refer to Chapter 4 and remove the ignition points and related parts (if equipped), then note which side of the point cam is facing out and slide it up, off the end of the crankshaft

7.75 Note how the wires to the coil are routed (it's a very good idea to draw a simple sketch). Mark the coil bracket and engine bosses with a scribe or center punch, . . .

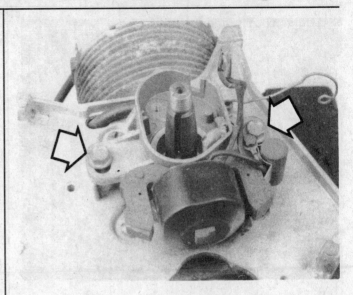

7.76 ... then remove the bolts (arrows) and detach the coil/spark plug wire assembly (note that this engine has the coil mounted under the flywheel; some engines are equipped with an ignition coil mounted outside the flywheel – the removal procedures are basically the same for both types).

7.77 If it's still in place, remove the screws and separate the reed plate from the engine – remove the gasket and discard it

7.78 Loosen the large cylinder head mounting screws in 1/4-turn increments – to avoid warping the head – then detach it from the engine. If it's stuck, don't pry on it – use a soft-face hammer to dislodge it. Remove the old gasket as well. If a carbon ridge has formed in the top of the cylinder, scrape it out so the rings don't catch on it during piston removal.

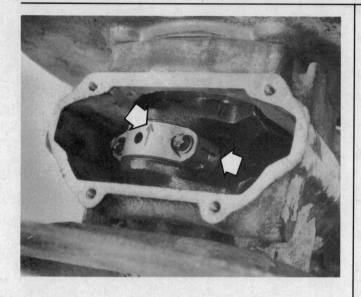

7.79 Look for match marks on the connecting rod and cap – if you can't see any, mark one side of the connecting rod and cap with a scribe or center punch (the parts must be reassembled in the exact same relationship to the crankshaft)

7.80 Loosen the connecting rod cap bolts in 1/4-turn increments until they can be removed by hand – on some engines, a special no. Six Torx socket (shown here) is needed for the bolts

7.81 Separate the cap from the connecting rod and remove the needle bearings and steel liner (used only with aluminum rods) from the cap

7.82 Push the piston/connecting rod assembly out through the top of the cylinder and finish removing the needle bearings. If the rod is aluminum, a steel liner is also installed in the connecting rod.

7.83 Remove the bolts and pull the bearing plate (engine top [shown here] or base plate) out of the crankcase, then remove the crankshaft. If the engine is equipped with ball-bearings, the crankshaft and plate will come out as an assembly. If the plate is stuck, tap it carefully with a soft-face hammer to break the gasket seal – DO NOT attempt to pry it off! Remove and discard the old gasket.

7.84 On some engines a separate base plate is bolted to the crankcase – it doesn't contain a bearing and doesn't have to be removed except to do a thorough cleaning job

Note: *If the crankshaft and ball-bearing must be separated from the bearing plate, heat the plate around the bearing race with a propane torch until it expands enough to release the bearing. If the bearing must be removed from the crankshaft, be sure to remove the retainer ring first (if used) and use a bearing splitter (this is a job for a dealer service department or an automotive machine shop). Before installing a new bearing, clean out the groove in the crankshaft and put liquid stud and bearing mount material in the groove (engines with a retainer ring don't require stud and bearing mount material). Press on the inner race only and support the crankshaft counterweight as pressure is applied.*

7.85   The reeds (arrow) must seat properly for the engine to run

7.86   Use a wooden tool to scrape the carbon out of the exhaust ports. Special chemicals are available to remove carbon – use them with care.

7.87   If the ball or needle roller bearings aren't in perfect condition, install new ones.

Inspection of components

After the engine has been completely disassembled, refer to Chapter 5 for the majority of the cleaning and component inspection procedures. **Note:** *Special test equipment is needed to check the ignition coil/electronic ignition module. If you suspect the coil/module is causing ignition problems, have it checked by a dealer service department.*

Check the reed valves and seats to make sure they're clean and undamaged. They must not rest more than 0.010-inch away from the seats or they're distorted **(see illustration 7.85)**. Do not disassemble the reed valves unless new parts are required. Replacement reeds have smudge marks on the smooth side, which must be installed next to the seats. If you can't see the marks, feel the edge of the reed and install them with the rough edge facing away from the seats.

Remove all built-up carbon from the exhaust ports **(see illustration 7.86)** and check the muffler to make sure it's not clogged.

Check the ball or roller bearings for wear and corrosion **(see illustration 7.87)**. If they aren't in perfect condition, install new ones after removing the seals and pressing the old ones out of the crankcase bores.

The seals are held in place by wire retaining rings **(see illustration 7.88)**. The seals should be removed after taking out the retaining rings with a scribe or awl. Always install new crankshaft seals when overhauling an engine.

Once you've inspected and serviced everything and purchased any necessary new parts, reassembly can begin. **Note:** *You must use new gaskets and seals when reassembling the engine. Also, the seals must be correctly installed or the engine may not run well or at all.*

Proceed with engine reassembly as follows:

7.88   The seals can be removed after prying out the retaining rings (arrow)

Two-stroke engine reassembly

7.89   Lubricate the crankcase oil seal lip, the plain bearing (if applicable) or the roller bearing with clean engine oil or grease, then reposition the crankshaft in the crankcase. If the engine has a ball-bearing, install the crankshaft/bearing plate assembly. Be sure to use a new gasket on the bearing plate.

7.90   Lubricate the oil seal lip and bearing in the plate, then position the plate on the crankcase and install the mounting bolts. Tighten them to the specified torque (see Appendix A) in a criss-cross pattern to avoid warping the plate

7.91 Before installing the piston/connecting rod assembly, the cylinder must be perfectly clean and the top edge of the bore must be chamfered slightly so the rings don't catch on it. Stagger the piston ring end gaps 180-degrees apart. Lubricate the piston and rings with clean two-stroke oil, then attach a ring compressor to the piston. Leave the skirt protruding about 1/4-inch. Tighten the compressor until the piston cannot be turned, then loosen it until the piston turns in the compressor with resistance.

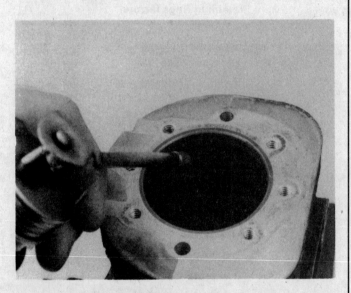

7.92 Rotate the crankshaft until the connecting rod journal is at TDC (Top Dead Center – top of the stroke) and apply a coat of two-stroke engine oil to the cylinder walls. If the piston has a "V" mark on the top, it must be in the 3 o'clock position when looking at the top of the engine with the exhaust port facing down. Make sure the match marks on the rod and cap will be facing the way they were originally when the rod/piston assembly is in place. Gently insert the piston/connecting rod assembly into the cylinder and rest the bottom edge of the ring compressor on the cylinder. Tap the top edge of the ring compressor to make sure it's making contact around its entire circumference.

7.93 Carefully tap on the top of the piston with the end of a wooden or plastic hammer handle while guiding the end of the connecting rod into place on the crankshaft journal. The piston rings may try to pop out just before entering the bore, so keep some pressure on the ring compressor. Work slowly – if any resistance is felt as the piston enters the cylinder, stop immediately. Find out what's hanging up and fix it before proceeding. Do not, for any reason, force the piston into the cylinder – you'll break a ring and/or the piston.

7.94 Position the steel liners (if used – the V-shape cutouts on the ends must match up) in the rod and cap, then install the needle bearings. If split needles are used, the blunt ends must be together and the tapered ends must face out. Use grease to hold the needle bearings in place as the parts are installed (new bearings come with a coating designed to hold them in place on the rod).

7.95 Lubricate the bearings with two-stroke engine oil, then install the connecting rod cap and bolts. Make sure the marks you made on the rod and cap (or the manufacturer's marks) are aligned and facing the same way they were originally.

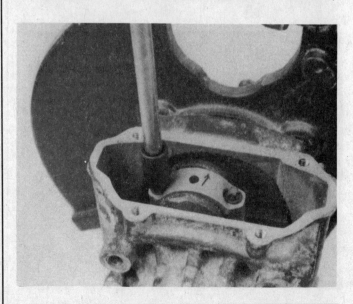

7.96 Tighten the bolts to the specified torque (see Appendix A). Work up to the final torque in three steps. Turn the crankshaft through two complete revolutions to make sure the rod doesn't hit the cylinder. If it does, the piston/connecting rod may be installed incorrectly.

Note: *If a ball-bearing equipped engine appears to be tight, and the flywheel was removed with a knock-off tool, the lower bearing may have been dislodged from the plate, causing the crankshaft to drag on the crankcase. To correct this condition, rap on the drive end of the crankshaft with a soft-face hammer to produce the required clearance.*

7.97   Install the reed plate and a new gasket and tighten the bolts to the specified torque (see Appendix A)

7.98   Install the cylinder head and a new gasket – no sealant is required. Tighten the screws to the specified torque (see Appendix A) in a criss-cross pattern. Work up to the final torque in two equal increments.

7.99   Install the ignition coil/spark plug wire assembly and align the marks on the coil bracket and crankcase bosses, then install the coil mounting bolts and tighten them securely.

Note: *If the coil is mounted on the outside of the fly-wheel, don't tighten the bolts completely – just snug them up. The bolt holes are slotted; move the coil as far away from the flywheel as possible before snugging up the bolts. Be sure to reroute the wires from the ignition coil properly.*

7.100 Refer to Chapter 4 and install the point cam and ignition points (if equipped), then make sure the tapered portion of the crankshaft and the inside of the flywheel hub are clean and free of burrs. Position the Woodruff key in the crankshaft keyway and install the flywheel. Install the starter cup, washer and nut. Tighten the nut to the specified torque.

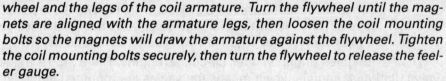

Note: *If the ignition coil is mounted outside the flywheel, turn the flywheel so the magnets are facing away from the coil assembly, then insert a feeler gauge equal to the thickness of the air gap (0.0125-inch) between the flywheel and the legs of the coil armature. Turn the flywheel until the magnets are aligned with the armature legs, then loosen the coil mounting bolts so the magnets will draw the armature against the flywheel. Tighten the coil mounting bolts securely, then turn the flywheel to release the feeler gauge.*

To install the remaining components, refer to Chapters 4 and 5 as necessary. **Caution:** *Be sure to fill the fuel tank with the correct gas/oil mixture before attempting to start the engine.*

8

Honda engines

Engine identification numbers/models covered

Honda G-series engines up to and including five horsepower are covered in this Chapter. Included are the GV150, GX110/140 and GXV120/160 (the GXV160 is actually rated at 5.5 horsepower, but it's nearly identical to the GXV120 in every way but physical size of some components).

The "G" denotes single cylinder, air-cooled engine. The GV150 is a side valve (flathead) engine, which means the valves are mounted in the engine block, while the others are overhead valve engines, which means the valves are mounted in the cylinder head. The "V" indicates the crankshaft is mounted vertically.

On vertical shaft engines, the model number is cast into the side of the crankcase **(see illustration 8.1)**. The serial number is stamped into the end of the crankcase **(see illustration 8.2)**. On horizontal shaft engines, both numbers are on the end opposite the cylinder head. Always have the model and serial numbers available when purchasing parts.

8.1   Engine model number (vertical shaft engine)

8.2   Engine serial number (vertical shaft engine)

Recoil starter rope replacement

If the rope breaks, the starter doesn't have to be disassembled to replace it, but it may be a good idea to take the opportunity to do a thorough cleaning job and check the spring and ratchet mechanism.

1   Hold the recoil starter housing in a vise or clamp it to the workbench so it doesn't move around as you're working on it. If necessary, use soft jaws in the vise to prevent damage to the housing. **Note:** *If you can't see the knot in the pulley end of the rope, the starter will have to be partially disassembled to install the new one. If you can see the knot, disregard the disassembly instructions and proceed to Step 3.*

2   Remove the bolt or nut and detach the friction plate or reel cover (see illustration 8.3).

3   If the rope isn't broken, pull it all the way out. Hold the pulley with Vise-Grip pliers or a C-clamp so the spring won't rewind and the pulley is held in position for installing the new rope (see illustration 8.4).

4   Pull the knot out of the cavity with needle-nose pliers, then cut the knot off and pull the rope out (see illustration 8.5). Note the type of knot used, then detach the handle – it can be used on the new rope.

5   Cut a piece of new rope the same length and diameter as the original.

6   Cauterize (melt) the ends of the nylon rope with a match to prevent fraying.

7   If the rope was broken, you'll have to wind up the spring before installing the new rope. Turn the pulley about three turns counterclockwise, then

8.3   Remove the bolt to detach the friction plate or reel cover from the recoil starter

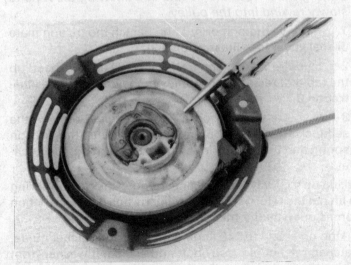

8.4   Restrain the recoil starter pulley with a C-clamp or Vise-Grips so the spring doesn't rewind

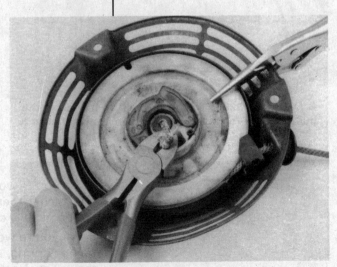

8.5   Cut the knot at the pulley to release the rope

Haynes small engine repair manual

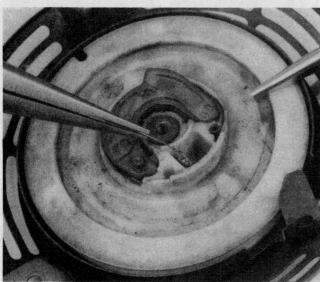

8.6   The rope is difficult to thread into the pulley, so attach it to a piece of wire and use the wire to pull it into place

8.7   On GXV120/160 engines, bend up the tab so the pulley can be removed from the recoil starter housing

add the following number of turns. Refer to Step 3 above to restrain the pulley after the spring is tensioned.

GV150 engine: 1-1/2 turns

GXV120/160 engines: 2-turns

GX110/140 engines: 3-turns

8   Position the pulley so the opening for the rope is as close to the opening in the housing as possible, then insert the rope into the housing opening and out through the pulley opening. This can be tricky – if the rope won't cooperate, hook a piece of wire through the end of the rope and bend it over with a pliers, then thread the wire through the holes and use it to pull the rope into place **(see illustration 8.6)**.

9   Tie a knot in the rope and manipulate it down into the cavity in the pulley.

10   Install the friction plate or reel cover and nut or bolt.

11   Release the Vise-Grips or C-clamp while holding the rope, then allow it to rewind slowly onto the pulley.

12   Attach the handle to the rope (make sure it's secure or the rope will disappear into the starter and you'll have to start over).

13   Check the starter for proper operation.

Recoil starter spring replacement

If the rope won't rewind and it isn't due to binding in the recoil starter, the spring may be broken. **Caution:** *Be sure to release the spring tension, if necessary, before disassembling the starter. This is done by cutting off or untying the knot in the handle and allowing the rope to slowly rewind into the pulley.*

1   Remove the bolt or nut and detach the friction plate or reel cover **(see illustration 8.3)**.

2   If you're working on a GXV120/160 engine, bend up the tab that restrains the pulley in the housing **(see illustration 8.7)**.

3   If you're working on a GV150 engine, remove the self-locking nut, the upper friction plate, the friction spring and the lower friction plate, then lift out the ratchet.

4   If you're working on a GXV120/160 engine, remove the friction spring and ratchet, then lift out the return spring **(see illustration 8.8)**. The friction spring usually comes out with the friction plate.

5   If you're working on a GX110/140 engine, remove the ratchet guide, friction spring, ratchet, ratchet pin, sub shaft and sub shaft washer from the pulley. Note how the parts fit together to simplify reassembly.

6   Lift out the pulley and detach it from the spring end (except GV150 engines).

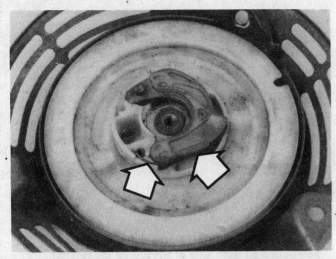

8.8 Remove the ratchet and return spring (arrows) from the pulley (GXV120/160 engine shown)

8.9 Make sure the recoil spring end is engaged in the housing slot (GXV120/160 engine shown)

7 **Caution:** *Wear gloves when handling the spring to avoid hand injuries.* Remove the spring from the starter housing. On GV150 engines, the spring will remain in the pulley recess. GX110/140 engines also have a spring case mounted between the spring and housing.

8 Remove the rope from the pulley. GV150 engines also have a bushing in the pulley bore that can be removed.

9 Clean the parts with solvent and dry them with compressed air, if available, or a clean cloth, then check them for wear and damage. If the spring is distorted, bent or broken, install a new one. On GV150 engines, apply a thin coat of grease to the faces of the new spring before installation.

10 Tie a knot in the end of the new rope, then thread it through the hole and wind it onto the pulley.

11 Position the spring in the housing and make sure the end is secured in the housing slot **(see illustration 8.9)**. On GX110/140 engines, Insert the hook in the outer end of the spring into the hole in the spring case, wind it to the right and insert the inner end into the slot in the housing near the center post. **Warning:** *Be careful not to let the spring fly out as it's being wound up – wear eye protection! If you're working on a GV150 engine, make sure the outer end of the spring is secured over the pulley lug, then wind the spring into place in the pulley recess.*

12 On GV150 engines, make sure the bushing is installed in the pulley bore – the tab fits into the pulley cutout. Apply a small amount of grease to the post that the pulley rotates on **(see illustration 8.10)**.

13 Install the pulley in the housing. Make sure the spring is properly engaged with the pulley and housing.

14 Thread the rope out through the opening in the housing and secure the handle to it.

15 On GV150 engines, apply a small amount of grease to the ratchet bore, then slide the ratchet onto the post. Install the lower friction plate, bevelled

8.10 Apply a small amount of grease to the post before installing the pulley

8.11   On GXV120/160 engines, make sure the return spring is properly positioned against the ratchet

8.12   The legs of the friction spring must be positioned on each side of the lug on the ratchet (GXV120/160 engine shown)

8.13   The rope can be positioned in the pulley cutout to wind up the spring

side out, followed by the friction spring and the upper friction plate, bevelled side in. The end of the spring fits into the hole in the ratchet and the curved section fits between the friction plate bevelled edges. Install a new self-locking nut and tighten it to 17 ft-lbs, then install the reel cover and outer nut.

16   On GX110/140 engines, lubricate the sub shaft and ratchet pin with a small amount of grease. Slip the sub shaft washer over the threaded post in the housing, followed by the sub shaft and friction spring. Insert the ratchet pin into the hole in the pulley, then install the ratchet and ratchet guide – the split end of the ratchet guide fits into the curved side of the ratchet. Install the friction plate – dished side in – and a new self-locking nut. Tighten the nut securely.

17   On GXV120/160 engines, position the ratchet and return spring in the pulley. The spring coil fits into the hole in the pulley and the end bears against the ratchet (see illustration 8.11). Install the friction spring over the housing post and position the legs on each side of the ratchet lug (see illustration 8.12). Install the friction plate and tighten the bolt securely. Bend the tab down to restrain the pulley, but make sure it doesn't rub on it.

18   Pull the rope out and position it in the pulley cutout (see illustration 8.13), then wind the spring up the number of turns specified in Step 7 under Recoil starter rope replacement.

19   Check the starter for proper operation.

Carburetor disassembly and reassembly

The following procedures describe how to disassemble and reassemble the carburetor so new parts can be installed. Read the sections in Chapter 5 on carburetor removal and overhaul before doing anything else.

In some cases it may be more economical (and much easier) to install a new carburetor rather than attempt to repair the original. Check with a dealer to see if parts are readily available and compare the cost of new parts to the price of a complete ready-to-install carburetor before deciding how to proceed.

1   While counting the number of turns, carefully screw the pilot air screw in until it bottoms, then remove it along with the spring **(see illustration 8.14)**. Counting and recording the number of turns required to bottom the screw will enable you to return it to its original position and minimize the amount of adjustment required after reassembly.

2   Detach the float bowl from the carburetor body. It's held in place with a bolt **(see illustration 8.14)**. Be sure to note the locations of any gaskets/washers used. Some carburetors also have a drain plug in the float bowl – it doesn't have to be removed.

3   Push the float pivot pin out of the carburetor body (you may have to use a small punch to do this) **(see illustration 8.1)**.

4   Remove the float assembly and the inlet needle valve (and spring, if used) by lifting the float straight up. Note how the inlet needle valve is attached to the float.

5   Remove the float bowl gasket.

6   Unscrew the main jet from the main nozzle casting in the carburetor body **(see illustration 8.14)**.

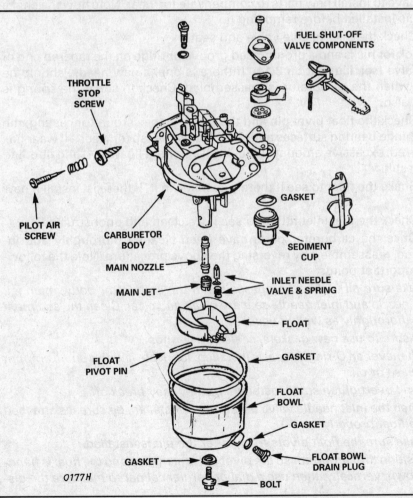

8.14 Typical carburetor components – exploded view

0177H

7   Turn the carburetor right-side-up and catch the main nozzle as it slides out.

8   Unscrew the sediment cup and remove the gasket (if equipped).

9   If the carburetor has an integral fuel shut-off valve mounted on it, remove the screws from the plate so the internal parts can be disassembled and cleaned. Note how they fit together to simplify reassembly – a simple sketch should be made if the parts could be confusing later.

10   Refer to Chapter 5 and follow the cleaning/inspection procedures outlined under *Carburetor overhaul*. **Note**: *Don't soak plastic or rubber parts in carburetor cleaner.*

11   Check the pilot air screw tip for damage and distortion. The small taper should be smooth and straight.

12   Check the throttle plate shaft for wear by moving it back-and-forth.

13   Check the throttle plate fit in the carburetor bore.

If there's play in the shaft, the bore is worn excessively, which may mean a new carburetor is required (on some carburetors, replacing the throttle plate shaft or plate, or both, may cure the problem – check with a dealer). The throttle plate and shaft don't have to be removed unless new parts are required. Note how the throttle plate is installed before removing it – if it is removed, make sure it's positioned exactly as it was originally.

14   Check the choke shaft for play in the same manner and examine the linkage holes to see if they're worn. Don't remove the choke shaft unless you have to install new parts to compensate for wear. Note how the choke plate is installed before removing it.

15   Check the inlet needle valve and seat.

Look for nicks and a pronounced groove or ridge on the tapered end of the valve **(see illustration 8.14)**. If there is one, a new needle should be used when the carburetor is reassembled. Check to see if the spring is weak also.

16   Check the float pivot pin and the bores in the carburetor casting, the float hinge bearing surfaces and the inlet needle tab for wear – if wear has occurred, excessive amounts of fuel will enter the float bowl and flooding will result.

17   Shake the float to see if there's gasoline in it. If there is, install a new one.

18   Check the fuel inlet fitting to see if it's clean and unobstructed.

19   Once the carburetor parts have been cleaned thoroughly and inspected, reassemble it by reversing the above procedure. Note the following important points:

Make sure all fuel and air passages in the carburetor body, main jet, main nozzle and inlet needle seat are clean and clear. Clean the sediment bowl thoroughly as well (if used).

Be sure to use new gaskets, seals and O-rings.

Whenever an O-ring or seal is installed, lubricate it with a small amount of grease or oil.

Don't overtighten small fasteners or they may break off.

When the inlet needle valve assembly is installed, be sure it's attached to the float properly.

Make sure the float pivots freely after the pin is installed.

Position the carburetor so the pivot pin is at the top and the float is hanging down, vertically, then use a dial or vernier caliper to measure the distance from the bottom of the float (the bottom surface when the carburetor is installed on the engine) to the carburetor body on the side directly opposite the pivot pin. It should be as specified in Appendix A. If it isn't, a new float and/or inlet needle valve must be installed – the height cannot be adjusted.

Turn the pilot air screw in until it bottoms lightly and back it out the number of turns required to restore it to its original position.

Carburetor adjustment

When making carburetor adjustments, the air cleaner must be in place and the fuel tank should be at least half full. The carburetor has a fixed main jet – no mixture screw is installed and no adjustment is required.

1   The pilot air screw should be backed out the specified number of turns after it's screwed in until it bottoms lightly:

GV150 engine: 2-1/8 turns
GX110 engine: 3-turns
GX140 engine: 1-5/8 turns
GXV120 engine: 3-turns
GXV160 engine: 2-turns

2   To adjust the idle speed, run the engine until it reaches normal operating temperature, then turn the THROTTLE STOP SCREW until the idle speed is as specified in Appendix A.

3   Turn the pilot air screw in or out in small increments until the engine runs at the highest speed.

4   Readjust the idle speed if necessary.

5   Since a tachometer is required, have the governed speed checked and adjusted by a dealer service department, if necessary.

Engine disassembly

The engine components should be removed in the following general order:

Engine cooling shroud/recoil starter
Fuel tank
Air cleaner
Carburetor/controls
Electric starter/control box (if used)
Muffler
Flywheel
Flywheel brake components (if equipped)
Ignition components
Cylinder head/rocker arms/pushrods
Oil pan/crankcase cover
Camshaft
Tappets
Piston/connecting rod assembly
Crankshaft
Governor components
Valves

Haynes small engine repair manual

For shroud/recoil starter, fuel tank, air cleaner, carburetor, muffler and cylinder head (GV150 engine only) removal, refer to Chapters 4 and 5 as necessary. The remaining components can be removed to complete engine disassembly by following the photo sequence shown here. Be sure to read the information in each caption. **Note:** *Use a ridge reamer to remove the carbon/wear ridge (if present) from the top of the cylinder bore after the cylinder head is off. Follow the manufacturer's instructions included with the tool.*

8.15   Restrain the flywheel with Vise-Grips and remove the large nut. After the nut is removed, the starter cup and plastic fan can be detached.
Note: *On GV150 engines, the fan and starter cup are attached to the flywheel with bolts and should be removed prior to loosening the flywheel nut.*

8.16   Note how the wires to the coil are routed (it's a very good idea to draw a simple sketch). Then remove the bolts (arrows) and detach the coil/spark plug wire assembly (note that this engine has the coil mounted outside the flywheel; some engines are equipped with an ignition coil mounted under the flywheel – the removal procedures are basically the same for both types).

8.17   In most cases the flywheel must be removed with a special puller (available from the engine manufacturer). In this example (GXV120/160 engine, type D1, N1, N4, N5 or N6), a commercially-available two or three-jaw puller can be used as long as the jaws are positioned away from the magnet on the flywheel. DO NOT pound on the end of the crankshaft with a hammer!

8.18   Remove the flywheel key and let it stick to the fly-wheel magnet so it doesn't get lost. If you're working on a GV150 engine, refer to Chapter 4 and remove the ignition points and related parts.

8.19   Remove the bolts and detach the crankcase breather plate, . . .

8.20   . . . then lift out the valve and wire mesh filter element

8.21   Remove the bolts (arrows) and separate the guide plate and tank bracket from the engine. Some engines have other brackets attached with bolts.

8.22   Remove the remaining two bolts and detach the cover from the cylinder head – you may have to tap it with a soft-face hammer to break the gasket seal

8.23   Unscrew the locknuts (arrows) and rocker arm pivots (adjusting nuts), then pull off the rocker arms. Store the intake parts separate from the exhaust parts – they should be returned to their original locations when the engine is reassembled.

8.24 Pull out the pushrods and store them with the other valvetrain parts

8.25 Loosen (and tighten) the cylinder head bolts in 1/4-turn increments in the sequence shown here until they can be removed by hand

8.26 Tap up on the head with a soft-face hammer to break the gasket seal, then detach it from the engine

8.27 Pull out the dowel pins, then use a scraper or putty knife to separate the old gasket from the top of the cylinder or the under side of the head

8.28 Note how it's positioned on the shaft (mark the shaft and arm if necessary), then remove the nut/bolt and detach the governor arm

8.29 Use emery cloth to remove rust and burrs from the drive end of the crankshaft so the bearing in the oil pan or cover can slide over it. Loosen the oil pan-to-engine block bolts in 1/4-turn increments to avoid warping the pan, then remove them – some engines have a crankcase cover instead of an oil pan (horizontal crankshaft engines); they're attached to the engine block with several bolts and removal is similar. Tap the oil pan/cover with a soft-face hammer to break the gasket seal, then separate it from the engine block and crankshaft – if it hangs up on the crankshaft, continue to tap on it with the hammer, but be very careful not to crack or distort it. If a thrust washer is installed on the camshaft, slide it off and set it aside.

8.30   Remove the clip and pull the governor shaft out of the oil pan bore (not used on GV150 engine)

8.31   Remove the mounting bolt and separate the governor/oil slinger assembly from the oil pan (GXV 120/160 engine)

8.32   Remove the plastic oil return tube (if equipped)

8.33 Turn the crankshaft until the marks on the timing gears are aligned, then lift out the camshaft

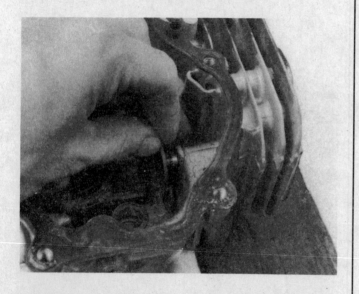

8.34 After the camshaft is removed, pull out the tappets and store them in marked containers so they can be returned to their original locations

8.35 Look for a raised rib (match mark) that extends across the rod and cap – if you can't see one, mark the side of the connecting rod and cap that faces out and note how the oil dipper (if used) is oriented (the parts must be reassembled in the exact same relationship to the crankshaft)

8.36 Loosen the connecting rod cap bolts in 1/4-turn increments until they can be removed by hand. Separate the cap from the connecting rod, move the end of the rod away from the crankshaft journal and push the piston/rod assembly out through the top of the bore. Pull out the crankshaft.

Note: *To get at the valve springs on GV150 engines, remove the tappet cover.*

8.37 Slotted retainers are used to hold the valve springs in place. Compress the intake valve spring and move the retainer to the side until the valve will slip through the larger hole, then withdraw the valve from the guide. Lift out the spring and retainer if necessary, then repeat the procedure for the exhaust valve.

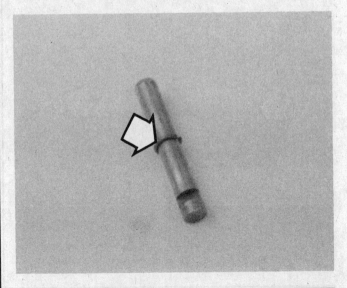

8.38 The governor assembly can be withdrawn from the shaft after the shaft is removed from the crankcase. Check the governor parts for wear and damage. If the shaft is replaced, make sure the retaining ring (arrow) is secured in the groove.

Note: *At this point, the GV150 engine oil pump can be disassembled. Remove the bolts and detach the cover and O-ring, then pull out the inner and outer rotors.*

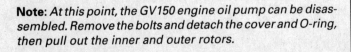

Inspection of components

After the engine has been completely disassembled, refer to Chapter 5 for the cleaning, component inspection and valve lapping procedures. Once you've inspected and serviced everything covered in Chapter 5 and purchased any necessary new parts, which should always include new gaskets and seals, follow the inspection procedures covered here before proceeding with engine reassembly. **Note:** *The oil pump used on GV150 engines must have the specified inner rotor-to-outer rotor and outer rotor-to-body clearances (see Appendix A).*

8.39   Check the rocker arm pivot stud threads for wear and damage. If new ones must be installed, they can be unscrewed from the cylinder head with a socket on the hex (arrow).

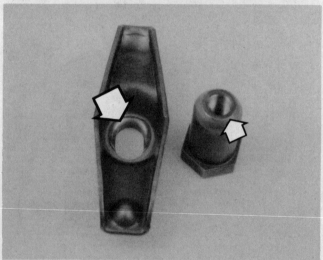

8.40   Check the rocker arm sockets and the pivot balls for wear and galling

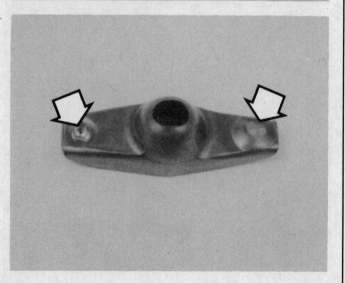

8.41   Check the rocker arm surfaces that contact the valves and pushrods for wear, galling and pitting

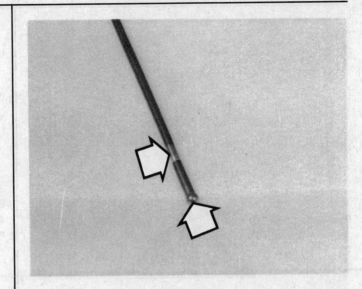

8.42 Check each pushrod for wear on the ends and where it rides in the guide (arrows). Look for any indication the pushrod is bent or otherwise distorted.

8.43 Check the tappet pushrod sockets for wear and galling

8.44 Check the ball-bearing(s) for radial and side-to-side play and make sure they turn smoothly. They must be securely mounted in the engine bores.

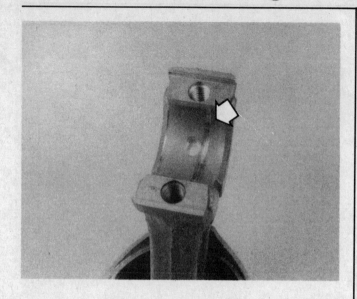

8.45 Check the connecting rod bearing surface as described in Chapter 5 – this one is scored and should not be reinstalled

8.46 The corresponding journal on the crankshaft is also damaged – it may be possible to salvage the crankshaft by dressing the journal with a fine file and emery cloth, but it would be a questionable approach

8.47 Assemble the connecting rod on the crankshaft and check the end play with a feeler gauge – If it's excessive, a new rod may correct it (the crankshaft may also be worn)

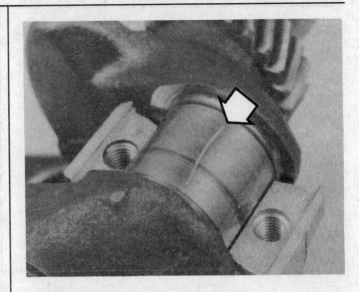

8.48 Lay a strip of Plastigage on the connecting rod journal, then install the rod and cap and carefully tighten the bolts to the specified torque – don't turn the rod as this check is done!

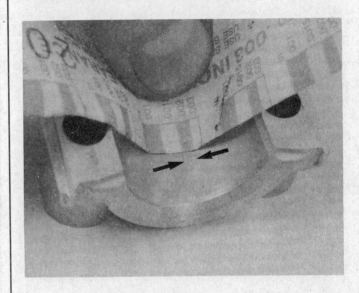

8.49 Remove the cap and check the width of the crushed Plastigage with the scale printed on the envelope – if the clearance is greater than it should be, a new rod may correct it (however, the crankshaft may also be worn excessively). Be sure to use the correct scale; standard (inch) and metric ones are both printed on the envelope.

8.50 Check the decompression mechanism on the camshaft to make sure it moves freely and the spring hasn't sagged

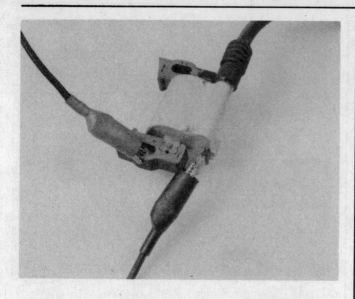

8.51 If the engine had no spark, check the ignition coil primary resistance by hooking up the ohmmeter leads as shown here

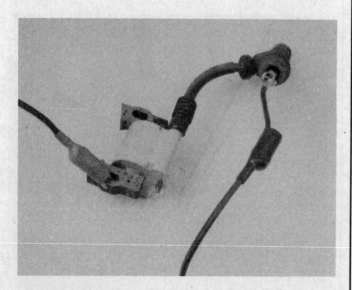

8.52 Check the ignition coil secondary resistance by hooking up the ohmmeter leads as shown here. If the coil resistance is not as specified, have it checked by a dealer service department to verify your findings before buying a new one.

8.53 Install a new governor shaft oil seal in the oil pan. Carefully pry the old one out and drive the new one in with a socket and hammer.

Engine reassembly

8.54 Install the governor/oil slinger assembly with the washer next to the engine boss, . . .

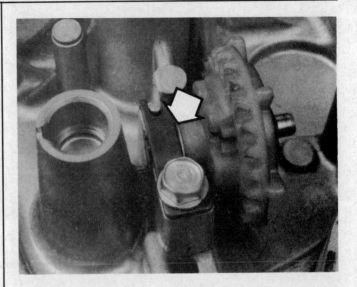

8.55 . . . then slip the thin blue washer . . .

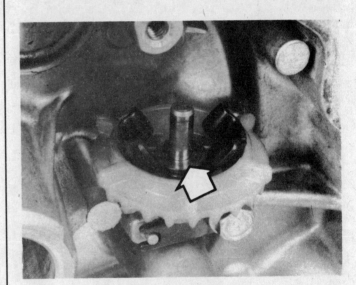

8.56 . . . and the slider over the opposite end of the shaft

8.57   Apply clean engine oil or grease to the magneto side oil seal . . .

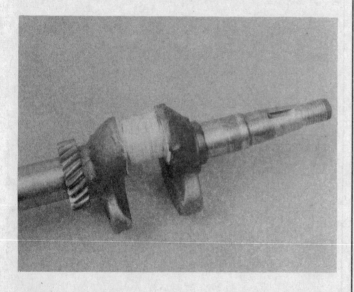

8.58   . . . and the connecting rod journal on the crankshaft, then install the crankshaft in the engine

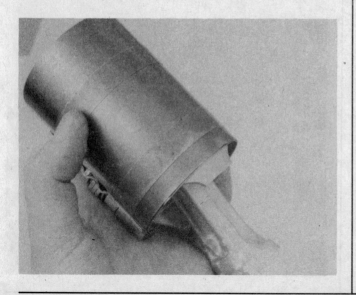

8.59   Before installing the piston/connecting rod assembly, the cylinder must be perfectly clean and the top edge of the bore must be chamfered slightly so the rings don't catch on it. Stagger the piston ring end gaps. Lubricate the piston and rings with clean engine oil, then attach a ring compressor to the piston. Leave the skirt protruding about 1/4-inch. Tighten the compressor until the piston cannot be turned, then loosen it until the piston turns in the compressor with resistance.

8.60 Rotate the crankshaft until the connecting rod journal is at TDC (Top Dead Center – top of the stroke) and apply a coat of engine oil to the cylinder walls. The triangular mark in the top of the piston must face the pushrod side of the engine. Make sure the match marks on the rod and cap will be facing out when the rod/piston assembly is in place. Gently insert the piston/connecting rod assembly into the cylinder and rest the bottom edge of the ring compressor on the engine block. Tap the top edge of the ring compressor to make sure it's contacting the block around its entire circumference.

8.61 Carefully tap on the top of the piston with the end of a wooden or plastic hammer handle while guiding the end of the connecting rod into place on the crankshaft journal. The piston rings may try to pop out just before entering the bore, so keep some pressure on the ring compressor. Work slowly – if any resistance is felt as the piston enters the cylinder, stop immediately. Find out what's hanging up and fix it before proceeding. Do not, for any reason, force the piston into the cylinder – you'll break a ring and/or the piston.

8.62 When the piston/rod assembly is installed correctly, the triangular mark on the piston crown will be pointing at the pushrod side of the engine

8.63 Install the connecting rod cap and the bolts. Make sure the marks you made on the rod and cap (or the manufacturer's rib) are aligned and facing out and the oil dipper (if used) is oriented correctly. Tighten the bolts to the specified torque (see Appendix A). Work up to the final torque in three steps. Temporarily install the camshaft and turn the crankshaft through two complete revolutions to make sure the rod doesn't hit the cylinder or camshaft. If it does, the piston/connecting rod is installed incorrectly.

8.64 Lubricate the magneto side ball-bearing with clean engine oil

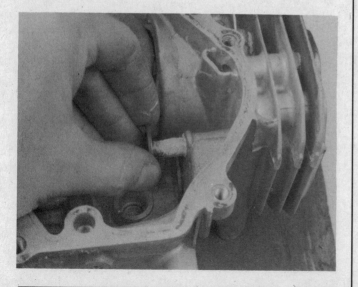

8.65 Apply clean engine oil, moly-base grease or engine assembly lube to the tappets, then reinstall them – make sure they're returned to their original locations

8.66 Apply clean engine oil, moly-base grease or engine assembly lube to the camshaft lobes and the lower bearing journal

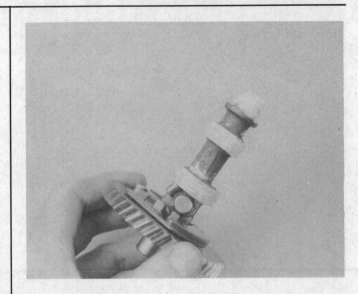

8.67 Align the timing marks on the gears and install the camshaft – this is very important! The marks are usually dimples/lines or bevelled teeth (or a combination of them) near the outer edge of the gears. Lubricate the main bearing journal on the crankshaft and the upper journal on the camshaft before proceeding.

8.68 Install the oil return tube (if used), . . .

8.69   . . . then lubricate the governor shaft and install it in the crankcase, along with the washer (on the inside of the case)

8.70   Make sure the dowel pins are in place and the governor shaft arm is vertical, then position a new gasket on the crankcase (the dowel pins will hold it in place)

8.71   Lubricate the lip on the oil seal in the oil pan (or crankcase cover) with clean engine oil, moly-base grease or engine assembly lube. If a ball-bearing is used in the cover, lubricate it with clean engine oil. Carefully lower the oil pan (or crankcase cover) into place over the end of the crankshaft until it seats on the crankcase. DO NOT damage the oil seal lip or leaks will result!

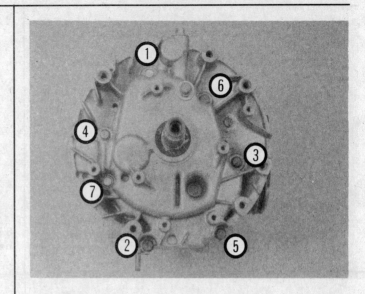

8.72   Install and tighten the oil pan mounting bolts to the specified torque. Follow a criss-cross pattern and work up to the final torque in three equal steps to avoid warping the oil pan. Attach the governor lever to the outer end of the shaft and tighten the nut/bolt securely.

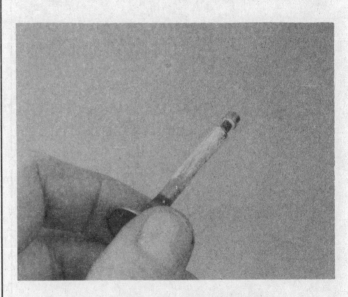

8.73   Coat the intake valve stem with clean engine oil, moly-base grease or engine assembly lube, then reinstall it. Make sure it's returned to its original location.

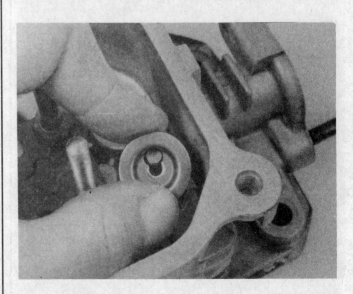

8.74   Compress the spring on the intake valve with the retainer in place, then push the valve through the large hole and move the retainer to the side to engage it on the valve stem. Repeat the procedure for the exhaust valve.

8.75   Make sure the dowel pins are in place, then position a new gasket on the head – DO NOT use sealant on the gasket

8.76   Install the cylinder head and the bolts, then tighten the bolts to the specified torque (see illustration 8.25 for the sequence to follow). Work up to the final torque in three equal steps.

8.77   Install the pushrods and make sure they're engaged in the tappet sockets, then lubricate the pushrod and valve stem ends with grease

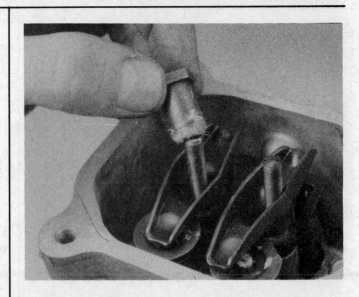

8.78 Position the rocker arms, then lubricate and install the pivots

8.79 Thread the locknuts onto the studs, then refer to Chapter 4 and adjust the valve clearances

8.80 Install the cylinder head cover and a new gasket, then thread the lower bolts into the holes, but don't tighten them completely until the cooling shroud and upper bolts are installed. Install the fuel tank bracket and guide plate next.

8.81 Position the crankcase breather wire mesh filter and the valve in the recess, . . .

8.82 . . . then install the cover and tighten the bolts securely

8.83 Make sure the key is in place and check the taper on the crankshaft to make sure it's clean, then install the flywheel, . . .

8.84 . . . the plastic fan (make sure the pegs fit into the holes in the flywheel) . . .

8.85 . . . and the starter cup (make sure the pegs in the flywheel fit into the cup holes)

8.86 Install the flywheel nut and tighten it to the specified torque

8.87   Position the ignition coil/spark plug wire assembly and install the coil mounting bolts.

Note: *If the coil is mounted on the outside of the flywheel, don't tighten the bolts completely. Turn the flywheel so the magnet is facing away from the coil assembly, then insert a feeler gauge equal to the thickness of the air gap listed in the specifications (Appendix A at the back of the manual) between the flywheel and the legs of the coil armature, then push the coil tightly against the feeler gauge. Tighten the coil mounting bolts securely, then turn the flywheel to release the feeler gauge.*

To install the remaining components, refer to Chapters 4 and 5 as necessary. **Caution:** *Be sure to fill the crankcase to the correct level with the specified oil before attempting to start the engine.*

Appendix A

Small engine service specifications

Briggs & Stratton engines

Engine oil type .... 30-weight, 10W30 or 10W40/SC, SD, SE or SF

Engine oil capacity
Aluminum engines
  Vertical crankshaft
    Series 100900, 130000 .... 1-3/4 pints
    All others .... 1-1/4 pints
  Horizontal crankshaft .... 1-1/4 pints
Cast-iron engines (horizontal crankshaft) .. 3 pints

Spark plug type
1-1/2 inch
  Champion .... CJ-8 or J-19LM
  Champion resistor .... RCJ-8 or RJ-19LM
  Autolite 235
  Autolite resistor 245
2-inch
  Champion .... J-8C or J-19LM
  Champion resistor .... RJ-8C or RJ-19LM
  Autolite 295
  Autolite resistor 306

Spark plug gap (all) .... 0.030 inch

Ignition point gap (all) .... 0.020 inch

Valve tappet clearance	Minimum	Maximum
Aluminum engines		
Intake	0.005 inch	0.007 inch
Exhaust*	0.007 inch	0.009 inch
Cast-iron engines		
Intake	0.007 inch	0.009 inch
Exhaust	0.014 inch	0.016 inch

* Some engines have been built with 0.005 to 0.007 inch exhaust valve clearance – the inside surface of the crankcase breather is stamped to indicate this

Appendix A

Briggs & Stratton engines (continued)

Valve seat width . . . . 3/64 to 1/16-inch

Coil armature air gap	**Two-leg**	**Three-leg**
Aluminum engines		
Series 100200, 100900, 13000	0.010 to 0.014 inch	0.012 to 0.016 inch
All others	0.006 to 0.010 inch	0.012 to 0.016 inch
Cast-iron engines	—————	0.012 to 0.016 inch

Maximum piston ring end gap

Aluminum engines	0.035 inch
Cast-iron engines	
Compression rings	0.030 inch
Oil control ring	0.035 inch

Connecting rod big-end bearing reject size

Aluminum engines	
Series 6B, 60000	0.876 inch
All others	1.001 inches
Cast-iron engines	
Series 5	0.752 inch
Series N, 6, 8	0.751 inch
Series 9	0.876 inch

Connecting rod piston pin bore reject size

Aluminum engines	
Series 100200, 100900	0.555 inch
All others	0.492 inch
Cast-iron engines	
Series 9	0.563 inch
All others	0.492 inch

Piston pin reject sizes

Aluminum engines	
Series 100200, 100900	0.552 inch
All others	0.489 inch
Cast-iron engines	
Series 9	0.561 inch
All others	0.489 inch

Piston pin bore (in piston) reject sizes

Aluminum engines	
Series 100200, 100900	0.554 inch
All others	0.491 inch
Cast-iron engines	
Series 9	0.563 inch
All others	0.491 inch

Small engine service specifications

Cylinder bore sizes

	Maximum	Minimum
Aluminum engines		
Series 6B, 60000 (before serial number 5810060)	2.3125 inches	2.3115 inches
Series 60000 (after serial number 5810030)	2.3750 inches	2.3740 inches
Series 8	2.3750 inches	2.3740 inches
Series 90000, 100700	2.5625 inches	2.5615 inches
Series 100200, 100900	2.500 inches	2.4990 inches
Series 11	2.7812 inches	2.7802 inches
Series 12	2.6885 inches	2.6875 inches
Series 13	2.5625 inches	2.5615 inches
Cast-iron engines		
Series 5, 5S, 6, N	2.000 inches	1.999 inches
Series 8, 9	2.250 inches	2.2490 inches

Crankshaft connecting rod journal reject sizes

Aluminum engines	
Series 6B, 60000	0.870 inch
All others	0.996 inch
Cast-iron engines	
Series 9	0.873 inch
All others	0.743 inch

Crankshaft main bearing journal reject sizes

	Drive side	Magneto side
Aluminum engines		
Series 100200, 100900, 130000	0.998 inch	0.873 inch
Series 100700, 120000	1.060 inches	0.873 inch
All others	0.873 inch	0.873 inch
Cast-iron engines		
Series 9	0.983 inch	0.983 inch
All others	0.873 inch	0.873 inch

Camshaft journal reject sizes

Aluminum engines	
Series 110000	
Magneto side	0.436 inch
Drive side	0.498 inch
All others	0.498 inch
Cast-iron engines	0.372 inch

Camshaft lobe height reject sizes

Aluminum engines	
Series 100200, 100900, 130000	0.950 inch
Series 110000	0.870 inch
All others**	0.883 inch
Cast-iron engines	
Series 9	1.124 inches
All others	0.875 inch

** On Series 100700 and 120000, replace the camshaft if the lobes are pitted or galled

Appendix A

Briggs & Stratton engines (continued)

Crankcase main bearing reject sizes

	Drive side	Magneto side
Aluminum engines		
Series 82000, 90000	0.878 inch***	0.780 inch
Series 100700, 120000	1.065 inches	0.878 inch
Series 100200, 100900, 130000	1.003 inches	0.878 inch
All others	0.878 inch	0.878 inch
Cast-iron engines		
Series 9	0.988 inch	0.988 inch
All others	0.878 inch	0.878 inch

*** Auxiliary drive models drive side bearing reject size is 1.003 inches

Torque specifications

Cylinder head bolts	140 in-lbs
Connecting rod bolts	
Series 9 cast-iron engines only	140 in-lbs
All others	100 in-lbs
Crankcase cover/oil sump bolts (aluminum engines)	
Series 100200, 100900, 130000	120 in-lbs
All others	85 in-lbs
Flywheel nut (aluminum engines)	
Series 100200, 100900, 130000	65 ft-lbs
All others	55 ft-lbs
Flywheel nut (cast-iron engines)	
Series 9	60 ft-lbs
All others	55 ft-lbs

Small engine service specifications

Tecumseh/Craftsman four-stroke engines

CROSS REFERENCE LIST FOR FOUR-STROKE ENGINES

How to use: Find engine horsepower and model number, then refer to proper column for desired specifications (see pages 271-274)

VERTICAL CRANKSHAFT ENGINES

2-1/2 H.P.

Model	Column
LAV25	1

3 H.P.

LAV30	1

7.75 C.I.

TVS75 (Prior to August, 1987)	1
TVS75 Ext. Ign. (Prior to 8/87)	1B

3-1/2 H.P.

LV35	3
LAV35	3

9.05 C.I.

TVS90	3
TVS90 External Ignition	2B

4 H.P.

LAV40	8
V40 External Ignition	4B
V40 thru V40B	7
VH40	7

10.0 C.I.

TVS100	5B
ECV100	5
ECV100 External Ignition	5B
TNT100	6
TNT100 External Ignition	5B

10.49 C.I.

TVS105	8
TVS105 External Ignition	4B

10.5 C.I.

ECV105	9

11.0 C.I.

ECV110	10

5 H.P.

LAV50	11
LAV50 External Ignition	6B
V50	14
VH50	14
VH50 External Ignition	7B

12.0 C.I.

ECV120	12
TNT120	13

12.04 C.I.

TVS120	11
TVS120 External Ignition	6B

12.18 C.I.

TVM125	14
TVM125 External Ignition	7B

6 H.P.

V60	15
VH60	15
VH60 External Ignition	8B

13.53 C.I.

TVM140	15
TVM140 External Ignition	8B

7 H.P.

V70	16
V70 External Ignition	9B
VH70	16
VH70 External Ignition	9B
VM70	16

17.16 C.I.

TVM170	17
TVM170 External Ignition	
Models ending in E	9B
Models ending in F and up	12B

8 H.P.

V80	18
*VM80	18 or 19
*VM80 External Ignition	13B

19.41 C.I.

TVM195	19
TVM195 External Ignition	
Models ending in A thru K	13B
Models ending in L and up	14B

10 H.P.

VM100	20

21.82 C.I.

TVM220	21
**TVM220 External Ignition	
Models ending in A thru F	15B
Models ending in G and up	16B

HORIZONTAL CRANKSHAFT ENGINES

2-1/2 H.P.

Model	Column
H25	1

3 H.P.

H30 (1982 and prior)	1
H30 (1983 Serial No.)	2

3-1/2 H.P.

H35 (1982 and prior)	3
H35 (1983 Serial No.)	4
H35 (1983 Serial No.) Ex. Ign.	3B

9.0 C.I.

ECH90	3

4 H.P.

H40	7
HH40	7
HS40	8
HS40 External Ignition	4B

5 H.P.

H50	14
H50 External Ignition	7B
HH50	14
HH50 External Ignition	7B
HS50	11
HS50 External Ignition	6B

6 H.P.

H60	15
H60 External Ignition	8B
HH60	13
HH60 External Ignition	8B

7 H.P.

H70	16
H70 External Ignition	9B
HH70	16
HH70 External Ignition	9B
HM70	17
HM70 External Ignition	
Models ending in C	10B
Models ending in D	11B
Models ending in E and up	12B

8 H.P.

H80	18
*HM80	18 or 19
**HM80 External Ignition	13B or 14B
HHM80	19
HHM80 External Ignition	13B

10 H.P.

*HM100	20 or 21
**HM100 External Ignition	15B or 16B

*CHECK TO DETERMINE BORE SIZE

**CHECK TO DETERMINE CRANKSHAFT BEARING DIAMETERS

All reference numbers followed by the letter "B" refer to the External Ignition chart.

Note: *Tecumseh/Craftsman engine specifications courtesy of and with permission of Tecumseh Products Company.*

CROSS REFERENCE LIST FOR FOUR-STROKE TABLE OF SPECIFICATIONS (continued)
(see pages 271-274)

CRAFTSMAN ENGINES

Craftsman Engine Models	See Column
143.201032 thru 143.203012	1
143.204022	5
143.204032 thru 143.204052	3
143.204062	5
143.204072 thru 143.204092	3
143.204102 143.204132	5
143.204162 thru 143.204182	3
143.204202	5
143.206012	15
143.206022	16
143.206032	15
143.207012 thru 143.207052	8
143.207062	9
143.207072	8
143.207082	9
143.213012 thru 143.213022	1
143.214012 thru 143.214032	3
143.214042 thru 143.214072	5
143.214082 thru 143.214252	3
143.214262 thru 143.214282	5
143.214292 143.214302	3
143.214312 143.214322	5
143.214332	3
143.214352	5
143.216012 thru 143.216022	16
143.216042 thru 143.216062	15
143.216092	16
143.216122	15
143.216132	18

Craftsman Engine Models	See Column
143.216142	15
143.216152 143.216162	
143.216172	18
143.216182	15
143.217012 thru 143.217032	9
143.217042 thru 143.217072	8
143.217092	9
143.217102	8
143.223012 thru 143.223052	1
143.224012 143.224022	3
143.224032	5
143.224062	3
143.224092 thru 143.224132	3
143.224142	1
143.224162 thru 143.224222	3
143.224232 143.224242	5
143.224252 thru 143.224282	3
143.224292 143.224302	5
143.224312 thru 143.224342	3
143.224352 143.224362	5
143.224372 thru 143.224422	3
143.224432	5
143.225012 143.225022	12
143.225032 thru 143.225052	14
143.225062 143.225072	12
143.225082 thru 143.225102	14
143.226012	15
143.226032	15

Craftsman Engine Models	See Column
143.226072	
143.226082	16
143.226092 thru 143.226122	18
143.226132	15
143.226142	16
143.226152 thru 143.226182	15
143.226192	18
143.226202	
143.226212	16
143.226222 thru 143.226262	15
143.226272	
143.226282	16
143.226292	18
143.226302	16
143.226312	18
143.226322	
143.226332	15
143.226342	16
143.226352	18
143.227012 thru 143.227072	10
143.233012 thru 143.233042	1
143.234022 thru 143.234052	3
143.234062 thru 143.234092	5
143.234102 thru 143.234162	3
143.234182	5
143.234192 143.234202	3
143.234212 thru 143.234232	5
143.234242 thru 143.234262	3
143.235012 143.235022	12
143.235032	11
143.235042 143.235052	12
143.235062	14
143.235072	11

Craftsman Engine Models	See Column
143.236012	15
143.236022 thru 143.236032	18
143.236052	15
143.236062 143.236072	18
143.236082	15
143.236092	16
143.236102 143.236112	15
143.236122	16
143.236132	15
143.236142	18
143.236152	15
143.236162 143.236172	16
143.237012 143.237022	10
143.237032	9
143.237042	8
143.243012 thru 143.143082	1
143.244012 thru 143.244032	3
143.244042 143.244052 143.244062	5
143.244072 thru 143.244112	3
143.244122 thru 143.244142	5
143.244202	3
143.244212	5
143.244222 143.244232	3
143.244242 143.244252	5
143.244262 thru 143.244282	3
143.244292 thru 143.244332	5
143.245012	11
143.245042	14
143.245052 thru 143.245082	12
143.245092	11

All reference numbers followed by the letter "B" refer to the External Ignition chart.

Small engine service specifications

CROSS REFERENCE LIST FOR FOUR-STROKE TABLE OF SPECIFICATIONS (continued)
(see pages 271-274)

CRAFTSMAN ENGINES

Craftsman Engine Models	See Column	Craftsman Engine Models	See Column	Craftsman Engine Models	See Column	Craftsman Engine Models	See Column
143.245102 thru 143.245132	12	143.254232 thru 143.254292	5	143.264352 thru 143.264372	5	143.266462 143.266472	20
143.245142 143.245152	11	143.254302 143.254312	3	143.264382	3	143.266482	18
143.245162	12	143.254322	5	143.264392 thru 143.264412	5	143.267012 thru 143.267042	8
143.245172 143.245182	11	143.254332	3	143.264422	3	143.274012 thru 143.274072	5
143.245192	12	143.254342 143.254352	5	143.264432	5	143.274092 thru 143.274132	3
143.246012	15	143.254362	3	143.264472	3	143.274142 143.274152	5
143.246022 143.246032	18	143.254372 143.254382	5	143.264482	5	143.274162 thru 143.274182	3
143.246042	15	143.254392	3	143.264492		143.274192 thru 143.274242	5
143.246052 thru 143.246072	16	143.254402 143.254412	5	143.264502	3	143.274252	3
143.246082 143.246092	18	143.254432	3	143.264512	5	143.274262	5
143.246102 143.246112	16	143.254442	5	143.264522 143.264542	3	143.274272 thru 143.274332	3
143.246122	18	143.254452	3	143.264562 thru 143.264652	5	143.274342	5
143.246132 143.246142	16	143.254462	5	143.264662	3	143.274352	3
143.246152 thru 143.246212	18	143.254472 143.254482	3	143.264672	5	143.274362	5
143.246222	16	143.254492	5	143.264682	3	143.274372	3
143.246232	18	143.254502 thru 143.254532	3	143.265012 thru 143.265192	11	143.274392	5
143.246242	16	143.255012 thru 143.255112	11	143.266012 143.266022	18	143.274402 thru 143.274462	5
143.246252	18	143.256012	18	143.266032	15	143.274472	3
143.246262	16	143.256022	15	143.266042		143.274482	5
143.246272 thru 143.246292	18	143.256032	16	143.266052	16	143.274492	3
143.246302 143.246312	16	143.256042	18	143.266062 143.266082	15	143.274502 thru 143.274542	5
143.246322 143.246332	18	143.256052	15	143.266092 thru 143.266132	16	143.274552	3
143.246342	16	143.256062 143.256072	18	143.266142 thru 143.266242	18	143.274562 143.274582	5
143.246352	15	143.256082 143.256092	15	143.266252	15	143.274592	3
143.246362 143.246382	20	143.256102	16	143.266262	18	143.274602 thru 143.274632	5
143.246392	15	143.256112	18	143.266272 thru 143.266302	16	143.274642	3
143.254012 thru 143.254052	3	143.256122	15	143.266312 143.266322	18	143.274652	5
143.254062	5	143.256132	16	143.266332	16	143.274662	3
143.254072 thru 143.254122	3	143.257012 thru 143.257072	8	143.266342	18	143.274672	5
143.254142 thru 143.254192	5	143.264012 thru 143.264042	3	143.266352	16	143.274682	3
143.254212 143.254222	3	143.264052 thru 143.264082	5	143.266362	18	143.274692	5
		143.264092	3	143.266372 thru 143.266412	15	143.274702	3
		143.264102	5	143.266422	18	143.274722 thru 143.274762	5
		143.264232 thru 143.264342	3	143.266432 thru 143.266452	15		

All reference numbers followed by the letter "B" refer to the External Ignition chart.

263

Appendix A

CROSS REFERENCE LIST FOR FOUR-STROKE TABLE OF SPECIFICATIONS (continued)
(see pages 271-274)

CRAFTSMAN ENGINES

Craftsman Engine Models	See Column	Craftsman Engine Models	See Column	Craftsman Engine Models	See Column	Craftsman Engine Models	See Column
143.274772	3	143.284052		143.286042		143.294242	
143.274782	5	143.284062	2	143.286052	20	143.294252	
143.274792	3	143.284072	5	143.286062	16	143.294262	
143.275012		143.284082		143.286072		143.294272	
thru		143.284092	3	thru		143.294282	
143.275082	11	143.284102	5	143.286092	18	143.294292	
143.276022	20	143.284112		143.286102	20	143.294302	
143.276032		thru		143.286112		143.294312	
143.276042	18	143.284182	3	143.286122	18	143.294322	2B
143.276052	20	143.284212	5	143.286132	16	143.294332	5B
143.276062	18	143.284222	1	143.286142		143.294342	2B
143.276092		143.284232		thru		143.294352	
thru		thru		143.286182	18	143.294362	
143.276112	16	143.284252	3	143.286192	20	143.294372	
143.276132	20	143.284262	5	143.286202	18	143.294382	
143.276142		143.284272	3	143.286212	20	143.294392	
thru		143.284282		143.286222	16	143.294402	
143.276162	18	thru		143.286232		143.294412	
143.276172	16	143.284322	3	143.286242	20	143.294422	5B
143.276182	15	143.284332		143.286252	16	143.294432	
143.276192	16	thru		143.286262		143.294442	
143.276202	15	143.284382	5	143.286272	20	143.294452	
143.276212		143.284392		143.286282	16	143.294462	2B
thru		143.284422	3	143.286292	20	143.294472	
143.276222	16	143.284432	5	143.286312	18	143.294482	5B
143.276232		143.284452		143.286322		143.294492	
thru		thru		143.286332	16	143.294502	
143.276242	18	143.284472	5	143.286342	15	143.294512	
143.276252	15	143.284482	3	143.286352	18	143.294522	
143.276262		143.284492		143.286362	20	143.294532	2B
143.276272	18	143.284502	5	143.287012		143.294542	5B
143.276282	16	143.284512		thru		143.294552	
143.276292		143.284522	3	143.287032	8	143.294562	4B
143.276302	18	143.284532	5	143.293012	1B	143.294572	
143.276322		143.284542		143.294012		143.294582	
thru		thru		143.294022		143.294592	5B
143.276342	16	143.284572	3	143.294032		143.294602	
143.276352	18	143.284582	5	143.294042		143.294612	2B
143.276362	20	143.284592	3	143.294052		143.294622	
143.276372		143.284602		143.294062		143.294632	
thru		thru		143.294072		143.294642	4B
143.276392	16	143.284622	5	143.294092		143.294652	2B
143.276402	20	143.284632	3	143.294102		143.294662	
143.276412	15	143.284642	5	143.294112		143.294672	
143.276422	16	143.284652		143.294122		143.294682	5B
143.276432		143.284662	3	143.294132	2B	143.294692	2B
thru		143.284672		143.294142		143.294702	4B
143.276472	18	thru		143.294152		143.294712	2B
143.276482	20	143.284702	5	143.294162		143.294722	
143.277012		143.284712		143.294172	5B	143.294732	
143.277022	8	thru		143.294182		143.294742	5B
143.284012	3	143.284732	3	143.294192		143.295012	
143.284022	3	143.284742		143.294202		143.295022	
143.284032	3	143.284752	5	143.294212	2B	143.295032	8
143.284042	5	143.284772		143.294222		143.295042	12
		143.284782	5	143.294232	5B	143.296012	18

All reference numbers followed by the letter "B" refer to the External Ignition chart.

Small engine service specifications

CROSS REFERENCE LIST FOR FOUR-STROKE TABLE OF SPECIFICATIONS (continued)
(see pages 271-274)

CRAFTSMAN ENGINES

Craftsman Engine Models	See Column
143.296022	20
143.296032	18
143.296042	20
143.296052	
143.296062	18
143.296072	20
143.296082	
143.296092	18
143.296102	
143.296112	
143.296122	
143.296132	20
143.296142	
143.296152	
143.296162	
143.296172	
143.296182	
143.296192	18
143.296202	
143.296212	20
143.296222	18
143.296232	20
143.296242	
143.296252	
143.296262	18
143.297012	4B
143.304012	2B
143.304032	
143.304042	5B
143.304052	2B
143.304072	5B
143.304092	2B
143.304102 thru	
143.304192	5B
143.304202 thru	
143.304272	2B
143.304282	
143.304292	5B
143.304302	2B
143.304312	
143.304322	
143.304332	
143.304342	
143.304352	5B
143.304362	3
143.305012 thru	
143.305032	12
143.305042	11
143.305052	12
143.305062	11
143.306012	18

Craftsman Engine Models	See Column
143.306022 thru	
143.306042	20
143.313012	
143.313022	1B
143.314012	
143.314022	5B
143.314032 thru	
143.314112	2B
143.314122 thru	
143.314172	5B
143.314182	2B
143.314192 thru	
143.314252	5B
143.314262 thru	
143.314302	2B
143.314312	5B
143.314322 thru	
143.314362	2B
143.314372	5B
143.314382	2B
143.314392	5B
143.314402	
143.314412	2B
143.314422	5B
143.314432	3
143.314442 thru	
143.314472	5B
143.314482	2B
143.314502	
143.314512	
143.314522	5B
143.314532	3
143.314542 thru	
143.314572	2B
143.314582	
143.314592	
143.314602	5B
143.34612 thru	
143.314692	5B
143.314702	3
143.314722 thru	
143.314772	2B
143.314782	5B
143.314792	2B

Craftsman Engine Models	See Column
143.314802	
143.314812	
143.315012	5B
143.315022	11
143.315032	
143.315042	4B
143.315052	12
143.315062	11
143.315072	4B
143.315082	12
143.315092 thru	
143.315122	11
143.315132	12
143.316022	18
143.316032	
143.316042	16
143.316052	
143.316062	
143.316082	18
143.316092	
143.316102	20
143.316112	18
143.316122 thru	
143.316142	20
143.316152	18
143.316162	20
143.316172	16
143.316182	18
143.316192	20
143.316202	20
143.316222 thru	
143.316252	18
143.316262	
143.316272	20
143.316282	
143.316292	18
143.316302	20
143.316312	18
143.321012	
143.321022	1B
143.324012	
143.324022	
143.324042	5B
143.324052	2B
143.324062 thru	
143.324102	5B
143.324112	
143.324122	2B
143.324132	5B
143.324142 thru	
143.324172	2B

Craftsman Engine Models	See Column
143.324182	4B
143.324192	2B
143.324202 thru	
143.324222	5B
143.326012 thru	
143.326112	19
143.326122 thru	
143.326182	15B
143.326192 thru	
143.326272	16
143.326282	
143.326292	15
143.326312	16
143.326322	17
143.326332	19
143.326342	19
143.326372	17
143.331012	
143.331022	1B
143.334022	
143.334032	2B
143.334042	5B
143.334052	4B
143.334062	
143.334072	2B
143.334082	
143.334102	5B
143.334112	
143.334122	2B
143.334132	5B
143.334142	
143.334152	
143.334162	2B
143.334172	
143.334182	5B
143.334192	3
143.334202	2B
143.334212 thru	
143.334252	5B
143.334262 thru	
143.334312	2B
143.334322	5B
143.334332	2B
143.334342	5B
143.334352 thru	
143.334382	2B
143.335012	
143.335022	12

All reference numbers followed by the letter "B" refer to the External Ignition chart.

CROSS REFERENCE LIST FOR FOUR-STROKE TABLE OF SPECIFICATIONS (continued)
(see pages 271-274)

CRAFTSMAN ENGINES

Craftsman Engine Models	See Column
143.335032	
143.335042	11
143.335052	6B
143.336012	15
143.336022	
143.336032	
143.336042	15B
143.344022	
143.344032	
143.344042	2B
143.344052	
143.344062	5B
143.344072	2B
143.344082	
143.344092	5B
143.344102	2B
143.344112	4B
143.344122	
143.344132	5B
143.344142	2B
143.344152	5B
143.344162	2B
143.344172	5B
143.344182 thru 143.344222	2B
143.344232	
143.344242	
143.344252	
143.344262	5B
143.344272 thru 143.344302	5B
143.344322 thru 143.344392	5B
143.344402	
143.344412	4B
143.344422	
143.344432	2B
143.344442	4B
143.344452	5B
143.344462	4B
143.344472	5B
143.345012	
143.345022	12
143.345032	6B
143.345042	11
143.345052	12
143.345062	12
143.346012	
143.346022	15B
143.346032	17
143.346042	
143.346052	13B

Craftsman Engine Models	See Column
143.346062	
143.346072	15B
143.346082	17
143.346092 thru 143.346132	13B
143.346142 thru 143.346192	15B
143.346202	14
143.351012	
143.351022	1B
143.354012	2B
143.354022	
143.354032	5B
143.354042	2B
143.354082	5B
143.354092	
143.354102	2B
143.354112	5B
143.354122	2B
143.354132	4B
143.354142	2B
143.354152	5B
143.354162 thru 143.354212	2B
143.354222	5B
143.354232	2B
143.354242 thru 143.354272	5B
143.354282	2B
143.354292	2B
143.354302	5B
143.354312	2B
143.354312 thru 143.354352	2B
143.354362 thru 143.354462	5B
143.354482 thru 143.354502	4B
143.355012	5B
143.355022	10
143.356012	15B
143.356022	7B
143.356032	13B
143.356042	15B
143.356052	13B
143.356062	7B
143.356072	13B

Craftsman Engine Models	See Column
143.356082	
143.356092	15B
143.356102	10B
143.356122	
143.356132	
143.356142	
143.356152	13B
143.356172	
143.356182	
143.356192	
143.356202	
143.356212	
143.356222	
143.356232	
143.356252	15B
143.356362	7B
143.361012	1B
143.364012	2B
143.364022	
143.364032	
143.364042	
143.364052	
143.364062	
143.364072	5B
143.364082	2B
143.364092	5B
143.364102	
143.364112	
143.364122	
143.364132	
143.364142	2B
143.364152	4B
143.364162	
143.364172	
143.364182	
143.364192	5B
143.364202	2B
143.364212	5B
143.364222	2B
143.364232	
143.364242	
143.364252	5B
143.364262	4B
143.364272	
143.364282	
143.364292	
143.364302	
143.364312	
143.364322	
143.364332	
143.364342	5B
143.364352	
143.364362	
143.364372	2B
143.364382	5B
143.364392	2B

Craftsman Engine Models	See Column
143.364402	4B
143.365012	
143.365022	12B
143.366022	14B
143.366032	16B
143.366042	14B
143.366052	
143.366062	
143.366082	7B
143.366102	14B
143.366112	
143.366122	
143.366132	16B
143.366152	14B
143.366172	16B
143.366182	7B
143.366192	
143.366222	16B
143.371012	
143.371022	1B
143.374012	
143.374022	
143.374032	
143.374052	
143.374062	
143.374072	
143.374082	2B
143.374092	
143.374102	
143.374112	
143.374122	
143.374132	
143.374142	
143.374152	
143.374162	
143.374172	
143.374182	
143.374192	
143.374202	5B
143.374212	
143.374222	
143.374282	
143.374302	2B
143.374312	4B
143.375012	
143.375022	12B
143.376022	16B
143.376042	14B
143.376052	16B
143.376062	14B
143.376092	16B
143.381012	
143.381022	2B
143.384012 thru 143.384082	2B

All reference numbers followed by the letter "B" refer to the External Ignition chart.

Small engine service specifications

CROSS REFERENCE LIST FOR FOUR-STROKE TABLE OF SPECIFICATIONS (continued)
(see pages 271-274)

CRAFTSMAN ENGINES

Craftsman Engine Models	See Column	Craftsman Engine Models	See Column	Craftsman Engine Models	See Column	Craftsman Engine Models	See Column
143.384092 thru 143.384122	5B	143.614012 thru 143.614032	3	143.627012 thru 143.627042	8	143.651012 thru 143.651072	1
143.384172	5B	143.614042 143.614052	3	143.631012 thru 143.631092	1	143.654022 thru 143.654312	3
143.384272 thru 143.384312	2B	143.614062 thru 143.614162	3	143.634012 thru 143.634032	3	143.655012 143.655032	11
143.384322	5B	143.615012 thru 143.615092	14	143.635012 143.635022	14	143.656012 thru 143.656052	15
143.384332	5B	143.616012	16	143.635032	11	143.656062	16
143.384342	2B	143.616042 thru 143.616112	15	143.635042 143.635052	14	143.656072 143.656082	18
143.384352 143.384362		143.616122	16	143.636012		143.656092	15
143.384372	5B	143.617012 thru 143.617182	8	143.636022	18	143.656102	16
143.384382 143.384392	2B	143.621012 thru 143.621092	1	143.636032	16	143.656112	15
143.384402 143.384412		143.624012 thru 143.624112	3	143.636042	18	143.656122 thru 143.656152	16
143.384422	4B	143.625012 thru 143.625132	14	143.636052	15	143.656162 thru 143.656182	15
143.384432	5B	143.626012	16	143.636062	16	143.656192	16
143.385012 143.385022		143.626022	15	143.636072	18	143.656202	15
143.385032	6B	143.626032	16	143.637012	8	143.656212	
143.386022	16B	143.626042	15	143.641012 thru 143.641062	1	143.656222	18
143.386042 143.386062	16B	143.626052		143.641072	3	143.656232	16
143.386072	14B	143.626062	16	143.644012 thru 143.644082	3	143.656242	18
143.386082	16B	143.626072	15	143.645012 thru 143.645032	11	143.656252	15
143.386122		143.626082 thru 143.626122	16	143.646012 thru 143.646032	16	143.656262 143.656272	16
143.386132	14B	143.626132	15	143.646042 143.646052	18	143.656282	18
143.386142	16B	143.626142		143.646062 thru 143.646102	16	143.657012 thru 143.657052	8
143.386172	16B	143.626152	16	143.646112	15	143.661012 thru 143.661062	1
143.601022 thru 143.601062	1	143.626162	15	143.646122 143.646132	16	143.664012 thru 143.664332	3
143.604012 143.604022 143.604032 143.604042 143.604052 143.604062 143.604072	3	143.626172	16	143.646142	18	143.665012 thru 143.665082	11
143.605012 143.605022 143.605052	14	143.626182	15	143.646152	16	143.666012 143.666022	16
143.606012 thru 143.606052	16	143.626192	16	143.646162	18	143.666032	18
143.606092	15	143.626202	15	143.646172		143.666042 thru 143.666072	16
143.606102	16	143.626212	16	143.646182	16	143.666082 143.666092	18
143.607012 thru 143.607032	8	143.626222 thru 143.626262	15	143.646192	15	143.666102 thru 143.666142	15
143.607042 thru 143.607062	8	143.626282	18	143.646202	16		
		143.626292	16	143.646212 thru 143.646232	18		
		143.626302	15	143.647012 thru 143.647062	8		
		143.626312 143.626322	16				

All reference numbers followed by the letter "B" refer to the External Ignition chart.

CROSS REFERENCE LIST FOR FOUR-STROKE TABLE OF SPECIFICATIONS (continued)
(see pages 271-274)

CRAFTSMAN ENGINES

Craftsman Engine Models	See Column	Craftsman Engine Models	See Column	Craftsman Engine Models	See Column	Craftsman Engine Models	See Column
143.666152		143.676222	18	143.701012		143.716162	14
143.666162	18	143.676232		143.701022	1	143.716172	
143.666172		143.676242	15	143.704022		thru	
thru		143.676252	18	thru		143.716192	18
143.666202	15	143.676262	20	143.704062	3	143.716202	16
143.666222	16	143.677012		143.706012		143.716212	20
143.666232	18	143.677022	8	143.706022	15	143.716222	18
143.666242	15	143.684012	3	143.706032		143.716232	15
143.666252	16	143.685012		143.706042		143.716242	14
143.666272	15	thru		143.706052	18	143.716252	16
143.666282	16	143.685032	11	143.706062	15	143.716262	20
143.666292	15	143.686012		143.706072		143.716272	
143.666302		143.686022	17	143.706082	18	143.716282	
143.666312	16	143.686032		143.706092	16	143.716292	
143.666322	18	thru		143.706102	15	143.716302	15
143.666332	20	143.686052	18	143.706112	16	143.716312	
143.666342	16	143.686062	16	143.706122	18	143.716322	16
143.666352	18	143.686072	14	143.706132	20	143.716332	20
143.666362	20	143.686082		143.706142	15	143.716342	17
143.666372	15	thru		143.706152	20	143.716352	15
143.666382	16	143.686102	18	143.706162	18	143.716362	16
143.667012		143.686112	14	143.706172		143.716372	
143.667022	8	143.686122	15	143.706182	16	143.716382	20
143.667032	11	143.686132	16	143.706212	14	143.716392	18
143.667042		143.686142	18	143.706222	18	143.716402	
thru		143.686152	20	143.706232	20	143.716412	15
143.667082	8	14.686162	15	143.707012	11	143.716422	14
143.674012		143.686172	20	143.707042	8	143.716432	20
thru		143.686182	15	143.707052	11	143.716012	
143.674062	3	143.687012	8	143.707062	8	143.717022	
143.675012		143.687022		143.707072		143.717032	8
143.675022	11	143.687032	11	143.707082		143.717042	11
143.675032	14	143.687042	8	143.707092		143.717052	8
143.675042	11	143.694012		143.707132	11	143.717062	
143.675062	14	143.694022		143.711012		143.717072	
143.676012		143.694032	3	thru		143.717082	
143.676022	18	143.696012	15	143.711052	1	143.717092	11
143.676032	16	143.696032	18	143.714012		143.717102	8
143.676042		143.696042	15	thru		143.717112	11
143.676052	18	143.696052	16	143.714132	3	143.721012	
143.676062		143.696062	18	143.716012	17	143.712032	1
thru		143.696072	20	143.716022	18	143.724012	
143.676092	20	143.696082	11	143.716032		143.724022	
143.676102	16	143.696092	18	143.716042	15	143.724042	3
143.676112	15	143.696102	16	143.716052		143.724052	8
143.676122	16	143.696112	20	143.716062	17	143.725012	11
143.676132	15	143.696122	15	143.716072		143.726012	15
143.676142	18	143.696132	18	143.716082	18	143.726022	20
143.676152		143.696142	14	143.716092		143.726032	18
143.676162	20	143.696152	15	143.716102	20	143.726042	
143.676172	16	143.697012		143.716112		143.726052	16
143.676182	18	143.697022	11	143.716122		143.726082	15
143.676192	16	143.697032	8	143.716132		143.726092	14
143.676202	18	143.697042		143.716142	16	143.726102	20
143.676212	20	143.697052	11	143.716152	18		

All reference numbers followed by the letter "B" refer to the External Ignition chart.

Small engine service specifications

CROSS REFERENCE LIST FOR FOUR-STROKE TABLE OF SPECIFICATIONS (continued)

(see pages 271-274)

CRAFTSMAN ENGINES

Craftsman Engine Models	See Column	Craftsman Engine Models	See Column	Craftsman Engine Models	See Column	Craftsman Engine Models	See Column
143.726112		143.746082		143.776072	9B		
143.726132		143.746092	18 or 19	143.784012	4B		
143.726142	15	143.746102	20 or 21	143.784022			
143.726152	18	143.751012		143.784032	6B		
143.726182		143.751032		143.784042	4B		
thru		143.751042	2B	143.784052			
143.726212	16	143.754032		143.784062	3B		
143.726222	15	143.754042		143.784072	6B		
143.726232	20	143.754052	3B	143.784082			
143.726242	15	143.754062	6B	143.784092			
143.726252	16	143.756042		143.784102	3B		
143.726262	15	143.756052	9B	143.784112			
143.726282	16	143.756062	16B	143.784122	3B		
143.726292	20	143.756072	8B	143.784132	6B		
143.726302	14	143.756082	14B	143.786012			
143.726312		143.756092	8B	143.786022			
143.726322	20	143.756102	14B	143.786032	14B		
143.731012	2	143.756112	16B	143.786042	16B		
143.734012		143.756122	14B	143.786052	14B		
143.734022		143.756142	7B	143.786062			
143.734032	4	143.756152	16B	143.786072	16B		
143.734042	8	143.756162	9B	143.786082	8B		
143.735012		143.756172	16B	143.786092	14B		
143.735022	11	143.756182		143.786102	9B		
143.736032	15	143.756192	14B	143.786112	14B		
143.736042	18	143.756202	16B				
143.736052		143.756212	14B				
143.736062	15	143.756222	9B				
143.736072	14	143.756232	16B				
143.736082	18	143.764012	6B				
143.736092	16	143.764032	4B				
143.736102	20	143.764042	6B				
143.736112	14	143.764052	3B				
143.736122		143.764062					
143.736132	18	143.764072	6B				
143.736142	20	143.766012					
143.741012		143.766072					
thru		143.766082	14B				
143.741042	2	143.766092	16B				
143.741052		143.766102					
thru		143.766112	14B				
143.741092	2	143.766122	16B				
143.742032	18	143.766132	9B				
143.742042		143.766142	16B				
143.742052	14	143.766152	14B				
143.744012		143.774012	3B				
thru		143.774022	2B				
143.744082	4	143.774032					
143.744092	11	143.774042	3B				
143.744102	8	143.774052					
143.744112	11	143.774062					
143.744122	4	143.774062	2B				
143.746012	15	143.776012	14B				
143.746022	18	143.776022	9B				
		143.776042	14B				
		143.776052					
		143.776062	16B				

All reference numbers followed by the letter "B" refer to the External Ignition chart.

269

Appendix A

Tecumseh/Craftsman four-stroke engines
TORQUE SPECIFICATIONS

	INCH POUNDS	FT. POUNDS
Cylinder Head Bolts	160 - 200	13 - 16
Connecting Rod Bolts (All Types Except Durlok) 2.5 - 3.5 H.P. & ECH90, ECV100, TNT100	65 - 75	5.5 - 6.2
4 - 5 H.P. (Small) & ECV105, ECV110, ECV120, TNT120	80 - 95	6.6 - 7.9
5 H.P. (Medium) - 6 H.P.	86 - 110	7.1 - 9.1
7, 8 & 10 H.P.(Medium)	106 - 130	8.8 - 10.8
Connecting Rod Bolts (Durlok Type) TVS, TNT, ECV, LAV, H, HS	95 - 110	7.9 - 9.1
5 H.P. (Medium) - 6 H.P.	160 - 180	13.3 - 15
7, 8, 10 H.P. (Medium)	200 - 220	16.8 - 18.4
*Cylinder Cover or Flange to Cylinder	100 - 130	8.3 - 10.8
Flywheel Nut (Light Frame)	400 - 440	33 - 36.3
Flywheel Nut (Ext. Ign.) (Light Frame)	400 - 440	33 - 36.6
Flywheel Nut (Medium Frame) H50 thru HM100	430 - 500	35 - 41.6
Flywheel Nut (Ext. Ign., Medium Frame) V, H & HH50 thru VM & HM100	600 - 660	50 - 55
Ext. Ign. Mounting studs and screws	30 - 40	1.7 - 2.5
Spark Plug	220 - 280	18.3 - 23.3
Magneto Stator to Cylinder	40 - 90	3.3 - 7.5
Starter-Side Mount Plastic	75 - 95	6.2 - 7.9
Starter Top Mount Recoil	40 - 60	3.3 - 5
Starter Side Mount Recoil	50 - 70	4.1 - 5.9
Intake Pipe to Cylinder	72 - 96	6 - 8
Carburetor to Intake Pipe	48 - 72	4 - 6
Air Cleaner to Carburetor (Plastic)	8 - 12	1
TVS Air Cleaner to Carburetor TVS75,90,105,120	20 - 32	1 - 2.6
Muffler Mounting (Small Frame) (Basic)	20 - 35	1.6 - 2.9
Muffler Mounting (Medium Frame)	90 - 150	7.5 - 12.5
Plastic Tank to Housing Mount TVS75,90,105,120	12 - 20	1 - 1.6
Ball Bearing Retainer 2.5 - 5 H.P. (Small)	45 - 60	3.7 - 5
Ball Bearing Retainer 5 - 10 H.P. (Medium)	15 - 22	1 - 1.9
Electric Starter to Cylinder	50 - 80	4 - 6.6

*Medium Frame
  All VM, HM and TVM models with Powerlok Screws   110 - 140   9.1 - 11.6

"Torque specifications listed on this page should not be confused with the torque value observed on engines which have been run. Torque relaxation occurs on all engines from thermal expansion and contraction. The torque specifications take relaxation into account so a sufficient clamping force exists after an engine has been run."

Small engine service specifications

Tecumseh/Craftsman four-stroke engines

SMALL & MEDIUM FRAME
STANDARD POINT IGNITION

SPECIFICATIONS		1	2	3	4	5	6	7	8	9
Displacement		7.75	9.06	9.06	9.52	9.98	9.98	11.04	10.49	10.50
Stroke		1.844	1.844	1.844	1.938	1.844	1.844	2.250	1.938	1.938
Bore		2.3125 / 2.3135	2.5000 / 2.5010	2.5000 / 2.5010	2.5000 / 2.5010	2.6250 / 2.6260	2.6250 / 2.6260	2.5000 / 2.5010	2.6250 / 2.6260	2.6250 / 2.6260
Timing Dim. B.T.D.C.		.065	.035	.065	.035	.035	.035	.050	.035	.035
Point Setting		.020	.020	.020	.020	.020	.020	.020	.020	.020
Spark Plug Gap		.030	.030	.030	.030	.030	.030	.030	.030	.030
Valve Clearance		.008 Both	.008 Both	.008 Both	.008 Both	.008 Both	.008 Both	.008 Both	.008 Both	.008 Both
Valve Seat Angle		46°	46°	46°	46°	46°	46°	46°	46°	46°
Valve Seat Width		.035 / .045	.035 / .045	.035 / .045	.035 / .045	.035 / .045	.035 / .045	.042 / .052	.035 / .045	.035 / .045
Valve Guide Oversize Dim.		.2807 / .2817	.2807 / .2817	.2807 / .2817	.2807 / .2817	.2807 / .2817	.2807 / .2817	.3432 / .3442	.2807 / .2817	.2807 / .2817
Crankshaft End Play		.005 / .027	.005 / .027	.005 / .027	.005 / .027	.005 / .027	.005 / .027	.005 / .027	.005 / .027	.005 / .027
Crankpin Journal Dia.		.8610 / .8615	.8610 / .8615	.8610 / .8615	.9995 / 1.0000	.8610 / .8615	.8610 / .8615	1.0615 / 1.0620	.9995 / 1.0000	.9995 / 1.0000
Crankshaft Mag. Main Brg. Dia.		.8735 / .8740	.9985 / .9990	.8735 / .8740	.9985 / .9990	.8735 / .8740	.9985 / .9990	.9985 / .9990	.9985 / .9990	.9985 / .9990
Crankshaft P.T.O. Main Brg. Dia.		.8735 / .8740	.8735 / .8740	.8735 / .8740	.9985 / .9990	.8735 / .8740	.8735 / .8740	.9985 / .9990	.9985 / .9990	.9985 / .9990
Camshaft Bearing Dia.		.4975 / .4980	.4975 / .4980	.4975 / .4980	.4975 / .4980	.4975 / .4980	.4975 / .4980	.6230 / .6235	.4975 / .4980	.4975 / .4980
Conn. Rod Dia. Crank Brg.		.8620 / .8625	.8620 / .8625	.8620 / .8625	1.0005 / 1.0010	.8620 / .8625	.8620 / .8625	1.0630 / 1.0635	1.0005 / 1.0010	1.0005 / 1.0010
Piston Diameter		2.3092 / 2.3100	2.4952 / 2.4960	2.4952 / 2.4960	2.4952 / 2.4960	2.6202 / 2.6210	2.6202 / 2.6210	2.4945 / 2.4950	2.6210 / 2.6202	2.6202 / 2.6210
Ring Groove	1st & 2nd Comp.	.002 / .005	.002 / .005	.002 / .005	.002 / .005	.002 / .005	.002 / .005	.002 / .005	.002 / .005	.002 / .005
Side Clearance	(Bot.) Oil	.0005 / .0035	.0005 / .0035	.0005 / .0035	.0005 / .0035	.001 / .004	.001 / .004	.001 / .004	.001 / .004	.001 / .004
Piston Skirt Clearance		.0025 / .0043	.0040 / .0058	.0040 / .0058	.0040 / .0058	.0040 / .0058	.0040 / .0058	.0055 / .0070	.0040 / .0058	.0040 / .0058
Ring End Gap		.007 / .017	.007 / .017	.007 / .017	.007 / .017	.007 / .017	.007 / .017	.007 / .017	.007 / .017	.007 / .017
Cylinder Main Brg. Dia.		.8755 / .8760	1.0005 / 1.0010	.8755 / .8760	1.0005 / 1.0010	.8755 / .8760	1.0005 / 1.0010	1.0005 / 1.0010	1.0005 / 1.0010	1.0005 / 1.0010
Cylinder Cover/Flange Main Bearing Diameter		.8755 / .8760	.8755 / .8760	.8755 / .8760	1.0005 / 1.0010	.8755 / .8760	.8755 / .8760	1.0005 / 1.0010	1.0005 / 1.0010	1.2010 / 1.2020

Notes: (A) VM & HM80 - Displacement 19.41   (B) VM & HM80 - Bore 3-1/8"

Appendix A

Tecumseh/Craftsman four-stroke engines

SMALL & MEDIUM FRAME
STANDARD POINT IGNITION (cont.)

10	11	12	13	14	15	16	17	18	19	20	21
11.50	12.04	12.04	12.04	12.18	13.53	15.04	17.17	18.65	19.43 See Note A	20.20	21.82
1.938	1.938	1.938	1.938	2.250	2.500	2.532	2.532	2.532	2.532 See Note B	2.532	2.532
2.7500 2.7510	2.8120 2.8130	2.8120 2.8130	2.8120 2.8130	2.6250 2.6260	2.6250 2.6260	2.7500 2.7510	2.9375 2.9385	3.0620 3.0630	3.1250 3.1260	3.1870 3.1880	3.3120 3.3130
.035	.035	.035	.035	.080	.080	.080	.090	.090	.090	.090	.090
.020	.020	.020	.020	.020	.020	.020	.020	.020	.020	.020	.020
.030	.050	.030	.030	.030	.030	.030	.030	.030	.030	.030	.030
.008 Both	.008 Both	.008 Both	.008 Both	.010 Both	.010 Both	.010 Both	.010 Both	.010 Both	.010 Both	.010 Both	.010 Both
46°	46°	46°	46°	46°	46°	46°	46°	46°	46°	46°	46°
.035 .045	.035 .045	.035 .045	.035 .045	.042 .052	.042 .052	.042 .052	.042 .052	.042 .052	.042 .052	.042 .052	.042 .052
.2807 .2817	.2807 .2817	.2807 .2817	.2807 .2817	.3432 .3442	.3432 .3442	.3432 .3442	.3432 .3442	.3432 .3442	.3432 .3442	.3432 .3442	.3432 .3442
.005 .027	.005 .027	.005 .027	.005 .027	.005 .027 See Note F	.005 .027 See Note F	.005 .027 See Note F	.005 .027	.005 .027	.005 .027	.005 .027	.005 .027
.9995 1.0000	.9995 1.0000	.9995 1.0000	.9995 1.0000	1.0615 1.0620	1.0615 1.0620	1.1860 1.1865	1.1860 1.1865	1.1860 1.1865	1.1860 1.1865	1.1860 1.1865	1.1860 1.1865
.9990 .9995	.9985 .9990	.9985 .9990	.9985 .9990	.9985 .9990	.9985 .9990	.9985 .9990	.9985 .9990	.9985 .9990	.9985 .9990	.9985 .9990	.9985 .9990
.9985 .9990	.9985 .9990	.9985 .9990	.9985 .9990	.9985 .9990	.9985 .9990	.9985 .9990	1.1870 1.1875	1.1870 1.1875	1.1870 1.1875	1.1870 1.1875	1.1870 1.1875
.4975 .4980	.4975 .4980	.4975 .4980	.4975 .4980	.6230 .6235	.6230 .6235	.6230 .6235	.6230 .6235	.6230 .6235	.6230 .6235	.6230 .6235	.6230 .6235
1.0005 1.0010	1.0005 1.0010	1.0005 1.0010	1.0005 1.0010	1.0630 1.0635	1.0630 1.0635	1.1880 1.1885	1.1880 1.1885	1.1880 1.1885	1.1880 1.1885	1.1880 1.1885	1.1880 1.1885
2.7450 2.7455	2.8072 2.8080	2.8072 2.8080	2.8072 2.8080	2.6210 2.6215	2.6210 2.6215	2.7450 2.7455	2.9325 2.9335	3.0575 3.0585 See Note C	3.1195 3.1205	3.1815 3.1825	3.3090 3.3105
.002 .004	.002 .005	.002 .005	.002 .005	.002 .004	.002 .004	.002 .003	.002 .005	.002 .005	.002 .005	.002 .005	.002 .005
.001 .002	.001 .004	.001 .004	.001 .004	.002 .004	.002 .004	.001 .003	.001 .004	.001 .004	.001 .004	.001 .004	.001 .004
.0045 .0060	.0040 .0058	.0040 .0058	.0040 .0058	.0035 .0050 See Note D	.0035 .0050 See Note D	.0045 .0060 See Note E	.004 .006	.0035 .0055	.0045 .0065	.0045 .0065	.0015 .0040
.007 .017	.007 .017	.007 .017	.007 .017	.010 .020	.010 .020	.010 .020	.010 .020	.010 .020	.010 .020	.010 .020	.010 .020
1.0005 1.0010	1.0005 1.0010	1.0005 1.0010	1.0005 1.0010	1.0005 1.0010	1.0005 1.0010	1.0005 1.0010	1.0005 1.0010	1.0005 1.0010	1.0005 1.0010	1.0005 1.0010	1.0005 1.0010
1.0005 1.0010	1.0005 1.0010	1.0005 1.0010	1.0005 1.0010	1.0005 1.0010	1.0005 1.0010	1.0005 1.0010	1.1890 1.1895	1.1890 1.1895	1.1890 1.1895	1.1890 1.1895	1.1890 1.1895

(C) VM & HM80 Piston Dia. $\frac{3.1195}{3.1205}$ (D) VH50, 60 $\frac{.0015}{.0055}$ (E) VH70 $\frac{.0038}{.0073}$ (F) VH, HH50-70 Models $\frac{.003}{.031}$

Small engine service specifications

Tecumseh/Craftsman four-stroke engines

SMALL & MEDIUM FRAME EXTERNAL IGNITION

SPECIFICATIONS		1B	2B	3B	4B	5B	6B	7B
Displacement		7.75	9.06	9.52	10.49	9.98	12.04	12.18
Stroke		1.844	1.844	1.938	1.938	1.844	1.938	2.250
Bore		2.3125 / 2.3135	2.500 / 2.501	2.500 / 2.501	2.625 / 2.626	2.625 / 2.626	2.812 / 2.813	2.625 / 2.626
Air Gap Dimension		.0125	.0125	.0125	.0125	.0125	.0125	.0125
Point Setting (if required)		.020	.020	.020	.020	.020	.020	Does Not Apply
Spark Plug Gap		.030	.030	.030	.030	.030	.030	.030
Valve Clearance		.008 Both	.008 Both	.008 Both	.008 Both	.008 Both	.008 Both	.008 Both
Valve Seat Angle		46°	46°	46°	46°	46°	46°	46°
Valve Seat Width		.035 / .045	.035 / .045	.035 / .045	.035 / .045	.035 / .045	.035 / .045	.042 / .052
Valve Guide Oversize Dim.		.2807 / .2817	.2807 / .2817	.2807 / .2817	.2807 / .2817	.2807 / .2817	.2807 / .2817	.3432 / .3442
Crankshaft End Play		.005 / .027	.005 / .027	.005 / .027	.005 / .027	.005 / .027	.005 / .027	.005 / .027 Note (A)
Crankpin Journal Dia.		.8610 / .8615	.8610 / .8615	.9995 / 1.0000	.9995 / 1.0000	.8610 / .8615	.9995 / 1.0000	1.0615 / 1.0620
Crankshaft Mag. Main Brg. Dia.		.9985 / .9990	.9985 / .9990	.9985 / .9990	.9985 / .9990	.9985 / .9990	.9985 / .9990	.9985 / .9990
Crankshaft P.T.O. Main Brg. Dia.		.8735 / .8740	.8735 / .8740	.9985 / .9990	.9985 / .9990	.8735 / .8740	.9985 / .9990	.9985 / .9990
Camshaft Bearing Dia.		.4975 / .4980	.4975 / .4980	.4975 / .4980	.4975 / .4980	.4975 / .4980	.4975 / .4980	.6230 / .6235
Conn. Rod Dia. Crank Brg.		.8620 / .8625	.8620 / .8625	1.0005 / 1.0010	1.0005 / 1.0010	.8620 / .8625	1.0005 / 1.0010	1.0630 / 1.0635
Piston Diameter	Bottom of Skirt	2.3092 / 2.3100	2.4952 / 2.4960	2.4952 / 2.4960	2.6202 / 2.6210	2.6202 / 2.6210	2.8072 / 2.8080	2.6212 / 2.6220 Note (D)
Ring Groove Side Clearance	1st & 2nd Comp.	.002 / .005	.002 / .005	.002 / .005	.002 / .005	.002 / .005	.002 / .005	.002 / .005
	(Bot.) Oil	.0005 / .0035	.0005 / .0035	.0005 / .0035	.001 / .004	.001 / .004	.001 / .004	.001 / .004
Piston Skirt Clearance		.0025 / .0043	.0040 / .0058	.0040 / .0058	.0040 / .0058	.0040 / .0058	.0040 / .0058	.0030 / .0048 Note (B)
Ring End Gap		.010 / .020	.010 / .020	.010 / .020	.010 / .020	.010 / .020	.010 / .020	.010 / .020
Cylinder Main Brg. Dia.		1.0005 / 1.0010	1.0005 / 1.0010	1.0005 / 1.0010	1.0005 / 1.0010	1.0005 / 1.0010	1.0005 / 1.0010	1.0005 / 1.0010
Cylinder Cover/Flange Main Bearing Diameter		.8755 / .8760	.8755 / .8760	1.0005 / 1.0010	1.0005 / 1.0010	.8755 / .8760	1.0005 / 1.0010	1.0005 / 1.0010

Notes: (A) VH, HH50-70 models .003/.031   (B) VH, HH50-60 .0015/.0055   (C) VH, HH70 .0038/.0073

All reference numbers followed by the letter "B" refer to the External Ignition chart.

Appendix A

Tecumseh/Craftsman four-stroke engines

SMALL & MEDIUM FRAME
EXTERNAL IGNITION (cont.)

8B	9B	10B	11B	12B	13B	14B	15B	16B
13.53	15.04	17.17	17.17	19.43	19.43	19.43	21.82	21.82
2.500	2.532	2.532	2.532	2.532	2.532	2.532	2.532	2.532
2.625 / 2.626	2.750 / 2.751	2.9375 / 2.9385	2.9375 / 2.9385	3.125 / 3.126	3.125 / 3.126	3.125 / 3.126	3.312 / 3.313	3.312 / 3.313
.0125	.0125	.0125	.0125	.0125	.0125	.0125	.0125	.0125
Does Not Apply	Does Not Apply	Does Not Apply	Does Not Apply	Does Not Apply	Does Not Apply	Does Not Apply	Does Not Apply	Does Not Apply
.030	.030	.030	.030	.030	.030	.030	.030	.030
.010 Both	.010 Both	.010 Both	.010 Both	.010 Both	.010 Both	.010 Both	.010 Both	.010 Both
46°	46°	46°	46°	46°	46°	46°	46°	46°
.042 / .052	.042 / .052	.042 / .052	.042 / .052	.042 / .052	.042 / .052	.042 / .052	.042 / .052	.042 / .052
.3432 / .3442	.3432 / .3442	.3432 / .3442	.3432 / .3442	.3432 / .3442	.3432 / .3442	.3432 / .3442	.3432 / .3442	.3432 / .3442
.005 / .027 Note (A)	.005 / .027 Note (A)	.005 / .027	.005 / .027	.005 / .027	.005 / .027	.005 / .027	.005 / .027	.005 / .035 Note (F)
1.0615 / 1.0620	1.1862 / 1.1865	1.1860 / 1.1865	1.3740 / 1.3745	1.3740 / 1.3745	1.1860 / 1.1865	1.3740 / 1.3745	1.1860 / 1.1865	1.3740 / 1.3745
.9985 / .9990	.9985 / .9990	.9985 / .9990	1.3745 / 1.3750	1.3745 / 1.3750	.9985 / .9990	1.3745 / 1.3750	.9985 / .9990	1.3745 / 1.3750
.9985 / .9990	.9985 / .9990	1.1870 / 1.1875	1.3745 / 1.3750	1.3745 / 1.3750	1.1870 / 1.1875	1.3745 / 1.3750	1.1870 / 1.1875	1.3745 / 1.3750
.6230 / .6235	.6230 / .6235	.6230 / .6235	.6230 / .6235	.6230 / .6235	.6230 / .6235	.6230 / .6235	.6230 / .6235	.6230 / .6235
1.0630 / 1.0635	1.0630 / 1.0635	1.1880 / 1.1885	1.3760 / 1.3765	1.3760 / 1.3765	1.1880 / 1.1885	1.3760 / 1.3765	1.1880 / 1.1885	1.3760 / 1.3765
2.6212 / 2.6220 Note (D)	2.6212 / 2.6220 Note (E)	2.9325 / 2.9335	2.9325 / 2.9335	3.1195 / 3.1205	3.1195 / 3.1205	3.1195 / 3.1205	3.3090 / 3.3105	3.3098 / 3.3108
.002 / .005	.002 / .005	.002 / .005	.002 / .005	.002 / .005	.002 / .005	.002 / .005	.0015 / .0035	.0015 / .0035
.001 / .004	.001 / .004	.001 / .004	.001 / .004	.001 / .004	.001 / .004	.001 / .004	.001 / .004	.001 / .004
.0030 / .0048 Note (B)	.0030 / .0048 Note (C)	.004 / .006	.004 / .006	.0045 / .0065	.0045 / .0065	.0045 / .0065	.0015 / .0040	.0012 / .0032
.010 / .020	.010 / .020	.010 / .020	.010 / .020	.010 / .020	.010 / .020	.010 / .020	.010 / .020	.010 / .020
1.0005 / 1.0010	1.0005 / 1.0010	1.0005 / 1.0010	1.3765 / 1.3770	1.3765 / 1.3770	1.0005 / 1.0010	1.3765 / 1.3770	1.0005 / 1.0010	1.3765 / 1.3770
1.0005 / 1.0010	1.0005 / 1.0010	1.1890 / 1.1895	1.3765 / 1.3770	1.3765 / 1.3770	1.1890 / 1.1895	1.3765 / 1.3770	1.1890 / 1.1895	1.3765 / 1.3770

(D) VH, HH50-60 2.6235 / 2.6205   (E) VH, HH70 2.7462 / 2.7437   (F) TVM220 Ultra Balance .000 / .040

All reference numbers followed by the letter "B" refer to the External Ignition chart.

Small engine service specifications

Tecumseh/Craftsman two-stroke engines

ENGINE TYPE NUMBER AND LETTER REFERENCE

TYPE NO.	Column No.
Vertical Crankshaft Engines	
638 thru 638-100	6
639 thru 639-13A	13
640-02 thru 640-06B	21
640-07 thru 640-21-A	22
640-23	36
641 thru 641-14	11
642-01,A	9A
642-02, A thru G	9A
642-02E, F	9B
642-03, A, B	9A
642-04, A, B, C	9A
642-05, A, B	9A
642-06, A	9A
642-07, A, B	9A
642-07C	9B
642-08	9B
642-08A, B, C	9A
642-09 thru 642-14	9A
642-13 thru 14C	9B
642-15 thru 642-23	9B
642-24 thru 642-33	9C
642-35	34
643-01, A, 03, A	10A
643-03B, C	10B
643-04, 05A	10A
643-05B	10B
643-13,14	10A
643-14A, B, C	10B
643-15	10A
643-15A thru 643-32	10B
643-32A	32
643-33	33
643-34	33
643-35,A,B	37
650	14
653-01 thru 653-05	31
653-07 thru 653-10	38
660-11 thru 660-38	18
660-39,A	39
660-40	40
661-01 thru 661-29	29
661-30 thru 661-45	41
662-02	42
670-01 thru 670-109	8
Horizontal Crankshaft Engines	
1398 thru 1399	11
1400	11
1401 thru 1401F	16
1401G, H	17
1401J	27
1402 and 1402B	7
1425	7
1430A	7
1432, A	7
1440, A, B, C, D	1

TYPE NO.	Column No.
Horizontal Crankshaft Engines	
1442, A, B,	7
1444, A	7
1448 thru 1450	16
1450A, A, B, C, D, E	16
1450F	17
1454, A	1
1459	7
1460, A, B ,C, D, E, F	1
1462	1
1464, A, B	12
1465	1
1466, A	16
1471, A, B	5
1472, A, B, C	12
1473, A, B	1
1474	12
1475 thru 1476	1
1479	7
1482, A	16
1483	16
1484, A, B, C, D	3
1485	7
1486	4
1488, A, B, C, D	1
1489 thru 1490B	3
1491	12
1493, A	7
1494 and 1495A	2
1496	7
1497	1
1498	5
1499	16
1500	5
1501,A, B, C, D, E,F,G	1
1503, A, B, C, D	12
1506	16
1506B	17
1507	16
1508	7
1509	3
1510	12
1511	3
1512, A	2
1513	12
1515 thru 1516C	3
1517	5
1518	4
1519 thru 1521	1
1522	12
1523	1
1524	2
1525A	16
1527	3
1528,A,B	1
1529, A, B	3
1530, A, B	1
1531	3
1534A	17
1535B	3
1536	12
1537	1

TYPE NO.	Column No.
Horizontal Crankshaft Engines	
1538 thru 1541A	12
1542	5
1543 thru 1546	1
1547	3
1549	3
1550A	15
1551	16
1552	20
1553	16
1554, A	3
1555 and 1556	16
1557 thru 1560	15
1561	19
1562 thru 1571	15
1572	2
1573	3
1574 thru 1577	23
1575	24
1578	25
1581 thru 1582A	23
1583 thru 1599A	26
1600 thru 1617	28
1618 thru 1619	43
1620	30
1622 thru 1623A	42
1624 thru 1642	35
Vertical Crankshaft Engines	
200-183112	6
200-183122	6
200-193132	6
200-193142	6
200-193152	7
200-193162	7
200-203112	8
200-203172	8
200-203182	8
200-203192	8
200-213112	8
200-213122	8
200-213132	8
200-223112	41
200-233112	41
200-243112	8
200-283012	8
200-2131128	31
200-2132228	29
Craftsman Vertical Crankshaft Engines	
200-503111	16
200-583111	16
200-593121	16
200-602112	35
200-613111	16
200-633111	35
200-643121	35
200-672102	26
200-682102	26
200-692112	26
200-692122	26
200-692132	26

Appendix A

Tecumseh/Craftsman two-stroke engines

TABLE OF SPECIFICATIONS

(All measurements in inches)

Reference Column	1	2	3	4	5	6	7	8	9A	9B	9C
Bore	2.093 / 2.094	2.093 / 2.094	2.093 / 2.094	2.093 / 2.094	2.093 / 2.094	2.093 / 2.094	2.093 / 2.094	2.093 / 2.094	2.093 / 2.094	2.093 / 2.094	2.093 / 2.094
Stroke	1.250	1.410	1.410	1.410	1.410	1.500	1.500	1.500	1.500	1.500	1.500
Cu. In. Displacement	4.40	4.80	4.80	4.80	4.80	5.20	5.20	5.20	5.20	5.20	5.20
Point Gap	.017	.017	.017	.017	.017	.018	.017	.020	.018	.020	.020
Timing B.T.D.C.	.122	.100	.135	.100	.135	.100	.185	.070	.100	.085 See Note 1	.078 See Note 2
Spark Plug Gap	.030	.030	.030	.030	.030	.030	.030	.030	.030	.030	.030
Piston Ring End Gap	.007 / .017	.007 / .017	.006 / .011	.006 / .014	.006 / .011	.006 / .014	.007 / .017	.006 / .016	.007 / .017	.006 / .016	.006 / .016
Piston Diameter	2.0870 / 2.0880	2.0870 / 2.0880	2.0875 / 2.0885	2.0875 / 2.0885	2.0875 / 2.0885	2.0870 / 2.0880	2.0870 / 2.0880	2.0870 / 2.0880	2.0870 / 2.0880	2.0870 / 2.0880	2.0870 / 2.0880
Piston Ring Groove Width (Top)	.0655 / .0665	.0655 / .0665	.0655 / .0665	.0975 / .0985	.0655 / .0665	.0975 / .0985	.0655 / .0665	.0655 / .0665	.0655 / .0665	.0655 / .0665	.0655 / .0665
Piston Ring Groove Width (Bot.)	.0645 / .0655	.0645 / .0655	.0645 / .0655	.0955 / .0965	.0645 / .0655	.0955 / .0965	.0645 / .0655	.0645 / .0655	.0645 / .0655	.0645 / .0655	.0645 / .0655
Piston Ring Width	.0615 / .0625	.0615 / .0625	.0615 / .0625	.0925 / .0935	.0615 / .0625	.0925 / .0935	.0615 / .0625	.0615 / .0625	.0615 / .0625	.0615 / .0625	.0615 / .0625
Piston Pin Diameter	.4997 / .4999	.4997 / .4999	.4997 / .4999	.3750 / .3751	.4997 / .4999	.3750 / .3751	.4997 / .4999	.4997 / .4999	.4997 / .4999	.4997 / .4999	.4997 / .4999
Crank Pin Journal Diameter	.5611 / .5618	.5614 / .5621	.5614 / .5621	.6857 / .6865	.5611 / .5618	.6857 / .6865	.5611 / .5618	.8442 / .8450	.6857 / .6865	.8442 / .8450	.8442 / .8450
Crankshaft P.T.O. Side Main Brg. Dia.	.6691 / .6695	.6691 / .6695	.6691 / .6695	.6691 / .6695	.6691 / .6695	.8745 / .8750	.6690 / .6694	.9998 / 1.0003	.8745 / .8750	.9998 / 1.0003	.9998 / 1.0003
Crankshaft Magneto Side Main Brg. Dia.	.6691 / .6695	.6691 / .6695	.6691 / .6695	.6691 / .6695	.6691 / .6695	.7495 / .7500	.6690 / .6694	Ball .6691 / .6695 See Note A	.7495 / .7500	.7498 / .7503	.6691 / .6695
Crankshaft End Play	None	None	None	None	None	.003 / .016	None	None	.003 / .016	.003 / .016	None

NOTE 1:   642-08, 14A, 14B B.T.D.C. = = .110
           642-16D, 19A, 20A, 21, 22 B.T.D.C. = .078

NOTE 2:   642-24, 26, 29 B.T.D.C. = .087

NOTE A: Needle Bearing .7498 / .7503

Small engine service specifications

Tecumseh/Craftsman two-stroke engines

TABLE OF SPECIFICATIONS

(All measurements in inches)

10A	10B	11	12	13	14	15	16	17	18	19	Reference Column
2.093 / 2.094	2.093 / 2.094	2.093 / 2.094	2.093 / 2.094	2.375 / 2.376	2.093 / 2.094	2.4375 / 2.4385	2.093 / 2.094	2.093 / 2.094	2.093 / 2.094	2.093 / 2.094	Bore
1.750	1.750	1.750	1.410	1.680	1.500	1.750	1.500	1.500	1.750	1.410	Stroke
6.00	6.00	6.00	4.80	7.50	5.20	8.17	5.20	5.20	6.02	4.80	Cu. In. Displacement
.018 See Note 4	.020	.018	.017	.020	.018	.018	.017	.017	.020	.017	Point Gap
.090 See Note 3	.087	.100	.135	.095	.100	.100	.110	.110	.070	.100	Timing B.T.D.C.
.030	.030	.030	.030	.030	.030	.030	.030	.030	.030	.030	Spark Plug Gap
.007 / .017	.006 / .016	.006 / .014	.007 / .017	.005 / .013	.006 / .014	.007 / .017	.006 / .016	.006 / .016	.006 / .016	.007 / .017	Piston Ring End Gap
2.0870 / 2.0880	2.0870 / 2.0880	2.0873 / 2.0883	2.0870 / 2.0880	2.3685 / 2.3695	2.0870 / 2.0880	2.4302 / 2.4312	2.0875 / 2.0885	2.0880 / 2.0890	2.0870 / 2.0880	2.0870 / 2.0880	Piston Diameter
.0655 / .0665	.0655 / .0665	.0975 / .0985	.0655 / .0665	.0655 / .0665.	.0975 / 0985	.0655 / .0665	.0645 / .0655	.0645 / .0655	.0655 / .0655	.0655 / .0655	(Top) Piston Ring Grove Width
.0645 / .0655	.0645 / .0655	.0955 / .0965	.0645 / .0655	.0645 / .0655	.0955 / .0965	.0645 / .0655	.0645 / .0655	.0645 / .0655	.0645 / .0655	.0645 / .0655	(Bot.)
.0615 / .0625	.0615 / .0625	.0925 / .0935	.0615 / .0625	.0615 / .0625	.0925 / .0935	.0615 / .0625	.0615 / .0625	.0615 / .0625	.0615 / .0625	.0615 / .0625	Piston Ring Width
.4997 / .4999	.4997 / .4999	.4997 / .4999	.4997 / .4999	.4997 / .4999	.3751 / .3750	.4997 / .4999	.3751 / .3750	.4997 / .4999	.4997 / .4999	.4997 / .4999	Piston Pin Diameter
.6857 / .6865	.8442 / .8450	.6857 / .6865	.5614 / .5621	.6259 / .6266	.6957 / .6865	.6259 / .6266	.6857 / .6868	.6857 / .6865	.8442 / .8450	.5614 / .5621	Crank Pin Journal Diameter
.8745 / .8750	.9998 / 1.0003	.8745 / .8750	.6691 / .6695	.8650 / .8850	.8745 / .8750	.6691 / .6695	.6691 / .6695	.9998 / 1.0003	.6691 / .6695	.6691 / .6695	Crankshaft P.T.O. Side Main Brg. Dia.
.7495 / .7500	.7498 / .7503	.7495 / .7500	.6691 / .6695	.7495 / .7503	.7495 / .7500	.7495 / .7500	.7495 / .7500	.7495 / .7500	Ball 1.0003 / .9998 See Note A	.6691 / .6695	Crankshaft Magneto Side Main Brg. Dia.
.003 / .016	.003 / .016	.003 / .016	None	None	.003 / .016	None	None	None	None	None	Crankshaft End Play

NOTE 3: 643-13 B.T.D.C. = .095

NOTE 4: 643-03A, 05A, 13, 14 = .020

NOTE B: Needle Bearing .7498 / .7503

Appendix A

Tecumseh/Craftsman two-stroke engines

TABLE OF SPECIFICATIONS

(All measurements in inches)

Reference Column	20	21	22	23	24	25	26	27	28	29	30
Bore	2.093 2.094	2.4375 2.4385	2.437 2.438	2.093 2.094	2.093 2.094	2.093 2.094	2.093 2.094	2.093 2.094	2.093 2.094	2.093 2.094	2.093 2.094
Stroke	1.250	1.750	1.750	.1500	1.410	.1410	1.500	1.500	1.500	1.746	1.746
Cu. In. Displacement	4.40	8.17	8.17	5.20	4.80	4.80	5.20	5.20	5.20	6.0	6.0
Point Gap	.017	.020	.020	.017	.017	.020	.020	.017	.020	.020*	.020
Timing B.T.D.C.	.122	.118	.115	.110	.135	Fixed	.062	.100	Ext. Ignition	Ext. Ignition	.052
Spark Plug Gap	.030	.030	.030	.030	.030	.030	.030	.030	.030	.030	.030
Piston Ring End Gap	.007 .017	.007 .017	.007 .017	.006 .016	.007 .017	.007 .017	.006 .016	.006 .016	.006 .016	.007 .017	.006 .016
Piston Diameter	2.0870 2.0880	2.4302 2.4312	2.4302 2.4312	2.0870 2.0880	2.0870 2.0880	2.0870 2.0880	2.0870 2.0880	2.0875 2.0885	2.0875 2.0885	2.0865 2.0875	2.0875 2.0885
Piston Ring Groove Width (Top)	.0655 .0665	.0655 .0665	.0655 .0665	.0655 .0665	.0655 .0665	.0655 .0665	.0655 .0665	.0655 .0665	.0655 .0665	.0655 .0665	.0655 .0665
Piston Ring Groove Width (Bot.)	.0645 .0655	.0645 .0655	.0645 .0655	.0645 .0655	.0645 .0655	.0645 .0655	.0645 .0655	.0645 .0655	.0645 .0655	.0645 .0655	.0645 .0655
Piston Ring Width	.0615 .0625	.0615 .0625	.0615 .0625	.0615 .0625	.0615 .0625	.0615 .0625	.0615 .0625	.0615 .0625	.0615 .0625	.0615 .0625	.0615 .0625
Piston Pin Diameter	.4997 .4999	.4997 .4999	.4997 .4999	.4997 .4999	.4997 .4999	.4997 .4999	.4997 .4999	.4997 .4999	.4997 .4999	.4997 .4999	.4997 .4999
Crank Pin Journal Diameter	.5611 .5618	.6259 .6266	.6919 .6927	.6919 .6927	.5614 .5621	.5614 .5621	.6919 .6927	.6922 .6927	.6922 .6927	.8113 .8118	.8113 .8118
Crankshaft P.T.O. Side Main Brg. Dia.	.6691 .6695	.6691 .6695	.6691 .6695	.6691 .6695	.6691 .6695	.6691 .6695	.7498 .7503	.6691 .6695	.7498 .7503	.9998 1.0003	.7498 .7503
Crankshaft Magneto Side Main Brg. Dia.	.6691 .6695	.8745 .8750	.8748 .8753	.7498 .7503	.6691 .6695	.6691 .6695	.6691 .6695	.7498 .7503	.6695 .6699	.6695 .6699	.6695 .6699
Crankshaft End Play	None	None	None	None	None	None	None	.003 .016	None	None	None

* Does not apply to units with Solid State Ignition.

Small engine service specifications

Tecumseh/Craftsman two-stroke engines

TABLE OF SPECIFICATIONS

(All measurements in inches)

Reference Column	31	32	33	34	35	36	37	38	39	40	41
Bore	2.093 2.094	2.093 2.094	2.093 2.094	2.093 2.094	2.093 2.094	2.437 2.438	2.093 2.094	2.093 2.094	2.093 2.094	2.093 2.094	2.093 2.094
Stroke	1.500	1.746	1.746	1.500	1.746	1.750	1.828	1.500	1.828	1.746	1.746
Cu. In. Displacement	5.20	6.0	6.0	5.20	6.0	6.0	6.0	5.20	6.0	6.0	6.0
Point Gap	.020	.020	.020	.020	*.020	.020	.020	*	.020	.020	*
Timing B.T.D.C.	Ext. Ignition	.088	.073	.078	Ext. Ignition	.112	.088	Ext. Ignition	.088	.070	Ext. Ignition
Spark Plug Gap	.030	.030	.030	.030	.030	.030	.030	.030	.030	.030	.030
Piston Ring End Gap	.006 .016	.006 .016	.006 .016	.006 .016	.006 .016	.007 .017	.006 .016	.006 .016	.006 .016	.006 .016	.006 .016
Piston Diameter	2.0865 2.0875	2.0865 2.0875	2.0865 2.0875	2.0865 2.0875	2.0882 2.0887	2.4307 2.4317	2.0880 2.0885	2.0880 2.0885	2.0880 2.0885	2.0880 2.0885	2.0880 2.0885
Piston Ring Groove Width (Top)	.0655 .0665	.0655 .0665	.0655 .0665	.0655 .0665	.0655 .0665	.0655 .0665	.0655 .0665	.0655 .0665	.0655 .0665	.0655 .0665	.0655 .0665
Piston Ring Groove Width (Bot.)	.0645 .0655	.0645 .0655	.0645 .0655	.0645 .0655	.0645 .0655	.0645 .0655	.0645 .0655	.0645 .0655	.0645 .0655	.0645 .0655	.0645 .0655
Piston Ring Width	.0615 .0625	.0615 .0625	.0615 .0625	.0615 .0625	.0615 .0625	.0615 .0625	.0615 .0625	.0615 .0625	.0615 .0625	.0615 .0625	.0615 .0625
Piston Pin Diameter	.4997 .4999	.4997 .4999	.4997 .4999	.4997 .4999	.4997 .4999	.4997 .4999	.4997 .4999	.4997 .4999	.4997 .4999	.4997 .4999	.4997 .4999
Crank Pin Journal Diameter	.8113 .8118	.8445 .8450	.8113 .8118	.8445 .8450	.8113 .8118	.6922 .6927	.8445 .8450	.8113 .8118	.8113 .8118	.8445 .8450	.8113 .8118
Crankshaft P.T.O. Side Main Brg. Dia.	.9998 1.0003	.9998 1.0003	.9998 1.0003	.9993 1.0003	.7498 .7503	.6695 .6699	.9998 1.0003	.9998 1.0003	.9998 1.0003	.9998 1.0003	.9998 1.0003
Crankshaft Magneto Side Main Brg. Dia.	.7498 .7503	.6695 .6699	.6695 .6699	.6695 .6699	.6695 .6699	.8748 .8753	.6695 .6699	.7498 .7503	.6695 .6699	.6695 .6699	.6695 .6699
Crankshaft End Play	None	.003 .016	.003 .016	.003 .016	None	None	.003 .016	None	None	None	None

*Does not apply to units with Solid State Ignition.

Appendix A

Tecumseh/Craftsman two-stroke engines

TABLE OF SPECIFICATIONS

(All measurements in inches)

Reference Column	42	43										
Bore	2.093 2.094	2.093 2.094										
Stroke	1.746	1.500										
Cu. In. Displacement	6.0	5.20										
Point Gap	*	.020										
Timing B.T.D.C.	Ext. Ignition	Ext. Ignition										
Spark Plug Gap	.030	.030										
Piston Ring End Gap	.006 .016	.006 .016										
Piston Diameter	2.0885 2.0880	2.0885 2.0880										
Piston Ring Groove Width (Top) (Bot.)	.0655 .0665 .0645 .0655	.0655 .0665 .0645 .0655										
Piston Ring Width	.0625 .0615	.0625 .0615										
Piston Pin Diameter	.4999 .4997	.4999 .4997										
Crank Pin Journal Diameter	.8118 .8113	.6927 .6922										
Crankshaft P.T.O. Side Main Brg. Dia.	.7503 .7498	.7503 .7498										
Crankshaft Magneto Side Main Brg. Dia.	.6699 .6695	.6699 .6695										
Crankshaft End Play	None	None										

*Does not apply to units with Solid State Ignition.

"Torque specifications listed on this page should not be confused with the torque value observed on engines which have been run. Torque relaxation occurs on all engines from thermal expansion and contraction. The torque specifications take relaxation into account so a sufficient clamping force exists after an engine has been run."

Tecumseh/Craftsman two-stroke engines

TORQUE SPECIFICATIONS

	INCH POUNDS	FT. POUNDS
Cylinder Head Screws	80 - 100	6.6 - 8.3
Flywheel Nut	264 - 324	22 - 27
Connecting Rod Bolts		
Aluminum Rods	40 - 50	3.3 - 4.2
Steel Rods	70 - 80	5.8 - 6.7
Spark Plug	192 - 264	16 - 22
Fuel Tank Screws	12 - 20	1 - 1.7
Blower Housing Mounting Screws	80 - 100	6.7 - 8.3
Muffler Mounting Screws	80 - 100	6.7 - 8.3
Muffler Cover (Snowthrowers)	20 - 30	1.7 - 2.5
Stator to Base (Except Outboards)	80 - 100	6.6 - 8.3
External Screws to Laminations	30 - 40	2.5 - 3.3
Point Screw	15 - 25	1.3 - 2.1
Air Filter or Carburetor Baffle (Metal)	30 - 40	2.5 - 3.3
Air Filter (Plastic)	18 - 25	1.5 - 2.1
Carburetor Mounting Nuts	60 - 75	5 - 6.3
Reed Plate, Cover Plate	35 - 45	2.9 - 3.8
Reed Hold down	15 - 25	1.3 - 2.1
Compression Release Cover	30 - 40	2.5 - 3.3
Base to Block	80 - 100	6.6 - 8.3
Starter Mounting Screws (Metal)	50 - 70	4.2 - 5.8
Starter Mounting Screws (Plastic)	30 - 40	2.5 - 3.3
Stop Level to Head	80 - 100	6.6 - 8.3
Speed Control to Shroud Base	30 - 40	2.5 - 3.3
Compliance Brake Bracket to Cylinder	60 - 80	5 - 6.6
Compliance Brake Bracket to Base	35 - 50	2.9 - 4.2

Appendix A

Honda engines

Engine oil type .... 10W40/SE or SF

Engine oil capacity

GV150 .... 0.62 US quarts
GX110/140 .... 0.63 US quarts
GXV120/160 .... 0.65 US quart

Idle speed

GV150 .... 1550 to 1850 rpm
GX110/140 .... 1250 to 1600 rpm
GXV120 .... 1850 to 2150 rpm
GXV16 .... 1550 to 1850 rpm

Intake valve clearance

GV150 .... 0.002 to 0.004 inch
All others .... 0.005 to 0.007 inch

Exhaust valve clearance

GV150 .... 0.004 to 0.006 inch
All others .... 0.007 to 0.009 inch

Ignition point gap (GV150 only) .... 0.012 to 0.016 inch

Cylinder compression pressure

GV150 .... 71.1 psi at 600 rpm
GX110/140 .... 85 to 120 psi at 600 rpm
GXV120/160 .... 43 to 100 psi at 600 rpm

Float height

GV150 .... 0.260 to 0.380 inch
All others .... 0.480 to 0.600 inch

Spark plug type

GV150 .... NGK BPMR-6A
GX110/140 .... NGK BP6ES or BPR6ES
                                      ND W20EP-U or W20EPR-U
GXV120/160 .... NGK BP5ES or BPR5ES
                                      ND W16EP-U or W16EPR-U

Spark plug gap

GV150
  Breaker point ignition .... 0.024 to 0.028 inch
  CDI ignition .... 0.035 to 0.039 inch
All others .... 0.028 to 0.031 inch

Ignition coil resistance

GV150 (secondary windings) .... 6.6 K-ohms
All others
  Primary windings .... 0.7 to 0.9 ohms
  Secondary windings .... 6.3 to 7.7 K-ohms

Small engine service specifications

Ignition coil air gap .... 0.016 ± 0.008 inch

Cylinder bore diameter

	Standard	Service limit
GV150	2.520 to 2.521 inches	2.526 inches
GX110	2.24 inches	2.2505 inches
GX140	2.52 inches	2.5262 inches
GXV120	2.3622 inches	2.370 inches
GXV160	2.677 inches	2.680 inches

Piston diameter

	Standard	Service limit
GV150	2.518 to 2.519 inches	2.515 inches
GX110	2.2435 inches	2.2368 inches
GX140	2.5190 inches	2.5124 inches
GXV120	2.3616 inches	2.360 inches
GXV160	2.677 inches	2.675 inches

Piston-to-cylinder bore clearance

GV150	0.002 inch maximum	
All others	0.0006 to 0.002 inch	0.005 inch

Piston pin hole inside diameter

	Standard	Service limit
GV150	0.590 to 0.591 inch	0.592 inch
GX110	0.5119 inch	0.5137 inch
GX140	0.7087 inch	0.7105 inch
GXV120	0.5118 inch	0.514 inch
GXV160	0.7087 inch	0.7106 inch

Piston pin outside diameter

	Standard	Service limit
GV150	0.5903 to 0.5906 inch	0.5887 inch
GX110	0.510 inch	0.5099 inch
GX140	0.710 inch	0.7068 inch
GXV120	0.5118 inch	0.510 inch
GXV160	0.7087 inch	0.7069 inch

Piston-to-pin clearance

GX110, GXV120/160	0.0001 to 0.0006 inch	0.003 inch
GX140	0.0001 to 0.0006 inch	0.002 inch

Piston ring side clearance

GV150	0.0004 to 0.0020 inch	0.006 inch
GX110/140, GXV120	0.0006 to 0.0018 inch	0.006 inch
GXV160	0.0012 to 0.0026 inch	0.006 inch

Piston ring end gap

GV150	0.008 to 0.016 inch	0.039 inch
All others		
Compression rings	0.008 to 0.016 inch	0.040 inch
Oil control ring	0.006 to 0.014 inch	0.040 inch

Appendix A

Honda engines (continued)

Connecting rod small end inside diameter
GV150 .... 0.590 to 0.591 inch   0.593 inch
GX110 .... 0.512 inch   0.515 inch
GX140 .... 0.7087 inch   0.711 inch
GXV120 .... 0.5120 inch   0.519 inch
GXV160 .... 0.7089 inch   0.7107 inch

Connecting rod bearing oil clearance
GV150 .... 0.0016 to 0.0026 inch   0.005 inch
GX110/140 .... 0.0016 to 0.0026 inch   0.005 inch
GXV120/160 .... 0.0015 to 0.0025 inch   0.0047 inch

Connecting rod end play
GV150 .... 0.004 to 0.031 inch   0.047 inch
All others .... 0.004 to 0.028 inch   0.043 inch

Crankshaft connecting rod journal diameter
GV150 .... 1.0617 to 1.0622 inches   1.0204 inches
GX110 .... 1.024 inches   1.0262 inches
GX140 .... 1.182 inches   1.1837 inches
GXV120 .... 1.023 inches   1.020 inches
GXV160 .... 1.180 inches   1.1780 inches

Crankshaft main bearing journal diameter
GX110 .... 1.023 inches   1.020 inches
GX140 .... 1.180 inches   1.178 inches

Camshaft lobe height
GV150 .... 1.141 to 1.149 inches   1.132 inches
All others
    Intake .... 1.091 inches   1.081 inches
    Exhaust .... 1.093 inches   1.083 inches

Camshaft journal diameter
GV150 .... 0.699 to 0.700 inch   0.698 inch
GX110/140 .... 0.5506 inch   0.5479 inch
GXV120/160 .... 0.551 inch   0.548 inch

Camshaft bearing bore diameter
GX110/140 (only) .... 0.550 inch   0.5531 inch

Valve spring free length
GV150 .... 1.45 inches   1.39 inches
GX110/140 .... 1.34 inches   1.28 inches
GXV120/160 .... 1.339 inches   1.280 inches

Valve stem diameter
GV150
    Intake .... 0.2738 to 0.2744 inch   0.2679 inch
    Exhaust .... 0.2720 to 0.2726 inch   0.2661 inch

Small engine service specifications

All others
Intake	0.216 inch	0.2093 inch
Exhaust	0.214 inch	0.2077 inch

Valve guide inside diameter
GV150	0.2756 to 0.2762 inch	0.2787 inch
GX110/140	0.217 inch	0.2193 inch
GXV120/160	0.2165 inch	0.222 inch

Valve stem-to-guide clearance (GX110/140, GXV120/160)
Intake	0.0008 to 0.0016 inch	0.004 inch
Exhaust	0.002 to 0.0034 inch	0.005 inch

Valve seat width
GV150	1/32-inch	1/16-inch
All others	1/32-inch	5/64-inch

Oil pump (GV150 only)
Inner rotor-to-outer rotor clearance	0.006 inch	0.008 inch
Pump body-to-outer rotor clearance	0.006 inch	0.010 inch

Torque specifications

	Ft-lbs
Connecting rod cap bolts	
GV150	9
GX110/140	8 to 9.5
GXV120/160	7.2 to 10
Cylinder head bolts	
GV150	18
All others	16 to 19
Flywheel nut	
GV150	54
All others	51 to 58
Rocker arm pivot (adjusting nut)	6 to 9
Rocker arm stud	16 to 19
Ignition coil mounting bolts (GV150 only) .	7
Oil pan/crankcase cover bolts	
GV150	7
GX110	8 to 11
GX140	16 to 19
GXV120/160	7.2 to 10
Muffler nuts	
GV150	7
GX110/140	16 to 19
GXV120/160	6 to 9
Tappet cover bolts (GV150 only)	7
Oil drain plug	
GV150	33
All others	11 to 14.5
Recoil starter self-locking	
nut (GV150 only)	17

Index

Haynes small engine repair manual

Haynes small engine repair manual

Haynes Automotive Manuals

NOTE: If you do not see a listing for your vehicle, consult your local Haynes dealer for the latest product information.

HAYNES XTREME CUSTOMIZING
11101 **Sport Compact Customizing**
11102 **Sport Compact Performance**
11110 **In-car Entertainment**
11150 **Sport Utility Vehicle Customizing**
11213 **Acura**
11255 **GM Full-size Pick-ups**
11314 **Ford Focus**
11315 **Full-size Ford Pick-ups**
11373 **Honda Civic**

ACURA
12020 **Integra** '86 thru '89 & **Legend** '86 thru '90
12021 **Integra** '90 thru '93 & **Legend** '91 thru '95

AMC
Jeep CJ - see JEEP (50020)
14020 **Mid-size models** '70 thru '83
14025 **(Renault) Alliance & Encore** '83 thru '87

AUDI
15020 **4000** all models '80 thru '87
15025 **5000** all models '77 thru '83
15026 **5000** all models '84 thru '88

AUSTIN-HEALEY
Sprite - see MG Midget (66015)

BMW
18020 **3/5 Series** not including diesel or all-wheel drive models '82 thru '92
18021 **3-Series** incl. Z3 models '92 thru '98
18022 **3-Series**, E46 chassis '99 thru '05, Z4 models '03 thru '05
18025 **320i** all 4 cyl models '75 thru '83
18050 **1500 thru 2002** except Turbo '59 thru '77

BUICK
19010 **Buick Century** '97 thru '05
Century (front-wheel drive) - see GM (38005)
19020 **Buick, Oldsmobile & Pontiac Full-size** (Front-wheel drive) '85 thru '05
Buick Electra, LeSabre and Park Avenue; **Oldsmobile** Delta 88 Royale, Ninety Eight and Regency; **Pontiac** Bonneville
19025 **Buick Oldsmobile & Pontiac Full-size** (Rear wheel drive)
Buick Estate '70 thru '90, Electra'70 thru '84, LeSabre '70 thru '85, Limited '74 thru '79
Oldsmobile Custom Cruiser '70 thru '90, Delta 88 '70 thru '85,Ninety-eight '70 thru '84
Pontiac Bonneville '70 thru '81, Catalina '70 thru '81, Grandville '70 thru '75, Parisienne '83 thru '86
19030 **Mid-size Regal & Century** all rear-drive models with V6, V8 and Turbo '74 thru '87
Regal - see GENERAL MOTORS (38010)
Riviera - see GENERAL MOTORS (38030)
Roadmaster - see CHEVROLET (24046)
Skyhawk - see GENERAL MOTORS (38015)
Skylark - see GM (38020, 38025)
Somerset - see GENERAL MOTORS (38025)

CADILLAC
21030 **Cadillac Rear Wheel Drive** all gasoline models '70 thru '93
Cimarron - see GENERAL MOTORS (38015)
DeVille - see GM (38031 & 38032)
Eldorado - see GM (38030 & 38031)
Fleetwood - see GM (38031)
Seville - see GM (38030, 38031 & 38032)

CHEVROLET
24010 **Astro & GMC Safari Mini-vans** '85 thru '03
24015 **Camaro V8** all models '70 thru '81
24016 **Camaro** all models '82 thru '92
24017 **Camaro & Firebird** '93 thru '02
Cavalier - see GENERAL MOTORS (38016)
Celebrity - see GENERAL MOTORS (38005)
24020 **Chevelle, Malibu & El Camino** '69 thru '87
24024 **Chevette & Pontiac T1000** '76 thru '87
Citation - see GENERAL MOTORS (38020)
24027 **Colorado & GMC Canyon** '04 thru '06
24032 **Corsica/Beretta** all models '87 thru '96
24040 **Corvette** all V8 models '68 thru '82
24041 **Corvette** all models '84 thru '96
10305 **Chevrolet Engine Overhaul Manual**
24045 **Full-size Sedans** Caprice, Impala, Biscayne, Bel Air & Wagons '69 thru '90
24046 **Impala SS & Caprice and Buick Roadmaster** '91 thru '96
Impala - see LUMINA (24048)
Lumina '90 thru '94 - see GM (38010)
24048 **Lumina & Monte Carlo** '95 thru '05
Lumina APV - see GM (38035)

24050 **Luv Pick-up** all 2WD & 4WD '72 thru '82
Malibu '97 thru '00 - see GM (38026)
24055 **Monte Carlo** all models '70 thru '88
Monte Carlo '95 thru '01 - see LUMINA (24048)
24059 **Nova** all V8 models '69 thru '79
24060 **Nova and Geo Prizm** '85 thru '92
24064 **Pick-ups '67 thru '87** - Chevrolet & GMC, all V8 & in-line 6 cyl, 2WD & 4WD '67 thru '87; Suburbans, Blazers & Jimmys '67 thru '91
24065 **Pick-ups '88 thru '98** - Chevrolet & GMC, full-size pick-ups '88 thru '98, C/K Classic '99 & '00, Blazer & Jimmy '92 thru '94; Suburban '92 thru '99; Tahoe & Yukon '95 thru '99
24066 **Pick-ups '99 thru '03** - Chevrolet Silverado & GMC Sierra full-size pick-ups '99 thru '05, Suburban/Tahoe/Yukon/Yukon XL '00 thru '05
24070 **S-10 & S-15 Pick-ups** '82 thru '93, Blazer & Jimmy '83 thru '94,
24071 **S-10 & Sonoma Pick-ups** '94 thru '04, Blazer & Jimmy '95 thru '04, Hombre '96 thru '01
24072 **Chevrolet TrailBlazer & TrailBlazer EXT, GMC Envoy & Envoy XL, Oldsmobile Bravada** '02 and '03
24075 **Sprint** '85 thru '88 & **Geo Metro** '89 thru '01
24080 **Vans - Chevrolet & GMC** '68 thru '96
24081 **Chevrolet Express & GMC Savana** Full-size Vans '96 thru '05

CHRYSLER
25015 **Chrysler Cirrus, Dodge Stratus, Plymouth Breeze** '95 thru '00
10310 **Chrysler Engine Overhaul Manual**
25020 **Full-size Front-Wheel Drive** '88 thru '93
K-Cars - see DODGE Aries (30008)
Laser - see DODGE Daytona (30030)
25025 **Chrysler LHS, Concorde, New Yorker, Dodge** Intrepid, **Eagle Vision,** '93 thru '97
25026 **Chrysler LHS, Concorde, 300M, Dodge** Intrepid, '98 thru '03
25027 **Chrysler 300** '05 thru '07
25030 **Chrysler & Plymouth Mid-size** front wheel drive '82 thru '95
Rear-wheel Drive - see Dodge (30050)
25035 **PT Cruiser** all models '01 thru '03
25040 **Chrysler** Sebring, **Dodge** Avenger '95 thru '05

DATSUN
28005 **200SX** all models '80 thru '83
28007 **B-210** all models '73 thru '78
28009 **210** all models '79 thru '82
28012 **240Z, 260Z & 280Z** Coupe '70 thru '78
28014 **280ZX** Coupe & 2+2 '79 thru '83
300ZX - see NISSAN (72010)
28018 **510 & PL521 Pick-up** '68 thru '73
28020 **510** all models '78 thru '81
28022 **620 Series Pick-up** all models '73 thru '79
720 Series Pick-up - see NISSAN (72030)
28025 **810/Maxima** all gasoline models, '77 thru '84

DODGE
400 & 600 - see CHRYSLER (25030)
30008 **Aries & Plymouth Reliant** '81 thru '89
30010 **Caravan & Plymouth Voyager** '84 thru '95
30011 **Caravan & Plymouth Voyager** '96 thru '02
30012 **Challenger/Plymouth Saporro** '78 thru '83
30013 **Caravan, Chrysler Voyager, Town & Country** '03 thru '06
30016 **Colt & Plymouth Champ** '78 thru '87
30020 **Dakota Pick-ups** all models '87 thru '96
30021 **Durango** '98 & '99, **Dakota** '97 thru '99
30022 **Dodge Durango** models '00 thru '03
Dodge Dakota models '00 thru '03
30023 **Dodge Durango & Dakota** '04 thru '06
30025 **Dart, Demon, Plymouth Barracuda, Duster & Valiant** 6 cyl models '67 thru '76
30030 **Daytona & Chrysler Laser** '84 thru '89
Intrepid - see CHRYSLER (25025, 25026)
30034 **Neon** all models '95 thru '99
30035 **Omni & Plymouth Horizon** '78 thru '90
30036 **Dodge and Plymouth Neon** '00 thru'05
30040 **Pick-ups** all full-size models '74 thru '93
30041 **Pick-ups** all full-size models '94 thru '01
30042 **Dodge Full-size Pick-ups** '02 thru '05
30045 **Ram 50/D50 Pick-ups & Raider and Plymouth Arrow Pick-ups** '79 thru '93
30050 **Dodge/Plymouth/Chrysler RWD** '71 thru '89
30055 **Shadow & Plymouth Sundance** '87 thru '94
30060 **Spirit & Plymouth Acclaim** '89 thru '95
30065 **Vans - Dodge & Plymouth** '71 thru '03

EAGLE
Talon - see MITSUBISHI (68030, 68031)
Vision - see CHRYSLER (25025)

FIAT
34010 **124 Sport Coupe & Spider** '68 thru '78
34025 **X1/9** all models '74 thru '80

FORD
10355 **Ford Automatic Transmission Overhaul**
36004 **Aerostar Mini-vans** all models '86 thru '97
36006 **Contour & Mercury Mystique** '95 thru '00
36008 **Courier Pick-up** all models '72 thru '82
36012 **Crown Victoria & Mercury Grand Marquis** '88 thru '00
10320 **Ford Engine Overhaul Manual**
36016 **Escort/Mercury Lynx** all models '81 thru '90
36020 **Escort/Mercury Tracer** '91 thru '00
36022 **Ford Escape & Mazda Tribute** '01 thru '03
36024 **Explorer & Mazda Navajo** '91 thru '01
36025 **Ford Explorer & Mercury Mountaineer** '02 thru '06
36028 **Fairmont & Mercury Zephyr** '78 thru '83
36030 **Festiva & Aspire** '88 thru '97
36032 **Fiesta** all models '77 thru '80
36034 **Focus** all models '00 thru '05
36036 **Ford & Mercury Full-size** '75 thru '87
36044 **Ford & Mercury Mid-size** '75 thru '86
36048 **Mustang V8** all models '64-1/2 thru '73
36049 **Mustang II** 4 cyl, V6 & V8 models '74 thru '78
36050 **Mustang & Mercury Capri** all models Mustang, '79 thru '93; Capri, '79 thru '86
36051 **Mustang** all models '94 thru '03
36052 **Mustang** '05 thru '07
36054 **Pick-ups & Bronco** '73 thru '79
36058 **Pick-ups & Bronco** '80 thru '96
36059 **F-150 & Expedition** '97 thru '03, F-250 '97 thru '99 & **Lincoln Navigator** '98 thru '02
36060 **Super Duty Pick-ups, Excursion** '99 thru '06
36061 **F-150** full-size '04 thru '06
36062 **Pinto & Mercury Bobcat** '75 thru '80
36066 **Probe** all models '89 thru '92
36070 **Ranger/Bronco II** gasoline models '83 thru '92
36071 **Ranger** '93 thru '05 & **Mazda Pick-ups** '94 thru '05
36074 **Taurus & Mercury Sable** '86 thru '95
36075 **Taurus & Mercury Sable** '96 thru '05
36078 **Tempo & Mercury Topaz** '84 thru '94
36082 **Thunderbird/Mercury Cougar** '83 thru '88
36086 **Thunderbird/Mercury Cougar** '89 and '97
36090 **Vans** all V8 Econoline models '69 thru '91
36094 **Vans** full size '92 thru '05
36097 **Windstar Mini-van** '95 thru '03

GENERAL MOTORS
10360 **GM Automatic Transmission Overhaul**
38005 **Buick Century, Chevrolet Celebrity, Oldsmobile Cutlass Ciera & Pontiac 6000** all models '82 thru '96
38010 **Buick Regal, Chevrolet Lumina, Oldsmobile Cutlass Supreme & Pontiac Grand Prix** (FWD) '88 thru '05
38015 **Buick Skyhawk, Cadillac Cimarron, Chevrolet Cavalier, Oldsmobile Firenza & Pontiac J-2000 & Sunbird** '82 thru '94
38016 **Chevrolet Cavalier & Pontiac Sunfire** '95 thru '04
38020 **Buick Skylark, Chevrolet Citation, Olds Omega, Pontiac Phoenix** '80 thru '85
38025 **Buick Skylark & Somerset, Oldsmobile Achieva & Calais and Pontiac Grand Am** all models '85 thru '98
38026 **Chevrolet Malibu, Olds Alero & Cutlass, Pontiac Grand Am** '97 thru '03
38027 **Chevrolet Malibu** '04 thru '07
38030 **Cadillac Eldorado** '71 thru '85, **Seville** '80 thru '85, **Oldsmobile Toronado** '71 thru '85, **Buick Riviera** '79 thru '85
38031 **Cadillac Eldorado & Seville** '86 thru '91, **DeVille** '86 thru '93, **Fleetwood & Olds Toronado** '86 thru '92, **Buick Riviera** '86 thru '93
38032 **Cadillac DeVille** '94 thru '05 & **Seville** '92 thru '04
38035 **Chevrolet Lumina APV, Olds Silhouette & Pontiac Trans Sport** all models '90 thru '96
38036 **Chevrolet Venture, Olds Silhouette, Pontiac Trans Sport & Montana** '97 thru '05
General Motors Full-size Rear-wheel Drive - see BUICK (19025)

GEO
Metro - see CHEVROLET Sprint (24075)
Prizm - '85 thru '92 see CHEVY (24060), '93 thru '02 see TOYOTA Corolla (92036)

(Continued on other side)

Haynes North America, Inc., 861 Lawrence Drive, Newbury Park, CA 91320-1514 • (805) 498-6703

Haynes Automotive Manuals (continued)

NOTE: If you do not see a listing for your vehicle, consult your local Haynes dealer for the latest product information.

40030 Storm all models '90 thru '93
Tracker - see SUZUKI Samurai (90010)

GMC
Vans & Pick-ups - see CHEVROLET

HONDA
42010 Accord CVCC all models '76 thru '83
42011 Accord all models '84 thru '89
42012 Accord all models '90 thru '93
42013 Accord all models '94 thru '97
42014 Accord all models '98 thru '02
42015 Honda Accord models '03 thru '05
42020 Civic 1200 all models '73 thru '79
42021 Civic 1300 & 1500 CVCC '80 thru '83
42022 Civic 1500 CVCC all models '75 thru '79
42023 Civic all models '84 thru '91
42024 Civic & del Sol '92 thru '95
42025 Civic '96 thru '00, **CR-V** '97 thru '01, **Acura Integra** '94 thru '00
42026 Civic '01 thru '04, **CR-V** '02 thru '04
42035 Honda Odyssey all models '99 thru '04
42040 Prelude CVCC all models '79 thru '89

HYUNDAI
43010 Elantra all models '96 thru '01
43015 Excel & Accent all models '86 thru '98

ISUZU
Hombre - see CHEVROLET S-10 (24071)
47017 Rodeo '91 thru '02; **Amigo** '89 thru '94 and '98 thru '02; **Honda Passport** '95 thru '02
47020 Trooper & Pick-up '81 thru '93

JAGUAR
49010 XJ6 all 6 cyl models '68 thru '86
49011 XJ6 all models '88 thru '94
49015 XJ12 & XJS all 12 cyl models '72 thru '85

JEEP
50010 Cherokee, Comanche & Wagoneer Limited all models '84 thru '01
50020 CJ all models '49 thru '86
50025 Grand Cherokee all models '93 thru '04
50029 Grand Wagoneer & Pick-up '72 thru '91 Grand Wagoneer '84 thru '91, Cherokee & Wagoneer '72 thru '83, Pick-up '72 thru '88
50030 Wrangler all models '87 thru '03
50035 Liberty '02 thru '04

KIA
54070 Sephia '94 thru '01, **Spectra** '00 thru '04

LEXUS
ES 300 - see TOYOTA Camry (92007)

LINCOLN
Navigator - see FORD Pick-up (36059)
59010 Rear-Wheel Drive all models '70 thru '05

MAZDA
61010 GLC Hatchback (rear-wheel drive) '77 thru '83
61011 GLC (front-wheel drive) '81 thru '85
61015 323 & Protogé '90 thru '00
61016 MX-5 Miata '90 thru '97
61020 MPV all models '89 thru '94
Navajo - see Ford Explorer (36024)
61030 Pick-ups '72 thru '93
Pick-ups '94 thru '00 - see Ford Ranger (36071)
61035 RX-7 all models '79 thru '85
61036 RX-7 all models '86 thru '91
61040 626 (rear-wheel drive) all models '79 thru '82
61041 626/MX-6 (front-wheel drive) '83 thru '92
61042 626 '93 thru '01, **MX-6/Ford Probe** '93 thru '01

MERCEDES-BENZ
63012 123 Series Diesel '76 thru '85
63015 190 Series four-cyl gas models, '84 thru '88
63020 230/250/280 6 cyl sohc models '68 thru '72
63025 280 123 Series gasoline models '77 thru '81
63030 350 & 450 all models '71 thru '80

MERCURY
64200 Villager & Nissan Quest '93 thru '01
All other titles, see FORD Listing.

MG
66010 MGB Roadster & GT Coupe '62 thru '80
66015 MG Midget, Austin Healey Sprite '58 thru '80

MITSUBISHI
68020 Cordia, Tredia, Galant, Precis & Mirage '83 thru '93

68030 Eclipse, Eagle Talon & Ply. Laser '90 thru '94
68031 Eclipse '95 thru '01, **Eagle Talon** '95 thru '98
68035 Mitsubishi Galant '94 thru '03
68040 Pick-up '83 thru '96 & **Montero** '83 thru '93

NISSAN
72010 300ZX all models including Turbo '84 thru '89
72015 Altima all models '93 thru '04
72020 Maxima all models '85 thru '92
72021 Maxima all models '93 thru '04
72030 Pick-ups '80 thru '97 **Pathfinder** '87 thru '95
72031 Frontier Pick-up '98 thru '04, **Xterra** '00 thru '04, **Pathfinder** '96 thru '04
72040 Pulsar all models '83 thru '86
Quest - see MERCURY Villager (64200)
72050 Sentra all models '82 thru '94
72051 Sentra & 200SX all models '95 thru '04
72060 Stanza all models '82 thru '90

OLDSMOBILE
73015 Cutlass V6 & V8 gas models '74 thru '88
For other OLDSMOBILE titles, see BUICK, CHEVROLET or GENERAL MOTORS listing.

PLYMOUTH
For PLYMOUTH titles, see DODGE listing.

PONTIAC
79008 Fiero all models '84 thru '88
79018 Firebird V8 models except Turbo '70 thru '81
79019 Firebird all models '82 thru '92
79040 Mid-size Rear-wheel Drive '70 thru '87
For other PONTIAC titles, see BUICK, CHEVROLET or GENERAL MOTORS listing.

PORSCHE
80020 911 except Turbo & Carrera 4 '65 thru '89
80025 914 all 4 cyl models '69 thru '76
80030 924 all models including Turbo '76 thru '82
80035 944 all models including Turbo '83 thru '89

RENAULT
Alliance & Encore - see AMC (14020)

SAAB
84010 900 all models including Turbo '79 thru '88

SATURN
87010 Saturn all models '91 thru '02
87011 Saturn Ion '03 thru '07
87020 Saturn all L-series models '00 thru '04

SUBARU
89002 1100, 1300, 1400 & 1600 '71 thru '79
89003 1600 & 1800 2WD & 4WD '80 thru '94
89100 Legacy all models '90 thru '98
89101 Legacy & Forester '00 thru '06

SUZUKI
90010 Samurai/Sidekick & Geo Tracker '86 thru '01

TOYOTA
92005 Camry all models '83 thru '91
92006 Camry all models '92 thru '96
92007 Camry, Avalon, Solara, Lexus ES 300 '97 thru '01
92008 Toyota Camry, Avalon and Solara and Lexus ES 300/330 all models '02 thru '05
92015 Celica Rear Wheel Drive '71 thru '85
92020 Celica Front Wheel Drive '86 thru '99
92025 Celica Supra all models '79 thru '92
92030 Corolla all models '75 thru '79
92032 Corolla all rear wheel drive models '80 thru '87
92035 Corolla all front wheel drive models '84 thru '92
92036 Corolla & Geo Prizm '93 thru '02
92037 Corolla models '03 thru '05
92040 Corolla Tercel all models '80 thru '82
92045 Corona all models '74 thru '82
92050 Cressida all models '78 thru '82
92055 Land Cruiser FJ40, 43, 45, 55 '68 thru '82
92056 Land Cruiser FJ60, 62, 80, FZJ80 '80 thru '96
92065 MR2 all models '85 thru '87
92070 Pick-up all models '69 thru '78
92075 Pick-up all models '79 thru '95
92076 Tacoma '95 thru '04, **4Runner** '96 thru '02, **& T100** '93 thru '98
92078 Tundra '00 thru '02 & **Sequoia** '01 thru '02
92080 Previa all models '91 thru '95
92082 RAV4 all models '96 thru '02
92085 Tercel all models '87 thru '94
92090 Toyota Sienna all models '98 thru '02
92095 Highlander & Lexus RX-330 '99 thru '06

TRIUMPH
94007 Spitfire all models '62 thru '81
94010 TR7 all models '75 thru '81

VW
96008 Beetle & Karmann Ghia '54 thru '79
96009 New Beetle '98 thru '00
96016 Rabbit, Jetta, Scirocco & Pick-up gas models '75 thru '92 & Convertible '80 thru '92
96017 Golf, GTI & Jetta '93 thru '98 & Cabrio '95 thru '98
96018 Golf, GTI, Jetta & Cabrio '99 thru '02
96020 Rabbit, Jetta & Pick-up diesel '77 thru '84
96023 Passat '98 thru '01, **Audi A4** '96 thru '01
96030 Transporter 1600 all models '68 thru '79
96035 Transporter 1700, 1800 & 2000 '72 thru '79
96040 Type 3 1500 & 1600 all models '63 thru '73
96045 Vanagon all air-cooled models '80 thru '83

VOLVO
97010 120, 130 Series & 1800 Sports '61 thru '73
97015 140 Series all models '66 thru '74
97020 240 Series all models '76 thru '93
97040 740 & 760 Series all models '82 thru '88
97050 850 Series all models '93 thru '97

TECHBOOK MANUALS
10205 Automotive Computer Codes
10206 OBD-II & Electronic Engine Management Systems
10210 Automotive Emissions Control Manual
10215 Fuel Injection Manual, 1978 thru 1985
10220 Fuel Injection Manual, 1986 thru 1999
10225 Holley Carburetor Manual
10230 Rochester Carburetor Manual
10240 Weber/Zenith/Stromberg/SU Carburetors
10305 Chevrolet Engine Overhaul Manual
10310 Chrysler Engine Overhaul Manual
10320 Ford Engine Overhaul Manual
10330 GM and Ford Diesel Engine Repair Manual
10340 Small Engine Repair Manual, 5 HP & Less
10341 Small Engine Repair Manual, 5.5 - 20 HP
10345 Suspension, Steering & Driveline Manual
10355 Ford Automatic Transmission Overhaul
10360 GM Automatic Transmission Overhaul
10405 Automotive Body Repair & Painting
10410 Automotive Brake Manual
10411 Automotive Anti-lock Brake (ABS) Systems
10415 Automotive Detailing Manual
10420 Automotive Electrical Manual
10425 Automotive Heating & Air Conditioning
10430 Automotive Reference Manual & Dictionary
10435 Automotive Tools Manual
10440 Used Car Buying Guide
10445 Welding Manual
10450 ATV Basics
10452 Scooters, Automatic Transmission 50cc to 250cc

SPANISH MANUALS
98903 Reparación de Carrocería & Pintura
98904 Carburadores para los modelos Holley & Rochester
98905 Códigos Automotrices de la Computadora
98910 Frenos Automotriz
98913 Electricidad Automotriz
98915 Inyección de Combustible 1986 al 1999
99040 Chevrolet & GMC Camionetas '67 al '87 Incluye Suburban, Blazer & Jimmy '67 al '91
99041 Chevrolet & GMC Camionetas '88 al '98 Incluye Suburban '92 al '98, Blazer & Jimmy '92 al '94, Tahoe y Yukon '95 al '98
99042 Chevrolet & GMC Camionetas Cerradas '68 al '95
99055 Dodge Caravan & Plymouth Voyager '84 al '95
99075 Ford Camionetas y Bronco '80 al '94
99077 Ford Camionetas Cerradas '69 al '91
99088 Ford Modelos de Tamaño Mediano '75 al '86
99091 Ford Taurus & Mercury Sable '86 al '95
99095 GM Modelos de Tamaño Grande '70 al '90
99100 GM Modelos de Tamaño Mediano '70 al '88
99106 Jeep Cherokee, Wagoneer & Comanche '84 al '00
99110 Nissan Camioneta '80 al '96, **Pathfinder** '87 al '95
99118 Nissan Sentra '82 al '94
99125 Toyota Camionetas y 4Runner '79 al '95

Over 100 Haynes motorcycle manuals also available

10-06

Haynes North America, Inc., 861 Lawrence Drive, Newbury Park, CA 91320-1514 • (805) 498-6703